RESILIENCE IN THE POST-WELFARE INNER CITY

Voluntary sector geographies in London, Los Angeles and Sydney

Geoffrey DeVerteuil

P

First published in Great Britain in 2016 by

Policy Press
University of Bristol
1-9 Old Park Hill
Bristol
BS2 8BB
UK
t: +44 (0)117 954 5940
pp-info@bristol.ac.uk
www.policypress.co.uk

North America office:
Policy Press
c/o The University of Chicago Press
1427 East 60th Street
Chicago, IL 60637, USA
t: +1 773 702 7700
f: +1 773 702 9756
sales@press.uchicago.edu
www.press.uchicago.edu

The author and publisher wish to thank John Wiley & Sons Ltd for permission to reproduce the images on page 157.

British Library Cataloguing in Publication Data
A catalogue record for this book is available from the British Library

Library of Congress Cataloging-in-Publication Data
A catalog record for this book has been requested

ISBN 978-1-4473-1664-0 paperback
ISBN 978-1-4473-2128-6 ePub
ISBN 978-1-4473-2129-3 Mobi

Cover design by Qube Design Associates, Bristol
Front cover image: Geoffrey DeVerteuil

To the voluntary-sector organisations for the gift of time, to Stephanie for the gift of patience, to Laurent-Joseph DeVerteuil (1916–2009) for the gift of perseverance and generosity, which moves the spirit of this book

'It is a vast labour – one must expend one's mind and soul generously, keeping nothing back'
Vasily Grossman, *Life and Fate*

'So, now vee may perhaps to begin, yes?'
Philip Roth, *Portnoy's Complaint*

'It is not those who can inflict the most but those who can endure the most who will prevail'
Mural, West Belfast (attributed to Terence MacSwiney, 1879–1920)

'There comes a time when the cup of endurance runs over ...'
Martin Luther King Jr

Contents

List of tables and figures

Tables

Figures

About the author

Geoff DeVerteuil (PhD Southern California, 2001) is senior lecturer at Cardiff University in the School of Planning and Geography. His research is at the grand intersection of inequality, its spatial expressions and its management within cities. He is interested more specifically in inequality as it manifests itself in terms of mental health, substance abuse treatment, homelessness, precarious migrants, gentrification and the voluntary sector. More recently, he has focused on the forces arrayed against inequality, including a critical articulation of social and spatial resilience, a focus which animates this book.

Acknowledgements

This book has had, even by academic standards, an unusually long gestation period. The personal motivations lay in my PhD work at the University of Southern California (1995–2001), where I immersed myself in the sage advice of Jennifer Wolch and Michael Dear, and future colleagues such as Robert Wilton, Wei Li, Jurgen von Mahs and Melissa Gilbert. Even back then, I was fascinated by phenomena from bygone (and perhaps more equitable) eras that uncannily persisted into the modern age in the deep recesses of the (global) city – how? Why? Why some phenomena and not others? And, in particular, why so many 'left-behinds' in the inner city, the antipode of where I grew up in suburban Montréal but an enduring source of fascination? When I came to the UK in 2007, I obtained funding from the Nuffield Foundation and the British Academy to pursue these questions, expanding to consider current, persistent and recurring threats to urban relics in the form of concentrated voluntary-sector hubs. Indeed, I could never have imagined that even the backwaters of Downtown Los Angeles, 10 years after my PhD research, could also be experiencing displacement pressure via gentrification. I began with a comparison of the spatial displacement of the voluntary sector in London and Los Angeles, which expanded to Sydney in 2011 with funding from the Worldwide Universities Network. The early ideas and proposals were critiqued at a variety of talks spanning three continents: the National University of Singapore (2011), the University of Alberta and the University of Calgary (2012), and King's College London (2013). Many thanks also to those publishers who rejected the proposed work but who further sharpened the arguments, leading to a variety of revelations that shifted the focus from displacement to resilience.

Once in the field – those places in the shadows of a gentrifying and glamorising inner city, in the ordinary spaces of the global city-region – I found myself grappling with the common issue of how, and how deeply, to 'know' a city, which is essential when undertaking comparative work (but whose complexities not always acknowledged, and the logistics of which can be tricky). I know LA well, to the point of obsession, London too, as it is but a 75-minute journey away, but am at a disadvantage with Sydney. So, in reverse order, the following thanks are due. In the Antipodes, I extend my profound gratitude to Thomas Baker, David Conradson, Luke Craven, Kurt Iveson, Robin Kearns and Wendy Shaw. In the UK, I am thankful to the following people: Nick Clarke, James Marshall, Jon May, Christine Milligan,

Andrew Power, Paul Watt and Andy Williams. Emily Watt and Laura Vickers at Policy Press have been especially helpful in getting the book to its final fruition. In particular, Emma Tompkins' seminars on resilience at the University of Southampton were helpful in developing my conceptual approach. Kanchana Ruwanpura's friendly chiding was also a source of inspiration. Finally, in Los Angeles, I extend my thanks to Ellen Reese and Ernest Savage, Lois Takahashi and Jennifer Wolch. Part of this work has already been published in *International Journal of Urban and Regional Research* (2010) *Urban Studies* (2011), *Urban Geography* (2011), *Social and Cultural Geography* (2011), *Area* (2012) and *Antipode* (2014). Gratitude to Elvin Wyly for writing a testimonial both pithy and coaxing.

A final thanks to my infinitely patient and long-suffering Stephanie. All solecisms, shibboleths and blandishments are mine alone.

Preface

The focal point for this book is the 'how' of resilience, the on-the-ground processes surrounding the fate of residual inner-city areas deemed 'service hubs' (for example, clusters of voluntary-sector organisations) faced with the threat of gentrification-induced displacement. Put as a question, what accounts for their resilience when other arrangements of collective consumption (especially social housing) have been severely curtailed or fallen by the wayside entirely? After all, even those most convinced of pervasive neoliberalism acknowledge that residual mechanisms of support, survival and 'staying put' from bygone eras persist in the city – it is just that they ignore or assume away the resilience inherent in this process, the actual means of resilience, the agents of resilience, the consequences of such resilience and how these tendencies may differ comparatively. These empirical and conceptual gaps will map on to five cornerstones that structure the book: neoliberalism and post-welfarism as the context and the threat; resilience as the response and the organising concept; the voluntary sector as the agent; the inner city as the territorial focus; and comparison as the method. Empirically and comparatively, I wish to see how processes of resilience play out across 10 different inner-city neighbourhoods in three global city-regions (London, Los Angeles and Sydney), in an attempt to learn from these places, alert to differences and similarities.

The book makes the following contributions. First, I will bring critical intent to the concept of resilience, the production of which is usually seen as regressively status quo, by developing what I deem a 'critical resilience of the residuals', whereby the relics of previously more equitable (Keynesian) arrangements are protected and defended. Second, I will present a more ambivalent, if not supportive, version of the voluntary sector. Third, I will advance a more complex interpretation of inner-city territory, one buffeted by multiple motivations that can breed resilience, rather than advancing a purely punitive representation. Fourth and finally, my comparative approach will valorise overlooked, ordinary agents and practices (of care, sustenance, abeyance) within global-city regions, and propose novel approaches to comparing the voluntary sector and resilience. Further, I will use the rich empirical material to explore the degree of similarity and difference across the Australian, UK and US welfare states and voluntary-sector settlements. The results suggested that the more uneven and autonomous, yet increasingly skeletal US welfare settlement contrasted with the more supported and centralised (yet relatively inflexible) Australian and UK systems. Resilience could never be assumed – it has become in and of itself a struggle, with advantages but also disadvantages for the voluntary sector and sometimes acting as a springboard to commons.

Geoffrey DeVerteuil
Cardiff, UK
October 2014

Part One
Introducing resilience in the post-welfare inner city: conceptual and methodological considerations

Cities nowadays are increasingly characterised by spatial splintering and polycentrism, as well as an apparently ascendant neoliberalism (MacLeod, 2011). Yet even in places as complex as London, Los Angeles and Sydney, there remains a remarkably coherent and centralised landscape of voluntary-sector organisations, a conspicuous clustering of helping agencies for downtrodden and vulnerable people. The persistence and supportiveness of service-rich inner-city areas such as Westminster, Hollywood, Downtown Skid Row, Kings Cross and Surry Hills counter the logics that assume the neoliberalised dismantlement of residual Keynesian arrangements, notably large-scale social housing (Hackworth, 2007), the displacement of homeless people through gentrification and punitive street clearances, and a more radical break between the Keynesian welfare city and the putative post-welfare city (DeVerteuil et al, 2009a). The main aim of the book is to investigate and interpret this 'how' of resilient service-rich inner-city areas (deemed service hubs), their local particularities, and crosscutting differences and similarities individually and comparatively through the specific lens of the voluntary sector and within a context of a consolidating but decidedly incomplete neoliberalism via the lens of gentrification. The results suggested a wide range of resilience strategies in the three global city-regions, with London generally proving more state supported than Los Angeles' more private and community-based strategies, and Sydney more in the middle of these extremes.

Part One introduces and explains the key concepts, gaps, contexts and methods, and grounds the resilience inherent in forthcoming case studies, the actual means of resilience, the agents of resilience, the consequences of such resilience, and how these may differ empirically and comparatively. Given the synthetic breadth of the proposed study – three global city-regions, 10 inner-city neighbourhoods, multiple and polysemous conceptual stances – this section is necessarily wide ranging. The title of the book plays on the tension between the practice of resilience and the promise of post-welfarism, and in particular how some residual arrangements prove resilient within a hostile yet

1

incomplete and uneven post-welfare environment. Chapter One introduces the five cornerstones of the book: neoliberalism and the post-welfare city as the context; resilience as the conceptual framework; the voluntary sector as the agent; the inner city as the territorial focus; and comparison as the methodology. Chapters Two, Three and Four serve to elaborate on these cornerstones, but also contextualise the empirical material in Part Two and the analysis in Part Three.

ONE

Introduction

This chapter begins with crucial extralocal contexts: the Keynesian welfare state[1] and its demise, prefiguring the focus on its stranded residuals within a context of consolidating yet incomplete neoliberalism and the uneven post-welfare city. As Esping-Andersen (1990: 3) noted, the welfare state seeks to de-commodify social goods and 'permit people to make their living standards independent of pure market forces'. At the same time, it is by nature a stratifying system to those unable or unwilling to avail themselves of the labour market, as Wacquant (1999: 1642) emphasised:

> for alongside market forces, welfare states are major producers and shapers of urban inequality and marginality. States not only deploy programmes and policies designed to 'mop up' the most glaring consequences of poverty and to cushion (or not) its social and spatial impact. They also help to determine who gets relegated, how, where and for how long. States are major engines of stratification in their own right and nowhere more so than at the bottom of the socio-spatial order … they provide or preclude access to adequate schooling and job training; they set conditions for labour market entry and exit via administrative rules for hiring, firing and retirement; they distribute (or fail to distribute) basic subsistence goods, such as housing and supplementary income; they actively support or hinder certain family and household arrangements; and they codetermine both the material intensity and the geographical exclusivity and density of misery through a welter of administrative and fiscal schemes.

At least in the Global North, the Keynesian period (1945–80) is now seen as a uniquely golden age, '… the culmination of a centuries-old struggle for social protection and security in the industrialised countries. It may justly be regarded as one of their proudest achievements in the post-war period' (Ghai, 1996: vii). At the urban scale, the Keynesian period was associated with expanding collective consumption underwritten by the state (Castells 1977; 1983). Collective consumption revolved around

3

what is termed publicly provided 'collective goods' such as education, health and social services. All of them 'improve the well-being of the community and would not be supplied by markets because their benefits are non-excludable, but similar to collective-implementation goods, they are supplied only through active forms of cooperation' (Hall & Lamont, 2013: 19). Neil Smith (2002: 85) identified the zenith of a distinctly Keynesian city of advanced capitalism in the 1960s and 1970s, 'in which the state underwrote wide swaths of social reproduction, from housing to welfare to transportation infrastructure', fusing the urban scale and social reproduction. The late 1970s and 1980s can be seen now as a crossroads in the administration of cities in the Global North, moving from a managerialist, (re)distributional and welfare-oriented Keynesian city to a more entrepreneurial and competitive one that increasingly shunned the provision of collective goods (for example, Peterson, 1981; Harvey, 1989; Zukin, 1995; MacLeod, 2011). This reflected broader shifts in welfare state governance, from a Keynesian model that promoted a redistributive and near-universalist approach to social goods while very much monopolising their provision, to a leaner, neoliberal and post-welfare model. It is to this new model that I now turn, as it provides the threatening context for the ensuing four cornerstones.

Neoliberalism and the post-welfare city as the context and the threat

Neoliberalism must be understood as contingent, a 'complex, multifaceted project of socio-spatial transformation [containing] not only a utopian vision of a fully commodified form of social life, but also a concrete vision of institutional modifications through which the unfettered rule of capital is to be promoted' (Brenner & Theodore, 2002: 16). Hodkinson (2011: 358–9) usefully defined neoliberalism in four ways: as (1) an ideological hegemonic project that serves as 'an ideological rejection of egalitarian liberalism and the Keynesian welfare state in particular' (Hackworth, 2007: 9); (2) a specific policy and programme that rolls back the previous arrangements while rolling out new ones; (3) a new state form with new modes of regulation and governance; and (4) a new form of diffuse governmentality, in the Foucauldian sense of introducing new spaces and subjectivities. I begin by recounting a largely regulationist account of neoliberalism before moving to some of its critiques. Further, I understand neoliberalism as (1) more a class project that favours the already powerful than a recipe for economic growth (Evans & Sewell, 2013), and (2) an intensely urban one, albeit incomplete and uneven. As Brenner and Theodore (2002: 2) contended, 'cities have become strategically crucial geographical arenas in which a variety of neoliberal initiatives – along with closely intertwined strategies of crisis displacement and crisis management – have been articulated', as well as exported (Massey, 2007).

Neoliberalism involves the active critique, repudiation and dismantlement of the public domain more generally, and previous welfare state arrangements more specifically. This is the essence of 'roll-back' neoliberalism, centrally concerned with hollowing out the (Keynesian) state through deregulation, devolution, privatisation and austerity measures (Peck & Tickell, 2002). From the 1980s onwards, it involved a process to 'abolish or weaken social transfer programs while actively fostering the "inclusion" of the poor and marginalised into the labor market, on the market's terms' (Peck, 2001a: 445). A 'hollowed out' welfare state was the result, generally hostile to redistribution and universality, magnifying rather than offsetting inequality, and epitomised by the 1996 US welfare reform (the Personal Responsibility and Work Opportunities Reconciliation Act, or PRWORA), the 1997 New Labour's 'Third Way' and the subsequent Coalition's 'Big Society' in the UK (Milbourne, 2013), and the 2006 'Welfare to Work' (*WorkChoices*) and 2014 'Welfare Reform' policies in Australia. Roll-back neoliberalism seeks the eventual *physical displacement* of Keynesian arrangements and a return to a more streamlined welfare state. Jessop (2002: 118) saw in neoliberalism a yearning for a partial return to the pre-welfare state, whereby 'arrangements should be instituted to encourage family, neighborhood, informal, or market-based and market-sustaining solutions to the problems of social reproduction', essentially reverting to a state of affairs in which the individual, family, community, and God were the primary support systems.

The consequences unleashed by roll-back neoliberalism were far reaching. Peck and Tickell (2002) saw from the 1990s onwards, and in response to some of the apparent failings of the 'roll-back' round of restructuring, a 'roll-out' phase in which the welfare state proactively deepened its interventions by re-regulating and micromanaging the poor through workfare, criminalisation and labour market flexibility. Far from weakening, the state was seen to be robustly disciplining the poor by 'enforcing [flexible] work while residualizing welfare' (Peck, 2001b: 10). The combined roll-back and roll-out phases yielded a conspicuously *post-welfare* city (Fairbanks, 2009) characterised by entrepreneurial policies that simultaneously promoted the marketing of the city while denigrating and punishing those who did not fit in to the new vision (Brenner & Theodore, 2002; Peck, 2003;

Hackworth, 2007). The post-welfare city is currently marked by 'a period of intensely coordinated activity to dismantle the liberal welfare state in accordance with the new ideological and political imperatives of market liberalism' (Fairbanks, 2009: 17). According to the regulationist account, there has been a shift from government to governance, the Keynesian welfare city of collective consumption to the entrepreneurial post-welfare city, redistribution to apparent revanchism, and accommodation of the 'public city' to its displacement and replacement (MacLeod, 2011).

Nonetheless, I treat this all-encompassing narrative with a certain scepticism, underlining the incomplete and uneven realities of current neoliberalism and the post-welfare city, one that is dutifully recognised even by strong adherents to the regulationist approach (Peck et al, 2009). Scholars such as Larner (2003), McGuirk and Dowling (2009), and Hodkinson (2011) have argued that neoliberalism is not a self-evident totality but rather an assemblage of disparate, hybridised and inherently precarious arrangements that exist side by side with residual arrangements from previous settlements, thereby negating any sense of a clear break into post-welfarism.[2] Viewing post-welfarism as incomplete, uneven and emerging accords with May and Cloke (2014: 894), who by building on Williams et al (2012), ascertained that

> ... neoliberalism itself is best understood as a dynamic and complex process; a messy and precarious fabrication of forms and practices which always remains open to different kinds of contestation and resistance, and that researchers need to be careful not to assume that the locally contextualized practices of providing welfare ... will simply mirror the neoliberal environment in which those contexts are staged.

More radically, Barnett (2005) and Castree (2006) argued that neoliberalism is more than just incomplete and contingent (or 'actually existing') – it is also fundamentally incoherent, with no extralocal and hegemonic 'neoliberalism in general' out there to guide, if not balance out, the locally impure and contingent projects. And so neoliberalism becomes amorphous and hybrid at all scales. While I believe that there is somewhat more coherency to neoliberalism than this (via the commonality of market fundamentalism), I remain convinced of its intrinsic messiness and lack of direction, avoiding reification of a cyclopean neoliberal ideal-type, and insisting on phenomena that exist in response to but also beyond neoliberalism (Gibson-Graham, 2006; McGuirk & Dowling, 2009).

Just as there is no immaculate version of neoliberalism, there is also no clearcut break between the Keynesian welfare city and the neoliberal post-welfare city. Even proponents of a 'neoliberal city', such as Hackworth (2007: 175), acknowledged that 'neoliberal urbanism is highly segmented and far from complete. Public housing, social welfare, and other Keynesian artifacts still exist, and their destruction is neither inevitable nor complete.' Inevitably, the post-welfare city contains important residues from Keynesianism while simultaneously removing the taken-for-granted nature of welfare and the role of the state in its provision. Fairbanks (2009) emphasised how previous welfare settlements, including the Keynesian, served as the foundation for current voluntary-sector practices and geographies. However, these residues are poorly understood and their on-the-ground persistence rarely studied. Thus, my overriding focus on the 'resilience of the residuals', which follows in Chapter Two, counters the clear-break thesis implied in the term 'post-welfare'.

With these qualifiers in mind, neoliberalism as context actively threatens (but has yet to completely overwhelm) Keynesian artefacts through displacement and replacement. As Harvey (2012: 11) noted, 'a process of displacement and dispossession ... lies at the core of the urban process under capitalism'; and with reference to London, Campkin (2013: 166) argued that displacement 'involves the imposition of elite perspectives on what a "good" or "world class" city is, and its accompanying social structures, proper functions and aesthetic attributes'. We can see the rise of displacement as an ominous harbinger of the new urban century (for example, Sassen, 2014). In Fullilove's words (2004: 5):

> I venture to propose that displacement is the problem the twenty-first century must solve. Africans and aborigines, rural peasants and city dwellers have been shunted from one place to another as progress has demanded, 'Land here!' or 'People there!' In cutting the roots of so many people, we have destroyed language, culture, dietary traditions, and social bonds. We have lined the oceans with bones, and filled the garbage dumps with bricks.

The chronic – and some would say globalised – threat of neoliberalised displacement comes in many guises, but I will focus on gentrification-induced displacement, with more detail in the next subsection, Chapters

Three and Four, and wrapping up in Chapter Eleven. Hackworth's definition of gentrification (2002: 815) implicitly acknowledged the physical displacement inherent in the process: 'the production of space for progressively more affluent users', producing what Smith (1996: 39) called 'the class remake of the central urban landscape'. This broad understanding of gentrification therefore includes not just incumbent rehabilitation of existing stock, but also new-build redevelopment, entailing direct and indirect displacement respectively (Davidson & Lees, 2010).

Resilience as the response, resilience as the conceptual framework

Resilience is but one of many potential responses to the threat of neoliberalism, post-welfarism and their displacing logics – others can include resistance, reworking and disappearance (Hall & Lamont, 2013). At its most basic, resilience variously refers to 'the ability to recover and position elastically following a disturbance of some form' (Wrigley & Dolega 2011: 2345), the 'capacity of a system to absorb disturbance and reorganize while undergoing change to still retain essentially the same function, structure, identity, and feedbacks' (Walker et al, 2004: 1), and the 'ability to absorb change and disturbance and still maintain the same relationships that control a system's behavior' (Holling, 1973: 14). The commonalities are clear enough across these definitions: (1) a particular threat to a relatively stable system; (2) the capacity to bounce back to some degree of stability and previous identity after the shock; and (3), in bouncing back, perhaps showing some adaptability and capacity for innovation. Resilience shifts attention from risk and vulnerability to something more positive and prospective, on analysing the capacity of people (social resilience) and places (spatial resilience) to anticipate, persist with, adapt to and minimise the damage caused by change, risk and adversity. Cindi Katz (2004: 242) saw social resilience as differing from 'reworking' and 'resistance' (the latter being an overused and sometimes unhelpful term, especially for everyday processes that do not always involve spectacular displays of agency). Reworking involves altering the conditions of people's existence to enable more workable lives; resistance draws on and produces a critical conscience to confront and redress conditions of oppression and exploitation. For Katz (2004), resilience captures the 'autonomous initiative [and] recuperation', the 'getting by', protective care and mutual aid that enables survival in circumstances that do not allow changes to the causes that dictate survival.

My focus on resilience necessarily emphasises incrementalism and reformism (Fainstein, 2010) but, as I will further argue, these protective tendencies can still work against the (neoliberal) status quo and prop up the residual Keynesian arrangements that Castells (1983) saw as part of high Fordism. My focus on resilience is ultimately about its *process* and *production*, not its absence/presence – the 'how' rather than the 'whether', the interpretations of the process on the ground. Fairbanks argued persuasively (2009: 19) that the lineaments of the (uneven) post-welfare age behove us to study the 'how', and that 'such an orientation requires a suspension of the question, "what works"? ... with an investigation into the effective workings of social failure [or success]'. I want to explore the 'how' of this resilience: how it is secured, by whom and with what consequences, how it may differ comparatively, and what it may say about the incompleteness of neoliberalism and the unevenness of the post-welfare city. Finally, while I recognise that cities are naturally, if close to universally resilient (Vale & Campanella, 2005), this applies only to *entire* cities and not necessarily to specific urban spaces – many older urban forms have disappeared entirely, and others are under threat, such as the service hub, the subject of the next cornerstone.

The voluntary sector as the agent

I want to specifically apply notions of social and spatial resilience to the residual arrangement of 'service hubs' constituted of notable clusters of voluntary-sector organisations. The voluntary sector may be defined as a set of relationships dominated by voluntary action, and lying in tension among state, informal community and private market influences, but not reducible to their handmaidens (Brandsen et al, 2005; May & Cloke, 2014). Salamon and Anheier's definition (1997: 9) also followed this approach to foreground their own extensive, cross-national study of the voluntary sector:

> First they are *organised*, ie they possess some institutional reality. They are *private*, ie, institutionally separate from government. They are *non-profit-distributing*, ie not returning any profits generated to their owners or directors. They are *self-governing*, ie equipped to control their own activities. They are *voluntary*, at least in part, ie, they involve some meaningful degree of voluntary participation, either in the actual conduct of the agency's activities or in the management of its affairs.

So defined, the voluntary sector can cover a wide range of agents – including charities, faith-based organisations and not-for-profits – and activities, including direct service to vulnerable clients as well as advocating on their behalf, but also more general fundraising, research and so forth. I favour the voluntary sector as a bellwether of neoliberalism and post-welfarism, sensitive to impacts from gentrification-induced displacement and the deleterious financial impacts of welfare state retrenchment, both signature neoliberal tendencies. I do not see the voluntary sector as inherently (or exclusively) co-opted into the neoliberal 'shadow state' (Wolch, 1990), but nor do I see it as intrinsically positive or progressive as Castells (1983) did. Rather, I view it as somewhere in between, increasingly crucial in filling the gaps left behind by welfare state roll-back, providing a vehicle for social movements, citizenship and survival despite its notoriously asymmetrical, uncoordinated and uneven nature, best understood as a heterogeneous set of networks, sites and actors. So characterised, the voluntary sector can never hope to duplicate the Keynesian welfare state's near-universalist coverage, but asserts its role as a crucial substitute. Moreover, and building on work by Cloke et al (2010), I understand voluntary organisations as not just as sites of control or punitiveness, but *also* as potential and genuine sites of help, caring and sustenance for people who cannot be easily absorbed into the capitalist order, sometimes working *for*, *alongside* or providing an *alternative to* neoliberalism (and the welfare state more generally) in the city (DeVerteuil & Wilton, 2009). Thus, voluntary-sector organisations can also *enable* social resilience among their vulnerable clientele.

Service hubs are conspicuous concentrations of voluntary organisations, many of which emerged and prospered in the public domain of pre-Keynesian times (for example, the Salvation Army) but reached their apogee during the era of the Keynesian 'public city' in the 1970s (Dear, 1980), providing advantageous agglomeration effects for their clients, many of whom prize the maximised accessibility that a central location affords (Glaeser et al, 2000). Service hubs act as residual proxies for patterns of collective consumption established during the long 'public' period (Marquand, 2004) that spanned the 19th-century efforts at municipal socialism, voluntarism and early welfare, to the height of prosperity in post-war Keynesian times. Crucially, service hubs can be likened to a residual of the state (Martin & Pierce, 2013), constituting holdover spaces of social innovation, sanctuary and refuge, but also incubators for voluntarism and care/support. Given their pronounced centrality and high visibility, the survival of service hubs is always in question – several have disappeared entirely (for example, the Bowery in New York City, Main Stem in Chicago), and others are under increasing threat of displacement and dismantlement from gentrification. Beyond their obvious centrality and visibility, service hubs are also vulnerable due to their long-time stigmatisation, which produced an artificial rent gap that many are now keen to exploit in the name of profits, 'edginess' and 'creativity' (Sakizlioglu & Uitermark, 2014).

The inner city as the territorial focus

I want to privilege the 'how' of resilient service hubs under conditions of incomplete yet menacing neoliberalism within particular spaces of the city – the *inner city*. This ill-defined territory retains some usefulness when designating generally denser, older and more heterogeneous urban areas near the original core (Horvath, 2004). Hutton (2010: 303) provided the following definition, delineating a transitional zone adjacent to the dominant CBD/centre:

> incorporating 'industry' (manufacturing, craft production, warehousing and distribution) as well as older housing, comprising in many cities a mix of occupations and social classes, but with an emphasis on working-class residential communities and households, some of which had persisted in form, building types, and ethnicity since the early nineteenth century. The precise configuration of these inner city zones, within which both the ravages of restructuring in the latter decades of the twentieth century, and the reassertion of production since the early 1990s, took place, vary from place to place.

The idea of a fixed and delineable inner city is immediately challenged, however, by two sets of literatures. The first is the idea of postmodern and polycentric urbanism. Dear and Flusty (1998: 66) argued that there has been a radical break in urban structure, in which 'urbanization is occurring on a quasi-random field of opportunities … it is evident that the traditional, center-driven agglomeration economies that have guided urban development in the past no longer apply'. Once stripped of its outlandish neologisms, Dear and Flusty's spatial approach now appears somewhat prescient vis-à-vis urban form in the emerging urban century, at least for the more dynamic urban agglomerations.[3] In an acknowledgement of this 'LA School' approach, Roy (2009: 827) emphatically stated that 'the 21st century metropolis is a chameleon. It shifts shape and size; margins become centres; centres become frontiers ... the 21st century metropolis makes a fool of census jurisdictions, of the mappings of city and suburbs'. Under conditions of increasing metropolitan implosion, fragmentation and dispersion, it seems difficult to argue the case for a distinctive inner city. However, I can certainly argue for its existence as a *residual* of older, more monocentric, agglomeration-oriented development that characterised most cities in the Global North well in to the mid-20th century – even Los Angeles (Soja, 2000) – and in which the inner city was structured by the core's gravity. So the inner city is itself inertial when compared to emerging forms of 21st-century urbanism – the edge city, post-suburbia, gated community, splintering infrastructure and revitalised core – yet a critical residual in its own right that feeds off a lingering centrality. These residual forms tend to be blithely left out of accounts of cutting-edge urbanism that celebrate the newest reconfigurations of urban space to the detriment of persistent and crucial structures of bygone eras, the strong residues and legacies of agglomerative urban structures so deeply studied by early Marxist geographers (for example, Harvey, Soja, Scott, Storper).

The second challenge is the recent rise of relational urban geography, where one is cautioned against seeing any intra-urban zone as something discrete and bounded (Ward & McCann, 2010). While appreciative of the conceptual advances made by thinking beyond 'city-as-territory' over the past decade (Jacobs, 2012), and the sea change from 'city' territory to 'urban' relationality (Merrifield, 2013), my own spatial approach only partially takes up McCann and Ward's (2011) conceptualised relationship between fixity (territory) and flow (relational). My study is fixed to a singular territory (inner city) across multiple sites, and never explicitly engages with the actual flows among them, except at the scale of the national welfare state and voluntary sector regime. In this respect, I adhere to Clarke's (2012) admonition that territory and immobility must not be lost in the rush to relate cities and only see mobilities. But, by using global city theory and comparative methods, my spatial approach does implicitly embrace an understanding of urban space as '*both* open, internally heterogeneous, constituted through its place in myriad of connections and networks *and* as a territorially institutionalized object, the outcome of various "political" contestations and struggles' (Ward & McCann, 2011: 171). After all, the inner city frequently acts as a synecdoche of the global city itself, in all of its inward/immobile and outward/mobile connections.

Politically and socially, the inner city acts as a residual arena for collective consumption and Keynesian residuals, as well as tolerance of difference and perhaps even emancipation from the sterility of suburban life (Caulfield, 1994), but now increasingly as a transitional and contested 'frontier' space for roll-back and roll-out neoliberalism, workfarism and post-welfarism (Hackworth, 2007). He contended that 'the inner city – widely seen as a vestige of the Keynesian welfare state (Jessop 2002) – is an area of extreme transition. It has served as the focus of high-profile real estate investment, neoliberal policy experiments, and governance changes' (Hackworth, 2007, 13). Frontier space also implies a certain unruliness that invites state heavy-handedness and pacification measures (Smith, 1996; Blomley, 2003). The inner city has been a conspicuous laboratory and locus for policy currents and outcomes since at least the 1950s, a key scale for interventions ranging from massive urban renewal and collective consumption to efforts at mixed-use development and state-sponsored downtown regeneration (Wyly & Hammel, 2005). Currently, the inner city is seemingly dominated by two alternating logics of neoliberalism. On the one hand, the logic of roll-out neoliberalism sees the inner city through the lens of decline, dependency, depravity, crime and disorder, and has used these representations to punish and isolate the poor and marginalised (Wacquant, 2008). On the other hand, the neoliberal inner-city is increasingly seen to reflect the logics of revitalisation, gentrification and creativity, as a desirable place for re-investment and creativity (Florida, 2002; Slater, 2004). This new *zeitgeist* is captured by Butler (2007: 177), who argued that 'the inner city is no longer the pit of despair but – for a significant number – the catwalk of conspicuous consumption'. Many critical geographers have connected the two strands, notably Neil Smith (1996), who saw the rolling out of punitive measures as essential to 'taming' inner-city frontier space for subsequent gentrification, which invites the same sterility found in suburbs.

Crucially for the purposes of this book, the inner city remains home to a disproportionately large number (if not the majority) of voluntary-sector organisations, which seek, and greatly value, central locations to maximise accessibility to their clients and/or enhance their visibility. This enduring presence of service hubs has surprisingly been forgotten in the rush to understand new urban forms; as MacLeod (2011: 2651) contended, 'research on these ordinary spaces appears overshadowed by the downtown glitz and mega projects', forgotten spaces in the shadows of the globalising core (McNeill et al, 2005), prone to longstanding stigmatisation and rent gaps. I propose that the inner city conceivably breeds resilience, a result of the diversity and high concentration of organisations in close proximity (via the service hub). Inner-city space is therefore constitutive of the tension between displacement and resilience, rather than mere backdrop (Uitermark et al, 2012).

Comparison as the methodology

Methodologically and empirically, I wish to consider the previous cornerstones through a *comparative lens* among the inner cities of three global city-regions: Greater London, Los Angeles County and Metropolitan Sydney (Table 1.1). Within the larger literature on global urbanism (Brenner & Keil, 2006; McCann & Ward, 2011), Scott et al (2001: 11) defined global city-regions as 'essential spatial nodes of the global economy', encompassing not just the 'global city' – which is usually the highly visible yet quite small 'command and control' centre of the city-region – but also its constituent and proximate parts, providing explicit recognition of polycentricity.

The three global city-regions exhibit wider theoretical significance, essential touchstones for global city theory and formation, whether in terms of the clustering of global city industries (finance, advertising, law, accounting), polycentrism, bifurcated immigration patterns or the polarisation thesis (Sassen, 2001; Soja, 2010). Beyond their global city-region status, however, one may still wonder why London, Los

Table 1.1: Case study global city-regions

	Population, 2010/11	Area (km²)	Governance structure	Inner-city area units of analysis
Greater London	8.1 million (2011 census)	1,590	Greater London Authority (GLA) for regional issues; locally composed of the City of London and 32 Boroughs	Borough (Islington, Lambeth, Southwark, Tower Hamlets, Westminster)
Los Angeles County	9.8 million (2010 census)	10,507	County Board of Supervisors, 88 municipalities and unincorporated territories, 526 zip codes; part of Metropolitan Statistical Area of Los Angeles–Long Beach	Zip code (arranged into three areas: Downtown LA, Hollywood, Pico-Union)
Metropolitan (Greater) Sydney	4.4 million (2011 census)	12,367	43 Local Councils (Local Government Areas); no regional government	Census communities within the City of Sydney (arranged into two areas: Darlinghurst/Kings Cross, Surry Hills)

Angeles and Sydney are being compared, given that they share relatively few obvious commonalities.[4] In terms of built form, London is clearly a 19th-century city, while Los Angeles and Sydney are 20th-century creations. London and Sydney are the primary gateway cities for their respective national contexts, while Los Angeles is more secondary to New York City, albeit within a more competitive urban arena and performing gateway functions for the burgeoning Pacific Rim. Its sprawl and pervasive automobility contrasts sharply with New York City and other global cities, but certainly in line with the American model. Finally, the signature industries of London and Sydney are more finance-orientated when compared to Los Angeles. Yet some commonalities are also apparent, especially around their *polarised social orders and geographies*. A common challenge to all three global city-regions necessarily involves the management of substantial economic and social polarisation through collective consumption, the local welfare state settlement and, crucially, the voluntary sector (Keil, 1998). Polarisation places greater pressure upon the voluntary sector, responsibilities only hinted at in smaller cities but fully fledged in global city-regions. Polarisation and its implications for the social governance of global city-regions have been consistently downplayed in the wider literature, the process whereby 'new territorial forms are ... reproduced through everyday acts and struggles around consumption and social reproduction' (Jonas & Ward, 2007: 170).

But why the comparative approach in the first place? What work does comparison do? Empirically, I wanted to *learn* from these three global city-regions through describing the range of resilience both spatially and during a crucial period of (incomplete) neoliberal consolidation. I wanted to valorise ordinary agents (the voluntary sector) traditionally overlooked within hegemonic understandings of the neoliberal and punitive city *and* the global city, (1) generating ground-level results that could offer a window into the actualities of convergence and divergence of welfare state policies nationally and locally when compared to received wisdom, (2) analysing the multiscalar connections between the voluntary sector and the local and national welfare settlements that underpin it, and (3) applying the lessons of comparative urbanism to crossnational comparisons of the voluntary sector and to resilience. Here I am inspired by Nijman's (2007b) contention that all cities are unique, but that it is at least as interesting to compare unlike cities to find similarities than to compare very similar cities to find similarities (for example, comparing London with New York). In comparing London, Los Angeles and Sydney, I will apply several key methodological insights from the burgeoning literature on comparative urbanism. Notably, I am interested in using comparison as a strategy (McFarlane, 2010), in terms of providing a rare, street-level opportunity to compare Australian, British and American realities for the voluntary sector and its clientele, within a context of similarly restructuring (yet rarely converging) liberal welfare state regimes (Esping-Andersen, 1990; DeVerteuil, 2011b) and 'Anglo-American gentrification'.

Given the wide-ranging extent of the study, the level of detail is squarely at the meso-institutional scale, relying heavily on interviews with voluntary-sector organisations across ten inner-city areas in three global city-regions. Of course this kind of approach will lack the richness associated with in-depth, extended single case studies. Yet it also nimbly avoids the paralysis of particularism that pervades a certain post-structuralist/post-colonialist approach that, while providing a welcome rebuke to the fruitless search for so-called model (or paradigmatic) cities that invariably overemphasise Global North cities, sometimes muddles any sense of crosscutting regularities and learning from cities comparatively (Scott & Storper, forthcoming). Moreover, it is very much centred on the everyday resilience of marginal vehicles in thoroughly ordinary, if not parochial spaces usually overlooked in the global city-region literature. So my comparative approach seeks to fill in the blanks at the ground level, thickening our empirical descriptions and analyses, but also conceptually sharpening notions of resilience.

Overall approach of the book

I consider this book to be a work of *social geography*, embedded within and feeding off the four themes identified by Smith et al (2010): the emphasis on social relations and the spatial structures that underpin them, a preoccupation with the hard edge of inequality and the uneven experience of welfare, a drive to understand social justice, and a reputation for methodological eclecticism. Conversely, and at the risk of being cacophemistic, some of today's post-structuralism seems akin to 1970s progressive rock[5] – extravagant, virtuosic, opaque and obtuse, unmoored to a (material) world that is growing more unequal by the hour and thus lacking a critical edge (Heynen, 2006; Dennett, 2013). If this sounds similar to other critiques of what Smith (2005) deemed neo-critical geography, then I am guilty as charged. And yet, while my own approach is very much a mix of political economy, critical geography and humanism, I am nonetheless vigilant of overly deterministic, rigid, totalising and 'desktop' Marxist approaches, and of critical urban theory that presents pristine and clearcut representations of a messy, muddled reality. In other words, being critical of critical geography, but sympathetically rather than throwing it out entirely (see DeVerteuil, 2014), calling for a more *flexible critical geography* that can move beyond articles of faith found, for instance, in the deep suspicion to resilience (Chapter Two) and dystopian representations of current urban social policy (Chapter Three). So despite 'resilience' being prominently featured in the title – which perhaps implies passivity, a property rather than action – this book *is* a work of critical geography, understood as working against the status quo and of having both revelatory impulses to show injustice, as well as a radical, revolutionary side, 'not necessarily of the violent variant, but in its most basic sense of turning power around, however and whenever it corrodes the bonds of justice and humanity' (Castree et al, 2010: 3). What the book shows is that resilience can become a verb, not just a property: *producing resilience*, a site of struggle and learning that favours the active over the passive.

If my keynote contribution is to develop a more critical consideration of resilience, then I need to be clear about what constitutes critical geography at the urban scale, following Brenner et al (2009: 179):

> In the most general terms, critical approaches to urban studies are concerned: (a) to analyse the systemic, yet historically specific, intersections between capitalism and urbanisation processes; (b) to examine the changing balance of social forces, power relations, sociospatial inequalities and political-institutional arrangements that shape, and are in turn shaped by, the evolution of capitalist urbanisation; (c) to expose the marginalisations, exclusions and injustices (whether of class, ethnicity, 'race', gender, sexuality, nationality or otherwise) that are inscribed and naturalised within existing urban configurations; (d) to decipher the contradictions, crisis tendencies and lines of potential or actual conflict within contemporary cities, and on this basis, (e) to demarcate and to politicise the strategically essential possibilities for more progressive, socially just, emancipatory and sustainable formations of urban life.

I leave section (a) in the good hands of the many theorists who have examined capitalism and urbanisation (for example, Harvey, Lefebvre, Smith). Section (b) is very much the topic of the book, since I am attempting to critically insert the voluntary sector into the interstices of a highly uneven, post-welfare city. Section (c) is addressed through my revelations on class and the city (Mohan, 2000), of revealing a more nuanced viewpoint on the regulation of vulnerable populations (defined as surplus populations in Chapter Three), wary of certain myopias of the critical approach. Section (d) is unavoidable, given the post–2008 crisis and austerity, providing an acute version of neoliberalism (see Chapter Twelve) that contrasts with its chronic, everyday tendencies. Finally, section (e) is ultimately about revealing the world in order to identify the regressive and the progressive, and use the latter to transform the world. This is a prickly topic given the focus on resilience, which is by nature defensive and protective, and perhaps in the service of oppressive structures. Like Fainstein (2010: 5), I approached resilience as a way to keep 'to what appears feasible within the present context of capitalist urbanization in wealthy, formally democratic, Western countries'. Inevitably, this approach will lack immediate and far-reaching transformative potential, but in Chapter Twelve I recast service hubs as commons, springboards for potential transformation.

At least up until Chapter Twelve, then, mine is more a bare-bones, slogging, everyday and survival-mode approach to critical geography (Gilbert, 2001; Heynen, 2006; Reese, 2011), more rearguard action to hold one's ground in what is a bitter war of attrition over urban space, rather than a focus on spectacular calls for right to the (rebellious) city (see Harvey, 2012: 115–17 for a litany of current urban revolts), of what Shantz (2013: 13) called 'the movement as a scream, as an exhilarating act of hurling ourselves against the world of capital'. It is also patient, reflective, even reparative: resilience can be about *holding on* to previously hard-won gains, yet using them (through the spatial manifestation of the service hub) as the basis for challenging the status quo and *holding out* for incremental change. The focus on survival, whether of service hubs or of the clients that depend on them, aligns with what Heynen (2006: 920) called the 'really radical geography', a 'back to basics' approach about 'recognizing that life depends on meeting material basic needs like food, water, shelter, etc.'. One cannot transform the world without first securing – and ultimately anchoring, defending and protecting – the 'material foundations necessary for human survival' (Heynen 2006: 921). I can go back to Bunge (1971) as an early example of this kind of 'really radical geography', in its emphasis on hard-won survival in a declining Detroit. But rather than connect survival to 'right to the city' (Mitchell & Heynen, 2009), I join it to resilience. I contend that, in the act of enabling survival, resilience provides a prerequisite and precondition for eventual transformation. Feminist scholars on social reproduction have been keenly aware of this for two decades, both at the household and movement level (for example, Gilbert, 1998; Katz, 2001; Staeheli, 2012), but it is time that other critical geographers take more heed. So in both Chapters Two and especially Twelve, I will address how resilience can be against the neoliberal status quo, at least in an incremental way.

This book is very much crosscut by the desire to interrogate and interpret the overlooked and the residual. Accordingly, I also strive to employ and re-deploy theories both forward looking *and* backward looking, which necessarily stretches our sometimes short attention spans that underline the trendy-now. In particular, many concerns of this book – particularly the spatial resilience of residual service hubs – extend and revive welfare geography and public facility location theory, whose legacies remain woefully forgotten (DeVerteuil, 2000). Since the 1980s, the concept of welfare geography has been theoretically superseded by more Marxian, and then post-structuralist, tendencies in urban analysis that tend to over-valorise distracting novelties, and over-valorise neoliberalism's purported dominance (Hackworth, 2007). Public facility location theory very much combined the normative and the applied sides of social geography, concerning itself with the question of where best to locate public facilities given equity and efficiency constraints, involving issues of distance, accessibility and locational conflict. These areas of study will be revisited throughout the book, but especially in Chapters Three and Eleven. In the tradition of *Landscapes of Despair* (Dear & Wolch, 1987), I elaborate on concerns that crosscut the urban, the social and health, including the ongoing evolution of the welfare state, the resilience of service hubs that treat service-dependent populations, the 'voluntary turn' (Skinner & Power, 2011), and the role of accessibility and centrality of help in the uneven post-welfare (but also polycentric) city.

Organisation

The main aim of the book is to comparatively investigate and interpret this 'how' of resilient service hubs in the inner city through the specific lens of the voluntary sector and within a context of consolidating yet very much incomplete neoliberalism. The remainder of Part One will detail the cornerstones of the concept (resilience), agent (the voluntary sector) and method (comparison). In Chapter Two, I will develop my (critical) version of resilience through seven propositions, aiming to apply it to service hubs. In Chapter Three, I will outline the building block of the service hub – the voluntary sector – and its dualistic relationship with neoliberalism. In Chapter Four, I will sketch my methodological approach, including the sampling frame, the operationalisation of resilience, and comparative methods. Part Two presents the empirical and case study material that spans the three global-city regions. In Chapter Five, I will politically contextualise London, Los Angeles and Sydney – their respective extralocal and local welfare and voluntary-sector settlements – before turning to a crosscutting place-typology of the ten inner cities: established gentrified, mixed, pioneer gentrified and immigrant enclave. This typology introduces an added layer of nuance to the comparison, and will structure the ensuing empirical sections. In Chapters Six to Nine, each place-type will be examined in greater detail using two case studies each, focusing on the relationships among gentrification, displacement, resilience and the overall nature of the service hub. Chapter Six will focus on Westminster (London) and Surry Hills (Sydney). Chapter Seven will focus on Southwark (London) and Darlinghurst/Kings Cross (Sydney). Chapter Eight will focus on Downtown and Hollywood, both in Los Angeles. Chapter Nine will focus on the immigrant enclaves of Tower Hamlets (London) and Pico-Union (Los Angeles). Finally, in Chapter Ten, I will compare patterns of resilience using a tripartite categorisation of strategies (private, voluntary sector and political) across the four place-types and the three global-city regions. Part Three will return to the concept of resilience, but also suggest avenues that transcend some of its limitations, particularly how it alleviates but does not necessarily solve seemingly intractable inequalities. In Chapter Eleven, I will use my results to sift through the seven proposals outlined in Chapter Two, and emerging with the concept of the 'critical resilience of the residuals'. In Chapter Twelve I recast resilience by adopting a more forward-looking perspective, proposing that service hubs can act as 'commons' that preserve hard-won gains but also generate incremental, transformative potential.

Notes

[1]   The welfare state is usually defined from a broad perspective that sees all state provision to the population for their (indispensable) social reproduction as 'welfare' (Katz, 2001). Yet there is also a narrow approach that focuses on the specific income assistance, transfers and social services that usually accrue to the least well-off.

[2]   Most leading accounts of neoliberalism are very much Anglo-American, from places like the US, UK and Canada where it is rampant, but insufficiently interrogating the more incomplete versions found in Quebec, France, Scandinavia and so forth.

[3]   This being said, there are still a remarkable number of Global North cities that feature dominant centres, if not downright monocentric – think of Calgary and Montreal, Pittsburgh and Portland, Chicago and New York City, and all the capital cities of Australia.

[4]   Relatively few obvious commonalities, but certainly well linked: London Heathrow was the busiest international destination for flights out of LAX in 2013, with Sydney

third; for Sydney, LAX was fourth busiest in 2013; and for London Heathrow, LAX was seventh busiest. Given that no direct flights are possible between London Heathrow and Sydney, the numbers are rather small and capture only one-stop flights. Data are from the Airport International Council.

[5] With the exception of course of Rush. Thank you, Professor, for making my adolescence more bearable.

TWO

Resilience and residualism

In this chapter I develop a parsimonious concept of social and spatial resilience that is directly applicable to residual arrangements, which I take to be service hubs, while also opening up some critical intent for the term. It is this careful and singular focus on resilience that builds upon, but also sets my work apart from, others who have deployed resilience from a critical (yet more peripheral) perspective (for example, Katz, 2004; Cloke et al, 2010; May & Cloke, 2014). Before proceeding to working definitions of social and spatial resilience, I should make clear the obvious: that resilience has become an academic and political buzzword, and its popularity has soared in the past ten years, moving from the natural sciences to the social sciences with apparent (yet worrying) ease (Brown, 2014). Analysis of the Web of Science shows a dramatic rise of the use of resilience since 2000 (Brown, 2014). A search with Google Scholar revealed more than 991,000 results (as of December 2013), with more than 60,000 hits in 2013 alone. Raco and Street (2012) argued that resilience is overtaking 'sustainability' as the *mot du jour*, more suitable to the short-term ability to cope with what could be very long-term trends that are impossible to fully predict, comprehend or easily change. Resilience has also begun to leach in to the popular imagination with atheoretical coffee table and pop psychology books such as *Resilience: Why things bounce back* (Zolli & Healy, 2013) and *Resilience: How to cope when everything around you keeps changing* (Webb, 2013), respectively, to say nothing about the rash of academic journals: *Resilience: A Journal of the Environmental Humanities, Ecology and Society*; *Resilience: International Policies, Practices and Discourses*; *Resilience: Interdisciplinary Perspectives on Science and Humanitarianism*; and *Society and Natural Resources*. Perhaps because of its haphazard proliferation, maddening suppleness, conceptual patchiness and sprawling approach, resilience has attracted suspicion that it lacks operational clarity and unity, problematically transfers ecological concepts into societal contexts while under-theorising the social dimensions, underplays endogenous dynamics, and presents considerable methodological hurdles, thus edging close to 'misused concept' and 'chaotic concept' territory (Walker et al, 2006; Martin, 2012; Raco & Street, 2012; Ward, 2012; Brown, 2014). There are more conservative, if sinister, uses of resilience as well: as a reactionary way to sustain an inequitable *status quo ante* (for example, imposing the 'business-as-usual' that props up the existing yet highly inequitable power structure), as we are witnessing in the consolidating period since the 2008 global recession with 'zombie neoliberalism' (Peck, 2011); casting off actually 'needy' people and regions using the pretence that they are ostensibly resilient (or not); and a failure to recognise the socially contingent nature of resilience – that is, who is resilience for, and to what ends? Suffice it to say that resilience remains a contested and controversial term (Klein et al, 2003; MacKinnon & Derickson, 2013; Staeheli, 2013; Brown, 2014).

Rather than seeing these critiques and confusions as grounds for dismissing the concept *tout court*, I see it as a challenge and opportunity to bring some much needed clarity to the concept, and to take up the urgent task of critically appraising and applying resilience. In particular, the field of resilience in urban social geography and critical geography is still very much wide open, a tantalising opportunity for a certain amount of agenda setting. So my response is to retain the concept and proceed to interrogate, enable, clarify, claim and propose – as authors have done in their respective fields, such as Vale and Campanella (2005) in urban planning, Martin (2012) in economic geography, and Hall and Lamont (2013) in sociology. If, as some authors have contended (Brown, 2014), resilience is powerful, popular and 'here to stay', especially in policy and practice, then we must acknowledge that the concept itself may prove resilient for the time being. Building on literature in ecology (Holling, 1973; Klein et al, 2004; Walker et al, 2004; Eakin & Luers, 2006), economic geography (Wrigley & Dolega, 2011; Martin, 2012; Bristow & Healy, 2014), social geography (Adger, 2000; Katz, 2004; MacKinnon & Derickson, 2013), and planning (Raco & Street, 2012), I carve a singular and critically informed path through what are very malleable understandings of the term. The purpose of this chapter is therefore not to provide a panoptic overview of resilience across its tentacular disciplinary and conceptual threads; rather, it is a selective building-up and reconceptualisation that suggests uses for resilience across urban social geography and critical geography (Cole & Nightingale, 2011).

I conceptualise resilience as both social and spatial. For *social resilience*, I rely primarily on Katz's (2004: 242) definition, which she identified as one of many possible responses to the eroding effects of uneven, globalised capitalism: the 'autonomous initiative [and] recuperation', the 'getting by', care and mutual aid that enables survival in circumstances that do not allow changes to the causes that dictate survival. In instances where the overthrow or transformation of oppressive systems is not possible, or even desirable, social resilience emerges as defensive acts that can in themselves be both a struggle and a triumph (Katz, 2004). This definition extended the more descriptive, ecological and influential approach taken by Adger (2000: 347), in which resilience was 'the ability of groups or communities to cope with external stresses and disturbances as a result of social, political, and environmental change'. Social resilience imparts a sense of moving beyond the individual to the collective, from independence to interdependence (McDowell, 2004; Vale & Campanella, 2005; Eakin & Luers, 2006; Wilson 2012). This underlines the importance of social, institutional and political structures that may bolster resilience particularly and well-being more generally; conversely, individual resilience and its study is more the domain of psychology (Hing, 2013) and certainly not the focus of this book, despite the overarching influence of neoliberalism to treat everything individualistically (McDowell, 2004; Jenson & Levi, 2013).

For *spatial resilience*, I borrow from economic and urban geography, drawing on the cases of the persistence of retail clusters (Wrigley & Dolega 2011; Martin 2012) and the resilience of voluntary-sector organisations under pressure from gentrification-induced displacement (Newman & Wyly, 2006; DeVerteuil, 2012). Both informed the process of 'staying put' in the face of adversity and external pressure, whether global recessions or the displacing tendencies of an incomplete neoliberalism. Hartman (1984) elaborated on 'staying put' as voluntary immobility, of standing one's ground in the face of displacement to safeguard previous gains and preserve roots. This 'staying put' equals spatial resilience, but it is more than mere persistence in situ – as we shall see, resilient spatial arrangements increasingly show evidence of adaptability in the aftermath of disturbances, so some malleability is required of them, otherwise they will be too brittle to survive.

From these initial definitions of social and spatial resilience, I now wish to develop seven propositions around this complex and vexed term. Each claim builds upon the last, and as a whole constitutes the hallmark of my own critical approach (the 'critical resilience of the residuals'), to be revisited and reappraised in Chapter Eleven through the empirical results. With each claim, I nudge resilience closer to key concerns in urban social geography, as well as a more critical yet perhaps not entirely transformative approach, and away from more ecological, rigid and apolitical understandings found in works such as *The resilient city* (Vale & Campanella, 2005). Crucially, my focus on the 'how' of resilience rather than the 'whether' – in other words, the *production* of resilience, of how it is as much a process as a condition, property and outcome – will be taken up in the third proposition.

Resilience requires a threat (acute or chronic)

Resilience as an optic cannot exist without a potentially destabilising threat, shock or crisis – all definitions were clear on this point, and the rise of resilience as a concept may reflect the sense of increased risk, permeability and uncertainty of a consolidating yet incomplete neoliberalism. Threats are usually seen as exogenous to the system under study, external disturbances: these range from the 2008–10 recession (Wrigley & Dolega, 2011; Martin, 2012) to neoliberalisation (Hall & Lamont, 2013) to 'wounded cities' reeling from externally imposed violence and trauma (Vale & Campanella, 2005; Till, 2012). For the empirical material that follows in Chapters Five to Ten, I will consider what Wilson (2012: 213) called the 'post-rupture' period, that is after the first encounter with the threat. However, neoliberalism is not strictly a one-off, nor is it a natural disaster. As such, the applicability of the literature on resilience in the face of acute hazards and disasters (for example, Vale & Campanella, 2005; Wilson, 2013) is limited for my purposes. Rather, neoliberalism is a recurring, chronic, medium-intensity threat to community and collective well-being, and itself occasionally suffering from severe and immediate crises. And so the threat of neoliberalism takes on a dual form, representing both a chronic and an acute one. On the chronic, everyday side, neoliberalism is a big and slow-moving erosion of former values and spatial arrangements (Hall & Lamont, 2013). Chapters Three and Five will focus on neoliberalism as chronic threat, particularly in terms of the displacement and dismantlement of previous Keynesian arrangements through gentrification. However, the reader will need to wait until Chapter Twelve to consider neoliberalism as more of an acute threat, in the form of the post-2008 global recession and the emergence of 'austerity urbanism' (Peck, 2012). By its displacing and corroding nature, neoliberalism increases the need for resilience and therefore the need to study it.

While the focus of this book is the 'how' of resilience and its overall efficacy, there are instances when the threat effectively exceeds the production, provoking a radical break, deformation or collapse – Martin's (2012) negative-leaning hysteresis. According to Raco and Street (2012: 1067), 'resilient systems are defined in contrast to vulnerable systems where, in the wake of exposure to external stresses and shocks, places and/or systems suffer irreparable and irreversible damage'. This damage relates to what Walker et al (2004: 3) called exceeding the 'latitude', 'the maximum amount a system can be changed before losing its ability to recover (before crossing a threshold which, if breached, makes recovery difficult or impossible)'. A classic case of vulnerability may be illustrated by Castells' 'dependent city' thesis (1983: 211) whereby squatter settlements in Latin American cities were completely at the mercy of the local political structure, and therefore more vulnerable than resilient:

> Without the state's tolerance, or without some effective political support, they would not even have the right to their physical presence in the city. Their territoriality, as an exception to the formal functioning of the economy and of the legal institutions, is by itself, a patronising relationship. Only their reliance on the state's permissiveness entitles the squatters to the spatial basis of their daily existence.

A more recent example was New Orleans in the wake of Hurricane Katrina in 2005, where decades of governmental neglect, combined with a highly vulnerable environmental and social context, created weak resilience and subsequent rupture. Another example was highlighted by Klinenberg (2002) in the case of the deaths resulting from the 1995 Chicago Heat Wave, which he took as a sign of social breakdown across communities, neighbourhoods, networks, governmental agencies and the media. Further, Till's concept of 'wounded cities' (2012) suggested an exceeding of resilience thresholds. In all of these examples, resilience is never guaranteed, but what is guaranteed is the never-ending need for adaptation alongside persistence and endurance. It is these ideas that I explore in the next proposition.

Resilience can be adaptive, and is more than just 'bouncing back' or persisting

Second, I see resilience as potentially more than just bouncing back to a similar or original position before the threat. Resilience should impart a sense of adaptive capacity, a pro-activity and potential for learning – it is produced and earned rather than being an inherent property. Without this elasticity, resilience becomes too brittle to be useful to systems, more a case of passive persistence and inertia. To Folke (2006: 259), resilience was 'about the opportunities that disturbance opens up in terms of recombination of evolved structures and processes, renewal of the system and emergence of new trajectories'. This links to Klein et al's (2004) concept of 'adaptive capacity' and Martin's (2012: 5) idea of 'adaptive resilience': the 'ability of a system to undergo anticipatory or reactionary reorganisation of form and/or function so as to minimize impact of a destabilizing shock'. Inherent in the adaptive approach to resilience is self-organisation, anticipation and the ability to reconfigure on the fly. To adopt such a position also anticipates my third proposition – that shocks can be acute Schumpeterian and chronically recurring, and that resilience is evolutionary and path-dependent, a process rather than a static endpoint (Wrigley & Dolega, 2011; Martin 2012; Bristow & Healy, 2014).

This plasticity and elasticity very much *rejects* the older (and more ecological) school of thought on resilience that emphasised steady-state and equilibrium properties of the system (for example, Klein et al, 2004; Vale & Campanella, 2005). Conversely, I embrace the idea that resilience is more adaptive and dynamic, and dare I say, inherently creative. As Raco and Street (2012: 1069) explained, 'rather than seeing resilience as a process of bouncing back, a more radical deployment would, in line with broader shifts in environmental thinking, view it as a dynamic process in which change and constant reinvention provide the grounds for fundamental ... reform'. And as Klein et al (2004: 42) contended in the instance of natural hazards and cities, 'going back to the original state is undesirable, as it would leave the city just as vulnerable to the next disaster'. Hurricane Katrina and its aftermath certainly spoke to this vulnerability.

I therefore do not deploy the concept of persistent or inertial resilience, yet I am well aware that it is commonly used and understood as such. Persistence and inertia have been independently theorised by anthropologists such as Alan Smart (2001: 32), who developed five reasons for persistence in the urban governance of illegal built forms, highlighting the spatial trajectory of squatter settlements in Hong Kong:

> Market persistence occurs because continued demand for illegal goods and services creates profit opportunities. Ambiguous persistence results from the existence of informal social legitimacy. Managed persistence refers to cases where the government allows an illegal activity to continue in order to reap certain benefits. Rebellious persistence is supported by internal political actors who engage in or protect illegality to support their rebellion. When political actors external to the nation-state support illegal activities in order to undermine state control, subversive persistence pertains.

All of these permutations of persistence involved some pro-activity, but were more the results of non-activity and tolerated inertia – Smart

(2001: 41) even developed a potential sixth reason, under the rubric 'inertial persistence' that results from bureaucratic torpor and benign neglect. This was again explored by Castells (1983) with regard to squatter settlements in Latin America. Fairbanks (2009) applied managed persistence to explain how the Kensington neighbourhood in North Philadelphia enabled a persistent yet unlicensed and unregulated, and largely failure-prone, recovery house movement for addicts and alcoholics.

So while persistence and active resilience overlap and underpin each other, an overlap first identified by Holling (1973) in his approach to resilience as the ability to absorb change and yet persist (if not return to equilibrium), resilience can be *more* than just persistence. Persistence and especially inertia imply endurance, toleration and intactness, but crucially a lack of forethought, strategy and focus, and are usually presented as unfortunate. For me, resilience is not passive. It must be activated and assembled at all times, its production can never be taken for granted: 'resilience is the product of much more creative processes in which people assemble a variety of tools, including collective resources and new images of themselves, to sustain their well-being in the face of social change' (Hall & Lamont, 2013: 14). It is this emphasis on adaptation that makes resilience worthy of study, even though resilience itself tends to be slow moving and incremental, rather than radically transformative. This is a point that will be raised again in the sixth proposition, and one that necessarily divides an incremental, critical geography from a more radically transformational and utopian one. For the meantime, resilience is harder and more complex than it looks: it is a production and process requiring agency and activity rather than passivity and inertia. It is to this production and process of resilience that the next proposition attends to.

Resilience is a process, not an endpoint: the production of resilience

Third, and following up on the second proposal, I will be focusing on the intricacies of the *process* of producing resilience rather than on its presence or absence – I assume presence, but want to know and interpret the mechanics of persistence, and avoid the tautological thinking that something is resilient because it is resilient. Ultimately, my focus is on resilience as adaptive capacity, rather than seeing resilience as an endpoint or a stable condition, or even a desired state of affairs. Resilience is more defensive and protective than necessarily transformative, but the very act of defending and protecting is complicated and fraught, and never guaranteed. The emphasis is also more on proactive rather than reactive resilience, one that 'accepts the inevitability of change and tries to create a system that is capable of adapting to new conditions and imperatives' (Klein et al, 2004: 39).

Resilience is recursive, shapes and is shaped by social, political and economic determinants, and remains provisional – it must always be refreshed and recommitted (Martin, 2012). Methodologically, the process of resilience can be approached retrospectively, akin to a social autopsy approach (Klinenberg, 2002), a point that will be expanded upon in Chapter Four. Klinenberg outlined a retrospective approach that attempted to make sense of, in his case, the social conditions that produced more than 700 deaths during the 1995 Chicago heatwave – a clear case of vulnerability rather than resilience in those neighbourhoods that experienced the majority of the deaths, and the opposite in those that did not. So, rather than spotlight the meteorological conditions, Klinenberg focused *post-mortem* on the social factors that 'made it possible for hundreds of Chicago residents – most of them old, alone and impoverished – to die during the one-week heat spell' (2002: 18). Klinenberg explained why certain neighbourhoods amplified the negative effects of the heatwave, while others did not. The geography of death concentrated in just a few neighbourhoods, mostly west and south of the Loop. Most – but not all – were poor, with high proportions of people of colour, crime and (isolated) elderly people. The fact that not all poor neighbourhoods suffered from high death rates, however, prompted the author to use a small-scale, place-based social ecology study of two matched and equally impoverished neighbourhoods on Chicago's West Side: North and South Lawndale. Here, Klinenberg revealed a wide disparity in death rates, with the abandoned, violent, disorganised and African-American North Lawndale neighbourhood suffering much higher rates than the equally poor yet vibrant and Latino South Lawndale, with its active street and social life, all of which ensured more protection for the elderly. The mirror image – that of resilience – was explained (but not explicitly named) not just in terms of greater sociality in South Lawndale, but also in the protective layers of wealth, safe public spaces and low crime rates found in the northern parts of Chicago. Klinenberg's analysis further combined the chronic and the acute – the chronic inequalities in Chicago that created conditions of vulnerability and resilience prior to the heatwave, and then the acute event of the heatwave itself. His case studies implied that the neighbourhood level, however defined, can transfer and enable resilience to its inhabitants – a topic approached in the next proposition.

Resilience can be enabled, shared and transferred

Fourth, since resilience is produced both individually but also collectively, it can be *enabled and transferred* to and from individuals and collectives, through material support, sustenance and care, resulting in distinct patterns of survival. I emphasise the collective nature of resilience and the structures that enable it, and therefore how resilience is transferred and enabled from social structures to the individual. This raises the possibility that individual and collective resilience are simultaneously exogenous – coming from external sources, such as the voluntary sector and government (Klinenberg, 2002; Wilson, 2013). In a piece in *Political Geography* with Robert Wilton (DeVerteuil and Wilton, 2009), as well as my own work on immigrant survival (DeVerteuil, 2011b, 2011c), exogenously sourced resilience can make a crucial difference in terms of the survival of vulnerable groups.

In particular, giving care and providing sustenance are essentially a transfer of resilience, albeit in a protective rather than immediately transformative way. As Lawson (2009: 210) asserted:

> care ethics assert the absolute centrality of care to our human lives: we are all in need of care and of emotional connection to others. We all receive care, and throughout our lives, many of us will also give care. In short, care is society's work in the sense that care is absolutely central to our individual and collective survival.

Although the concept of care will be revisited in Chapter Three through the institutional platform of the voluntary sector, it is important to underline that it remains under-researched 'within debates about the marketplace, the spaces of the state, and the social contract' (Till, 2012: 8), but that its study could lead us towards a 'more humane human geography' (Ward, 2012: 20).

Goldstein (2011) argued that resilience can be a collaborative enterprise that involves society-wide and society-spanning institutions. Using Quebec as an example, Bouchard (2013) chronicled how a social resilience can be enabled by a strong safety net and institutional supports, including unions, community organisations and the voluntary sector. Moreover, Quebec has managed to insulate itself from – and resist the worst effects of – a seemingly pervasive neoliberalism sweeping North America, instituting a progressive sense of resilience. This state of affairs seized 'on the occasion to respond creatively to the challenge and to reinvent oneself through major innovations and progressive changes – in other words, to thrive in adversity and, in the process, "do better than expected" (2013: 267). Barnes and Hall (2013) identified key vehicles of social resilience within the structure of social relations, including social capital and connectedness, as well as collective action through democratic governance and trades unionism. In Chapter Three and beyond, I will speak to how the process of institutionalised, collective resilience is enabled to individuals through the platform of the voluntary sector. Finally, and given the focus of the book, I can argue that urban space in general – and inner-city space in particular – has a special role in transferring and sharing resilience, through hallmarks such as density, concentration, proximity, solidarity, collectivism, irreplaceability and motivation to preserve previous gains. This is threatened by chronic neoliberalism and gentrification that reject solidarity and collectivism, promoting instead individualism and suburban-like drive for privacy and privatisation (Deener, 2012) or weakly developed allusions to social capital (for example, the 'Big Society' in the UK).

'Everyday' resilience is a potential alternative to spectacular ' resistance' or 'reworking'

Fifth, using resilience can provide an alternative to the profligate application of resistance. If resilience is only now gaining momentum, then resistance has been well entrenched within critical social science for decades, a recurring feature of critical approaches to inequality, transgression and transformation (Sharp et al, 2000). Yet the frequently oblivious use of the term within critical geography remains problematic – as Katz (2004: 240) pleaded, there is need to unpack not 'only categories of people's response to capitalism's uneven developments, but the category of "resistance" as well'. She saw resistance as drawing upon and producing a critical consciousness to confront and redress conditions of oppression and exploitation. Associated to this was reworking, which involves altering the conditions of people's existence to enable more workable lives. Sharp et al (2000: 3) saw domination and resistance as integrally entangled; resistance is the power 'which attempts to set up situations, groupings and actions which resist the impositions of dominating power'. To Katz, Sharp and others (for example, Cresswell, 1996), not every or transgressive act equates resistance. Projecting resistance on to every defiant act, no matter how inconsequential and trivial, only clouds important issues of what can be changed and what cannot be changed, at least in the short term, and masks instances of resilience itself.

These insights build on previous work (DeVerteuil et al, 2009a; 2009b) in which resistance, especially the spectacular kind, was not always appropriate or useful in terms of why residual phenomena prove resilient. There have been tendencies in research on homeless people, for instance, to celebrate resistance, and the detection 'in all kinds of activities [of] the expression of a resistant spirit refusing to knuckle under the yoke of domination' (Sharp et al, 2000: 11). This approach ignores that much so-called resistant behaviour among the homeless is at best adaptive, resilient and transgressive, rather than representing an overturning of the social order (Cresswell, 1996). More broadly, critical geographers have been especially interested in spectacular instances of collective resistance and rebelliousness – whether the Arab Spring or mass protests among homeless people – but again this is too narrow and too rare to capture the mundane and adaptive resilience and 'everydayness' inherent in how residual phenomena stay put in urban space. Resilience downplays the spectacular, and elevates the mundane and more optimistic 'weak theory' (Hodkinson, 2010) as a way to compensate and counterbalance all of the hubbub around the big, the vocal, the cries and demands heard in public spaces (Harvey, 2012). Resilience must therefore be seen as a social and spatial foundation, an anchor for future resistance and reworking, not always a replacement but a necessary underpinning and precursor. This point will be refined in Chapter Twelve, when I supplement resilience with the concept of the 'commons'. The need to more deeply consider this vexed relationship between resilience and critical geography animates the next subsection.

Resilience can be critical, but perhaps not transformative

Sixth, and anticipated by some of the comments in the fifth proposition, many radical social scientists will see resilience as irretrievable – a 'rascal and a chaotic concept if ever there was one' (Ward, 2012: 20). In this viewpoint, and by its very definition, to be an apostle of resilience is to have foresworn transformative action and a critical mindset. Resilience may well be adaptive and persistent, a process without endpoint, but it cannot overthrow the current (inequitable) social order. Rather, and from this perspective, resilience can *only* be understood as reactionary, in at least three ways: perpetuating and reinforcing the neoliberal status quo; lacking any transformative promise for a better urban world; and, in an age of austerity, providing further pretence to abandon and de-fund residual, Keynesian arrangements (see Hall & Lamont, 2013; MacKinnon & Derickson, 2013; Slater, 2014b).

The most sustained critiques thus far have come from MacKinnon and Derickson (2013), who engaged in a systematic theoretical and political critique of place-based resilience from a radical geographical perspective. They focused on how the concept derives from ecology, which then becomes naturalistic and apolitical when applied to the social sphere: 'this apolitical ecology not only privileges established social structures, which are often shaped by unequal power relations and injustice, but also closes off wider questions of progressive social change which require interference with, and transformation of, established systems' (2013: 254). Crucially, the authors identified resilience as a neoliberal strategy, since by definition resilience necessarily props up whatever the current, hegemonic 'system' is. Resilience becomes part of neoliberal urban governance strategy, in which 'the vacuous yet ubiquitous notion that communities ought to be 'resilient' can be seen as particularly troubling in the context of austerity and reinforced neoliberalism' (2013: 262). Resilience becomes depoliticised, ignoring the 'powerful interests to protect against such a dynamic or adaptive strategy' (Brown, 2014: 109). The authors worried that resilience constituted a top-down process, rather than a grassroots one, which placed an unfair onus on communities. Finally, they identified capitalism as the scale that shapes resilience but also creates most of the disruption. In place of resilience, which is 'ill suited to the animation of more progressive and just social relations' (MacKinnon and Derickson 2013: 263), the authors propose 'resourcefulness', which more fully captures alternative and transformative visions of a better set of social relations.

So why bother with the term resilience if it can never escape its association with current power structures, particularly neoliberalism? Why not take on potentially more progressive terms like 'resourcefulness' (MacKinnon & Derickson, 2013)? My response is twofold. First, there is great utility in reclaiming a critical approach (see Chapter One) to resilience within urban social geography. Resilience is frequently assumed but neglected as a crucial stage in survival, the foundation for future transformation but in and of itself rarely explained or interpreted. The very prominence and popularity of resilience makes this task all the more important; it is too early to give up just yet on the term, to sink one's head below the sand and hope the term goes away on its own, to once again 'miss the boat'! More to the point, critical geographers should not cede the term without a fight, without trying to co-opt it for themselves – that is the arduous conceptual task I have set for myself in this book. This task necessarily involves an honest, critical and sustained engagement with the concept, deconstructing and reconstructing it rather than dismissing it with incisive and diversivolent potshots (see Slater, 2014b). Incisive as they are, potshots are still potshots, engaging only the most caricatured versions produced by media and policy think-tanks rather than studiously tackling the voluminous academic literature on resilience, some of which does engage important questions of radical geography (for example, Katz, 2004) to be revisited in Chapter Eleven.

Second, I argue that as a critical geographer, I can retain resilience with a clean conscience *if applied to the residues of a previous, more equitable power structure*. If resilience is irreparably tainted by its association with neoliberalism, then one way to remain 'critical' (but perhaps not transformative) is to promote the resilience of the residues of a previous system that was more redistributive, that is the Keynesian era, the still-potent 'Left Modernisms' that provided visions of opportunity and progress unsullied by the market (Campkin, 2013). In this way, I maintain my previous point about resilience having adaptive capacity, rejecting status quo resilience that justifies neoliberalism. By deeming neoliberalism as the threat rather than the system to be propped up by resilience, I am exercising a critical rather than anodyne approach to the concept.

Yet even if I associate resilience with a more equitable power structure, and show it to be dynamic and adaptive, it will never fully satisfy the more radical viewpoint because it was not, is not and cannot truly be *transformative* – what Katz (2004) would call 'reworking' and 'resistance'. As Rajan and Duncan (2013: 70) offered with regards to the small, incremental social change initiated through small-scale institutions:

> Arguably, with some specific exceptions, they do not make much of a dent on the wider political economic equations that, reworked, might define a just world ... they are not new social movements or novel forms of resistance, or even examples of popular protest and mobilization against bio-power in any form ... it is perfectly possible to dismiss such cases as historically uninteresting, because they are less likely to produce large-scale change. Indeed, in the history of Marxism, [such] interventions ... were dismissed as 'reformist', and criticized as being counter-revolutionary.

So I appreciate the suspicion of critical geographers to resilience, who prefer something more transformative and who have offered other, perhaps more politically progressive and socially just concepts such as 'resourcefulness', 'remaking', 'reworking', 'right to the city' and the always reliable but sometimes trite 'resistance'. For the time being, however, they will have to accept the more reformist and incremental (yet active) production of resilience while not foreclosing on the concept prematurely – in Chapters Eleven and Twelve I return to these concerns, of how resilience recast as 'commons' can provide a springboard to transformation.

Resilience can be usefully applied to residual arrangements

The final proposition picks up on a central point from the last subsection – that we can retain resilience in a critical sense precisely because it can be applied to the residues of a previous, more equitable power structure, rather than propping up current neoliberalism. So if one considers residual Keynesian arrangements such as social housing or clusters of voluntary-sector organisations as still-useful resources of collective consumption, then their very resilience under the threat of neoliberal displacement becomes something *positive*, neither reactionary nor supporting an inequitable status quo but a bulwark against it, its production still progressive and bottom up. A better everyday is thus sustained, fed by incremental adaptation. This ties in to the idea that there is always the *potential* that civil society, community organisations and social movements can deploy resilience in less regressive ways, 'as an organizing principle ... to challenge the status quo and to design and shape alternative futures' (Brown, 2014: 113).

I wish to apply resilience to residual arrangements of collective consumption and the public city, peaking during Keynesian times and under pressure from the displacing logics of current neoliberalism. While not everything about the Keynesian managerialist state can be considered positive, it certainly promoted a more equal vision of society and a more robust intervention to prop up social life. This contrasts with globalised, post-Fordist economic growth at present, which

> is based on an industrial complex that leads not to the expansion of a middle class but to increasing dispersion in the income structure and in the bidding power of firms and households. There is social and economic polarization, particularly strong in major cities which concentrate a large proportion of the new growth industries and create a vast direct and indirect demand for low-profit and low-wage jobs. (Sassen, 2001: 339)

Anticipating Castells and emerging out of public facility location theory in the 1970s (DeVerteuil, 2000), Michael Dear proposed the 'public city' as a speculative (and now obscure) concept to capture the prevailing tendency towards the 'spatial concentrations of service-dependent populations and helping agencies in the inner city' (1980: 219). These agencies agglomerated in devalued yet central areas to maximise accessibility to their clients. Dear was interested in the 'origins and consequences' of the public city, which for him included the costs associated with the sociospatial exclusion of service-dependent populations from mainstream society and the saturation of helping facilities. Despite this obvious drawback, several positive elements of the public city may be recovered. First, there is the supportive – and possibly redeeming – role of inner-city space, despite the saturation of services and clients (Masuda & Crabtree, 2010). Second, there is the crucial, if grudging, role of the state in supporting the de-commodification of urban space for the purposes of redistributive welfare and collective consumption. Third, the public city's central location maximises accessibility to its clientele; urban centrality thereby becomes crucial for the public city's continued survival, as many clients will not travel far to access services (Wolch, 1981). The public city would find its most obvious spatial expression in the emergence of service-dependent ghettoes for the deinstitutionalised psychiatric patients of the 1970s (Dear and Wolch, 1987).

That some of these concentrations of the public city survived into the neoliberal age to become marooned artefacts, relics and residuals is of central interest to this book, currently arranged in recurring patterns across the inner cities of the Global North. Martin and Pierce (2013) outlined a concept of 'residuals of the state', and I wish to activate several of its key aspects to buttress my own approach to residual arrangements. To the authors, the state is both heavily implicated in neoliberalism but also has within itself seeds of non-neoliberal 'residuals' sedimented from earlier eras, seeds 'which offer latent tools for a variety of activists and institutional actors against the dominance of neoliberal thinking and actions within governments at multiple scales' (Martin & Pierce 2013: 62). These latent tools can be the legal structures that enable social service agencies greater power to site necessary facilities in the face of exclusionary NIMBYism ('not in my back yard'), but can also include other residuals such vestigial, locally funded general relief welfare programmes that abetted the emerging recovery home system in North Philadelphia (Fairbanks, 2009). Crucially, these latent tools are tied to the residual welfare state, the leftovers from the more redistributive Keynesian era, pre-dating current neoliberalism yet contributing to 'a basket of state-supported outcomes somewhat orthogonal to the nominal goals of neoliberalism ... their continued existence is tolerated and even enrolled in contemporary economic projects' (Martin & Pierce, 2013: 68). These concepts introduce a more overtly political and politicised approach to resilience, one that rejects the clean slate of neoliberalism and embraces a more muddled post-welfare reality.

All of this reinforces an important point: just because the state is implicated and invested in neoliberalism does not mean that state policies are monolithically or even sympathetically neoliberal – some clearly sustain older forms of statecraft, whether by (expedient) design or inadvertently (Fairbanks, 2009). This suggests the presence of what Moyersoen and Swyngedouw (2013) referred to as 'cracks in the city', and what Hackworth (2007: 187) called a 'series of fissures' that challenges current models of urban governance. Neoliberalism does not displace, replace or appropriate everything from the past in waves of 'roll-back' and 'roll-out' (Kymlicka, 2013); it is inherently incomplete. Hackworth (2007: 190) acknowledged that one line of resistance to neoliberalism has been 'to protect or to preserve gains made under the Keynesian managerialist state' (see also Watt, 2009); but while he was reluctant to fully embrace such 'neo-Keynesian' efforts due to their highly localised and limited successes, I side with Martin and Pierce (2013), who saw residuals of the state as potentially productive to subvert the current power structure, or at least operate in a space partially beyond it and not always responding. Overall, then, I am interested in applying resilience to the legacies of Keynesian urban policy, conceptualised as a residual arrangement. Some residuals are more obscure, such as the 19th-century asylums that dot the exurban fringe of many cities, predating the Keynesian welfare state entirely (Moon et al, 2006). What is missing overall, however, is the interpretation of the production of resilience of residuals.

The particular residual arrangement that constitutes the focal point of this book is the *service hub*, a Keynesian (and sometimes pre-Keynesian) spatial arrangement that distils the essence of the public city and collective consumption. The service hub is a normative concept with on-the-ground manifestations and implications. Service hubs were conceptualised to 'reap the benefits of facility concentration while pushing for a more equitable dispersion of service agglomerations across the metropolitan area' (DeVerteuil, 2000: 63; see also Nelson & Wolch, 1985; Dear & Wolch, 1986; 1987; Dear et al, 1994). In principle, service hubs would avoid the saturation and exclusionary effects of over-saturation of services through a strategy of equitable dispersion, while still taking advantage of the benefits of agglomeration of helping facilities in the inner-city zone of dependence, what Lee (1994: 204) identified as 'providing access to a diverse service mix, easy referral and linkages between services, and multi-purpose trip making'. On the ground, the service hub is perhaps less successful, many still inequitably localised to just a few areas of the city. And yet service hubs retain the beneficial agglomeration that imparts a certain protective and sustaining set of institutions, a critical node in the geographies of help to vulnerable populations. Increasingly hemmed in, yet proving remarkably resilient, service hubs can play a 'brokerage role' (Moyersoen & Swyngedouw, 2013) between the rest of the city and the voluntary sector and its clients. The service hub is therefore the epitome of a Keynesian residue, the product of contentious (and conscientious) politics from a previous era, a 'socio-spatial-temporal but also implicitly and already (negotiated) *scalar* configuration of grievances, activists, claimants, and political resistances' (Martin, 2013: 90). A clear (if unacknowledged) example is The Block in Redfern, Sydney (Shaw, 2007: 47), a highly conspicuous concentration of housing and services that emerged as part of intense political contestations during the 1960s and 1970s over the creation of specifically Aboriginal space in inner Sydney that 'provided refuge for the most dispossessed, hungry and threatened'. Currently, The Block represents a tenacious product of self-help and survival, grudgingly supported by local government since the Keynesian era as a necessary but stigmatised space, invariably under threat. Another example is Vancouver's Downtown Eastside, a pre-Keynesian concentration of cheap housing and services for the downtrodden that, through subsequent Keynesian support, sheer density and activism, survived almost intact into the neoliberal phase (Blomley, 2003; Lees et al, 2008; Masuda & Crabtree, 2010; see also DeVerteuil, 2005 on the concept of 'welfare neighbourhoods').

There are of course instances where service hub resilience was not assured, and in this regard we should consider all service hubs as 'borrowed places' (Smart, 2001: 31), provisionally tolerated for the time being but without any future promise of state or market restraint. The 'Hobohemia' (that is, Main Stem) of Chicago virtually disappeared by the 1990s (Wright, 1997), while the Bowery District, once America's most prominent 'Skid Row', had been gentrified beyond recognition by the early 2000s (Isay & Abramson, 2000). In such locales, the intra-urban geography of helping facilities became increasingly dispersed, in parallel with the North American trend of urban sprawl since the 1960s (Yanos, 2007). Helping facilities have been scattered and become isolated, and in the process the advantages of co-location within the service-dependent ghetto have been lost (DeVerteuil & Evans, 2009). These spatial shifts suggest emerging lineaments of a distinctly (yet always uneven) post-welfare service hub geography, to which I return in Chapter Eleven, but armed with results from the three global city-regions.

In summary, I have developed seven propositions that will frame the empirical chapters as well as undergo critical reappraisal in Chapter Eleven, where I advance a unified concept of the 'critical resilience of the residuals'. I have articulated a critical approach to the production of resilience (resilience as a verb, akin to 'resist' and 'rework') that is process based and without a necessary endpoint, open to adaptive and persistent strategies, an alternative to resistance and reworking, enabled and transferable. By applying resilience to residual arrangements of a previously more redistributive system, resilience can become part of a critical approach; considering and prioritising resilience is not the same as being an apologist for neoliberalism. Service hubs produce resilience for themselves and their clientele. With my second cornerstone now fully introduced, it is time to consider the third: what is the agent of the service hub, who is social and spatial resilience for? This is the subject of Chapter Three.

THREE

The voluntary sector within the post-welfare city

As Chapter Two made clear, the (resilient) service hub pre-dates neoliberalism, but its primary agent and building block – the voluntary sector – is also deeply implicated in and influenced by neoliberalism. The voluntary sector owes some of its growth to neoliberalism while acting as a substitute for the Keynesian welfare state, unable to match the latter's scope, scale, coverage and universality. Rather, the voluntary sector is far more ad hoc, uncoordinated, asymmetrical and uneven, reflecting the vicarious nature of voluntary action and state support. So if the clustering of the voluntary sector in service hubs was Keynesian or even pre-Keynesian, the agents themselves have a complex relationship to both previous systems and the incompletely consolidating neoliberal one. The very complexity of this relationship animates two viewpoints on the voluntary sector: the dismissive, which sees it as a neoliberal stooge thoroughly enrolled in its projects, and the ambivalent to hopeful, which sees it as quasi-independent of the current governance structure, resilient and an important enabler of social resilience. This second viewpoint (which I favour) valorises agency, and in that respect I understand resilience as having a strong behavioural and adaptive aspect that further distances it from ecological and system-wide understandings (Bristow & Healy, 2014). This agency has led to very specific forms of spatial resilience and service hub geography, enabling both centrality and accessibility.

From the second viewpoint, the voluntary sector is distinguishable from the state by its independence; from the market by its emphasis on the non-profit principle, mutualism and altruism; and from the family/community by its formality (Milbourne, 2013). I do not see the voluntary sector as inherently (or exclusively) progressive/de-centred or co-opted into the 'shadow state' (Wolch, 1990) nor solely the means with which to absorb the most conspicuous shortfalls of the welfare system (for example, the 'roll-back' neoliberal argument). Along these lines, Trudeau and Veronis (2009) deemed the voluntary sector as a 'translation mechanism' that filters, if not occasionally deforms and restructures, welfare state policies and edicts into actual, on-the-ground service provision. Similarly, Elwood (2006) saw the voluntary sector as 'strategic actors' between the state and other local entities.

One common desire on the part of voluntary-sector organisations is to serve, though not exclusively, dependent and vulnerable people. These populations are usually ill-served by other structures, stemming from market and state failures to absorb them, and see the voluntary sector as a safety net of last resort (Clifford et al, 2012). The topic of abandoned populations – ranging from service-dependent populations (Dear & Wolch, 1987) to the post-industrial precariat (Wacquant, 2008) – is too sprawling to consider fully here. I limit my discussion to the unfortunate but increasingly necessary term *surplus populations* (Tyner, 2013) and their everyday survival in the face of supposed Agambenian abandonment to bare life and neoliberal exclusion (Li, 2010; Evans, 2011; Tyner, 2013). Li (2010) and Tyner (2013) both deployed Marx's concept of surplus populations as unable to fully avail themselves of wage labour (or a living wage) and, at the very bottom reaches, suffering from pauperism. To be a part of the surplus populations is to be vulnerable and place-dependent (Wolch, 1979; 1980; 1981), seeking alternative means of support through informal community, the state or the voluntary sector (if one exists) to protect against dispossession (Li, 2010). In response to this need, 'voluntary-sector organizations maintain a critical layer of social protection that … can mean the difference between life and death' (Evans, 2011: 24), helping to structure complex 'geographies of survival' (Mitchell & Heynen, 2009). Working through a sense of obligation for surplus populations, voluntary-sector spaces also function as crucial and potentially alternative spaces of citizenship by taking in and tolerating/ sustaining those excluded by neoliberalism as non-producing and non-consuming (Trudeau 2008a; Evans, 2011). So the voluntary sector can be a force in the creation of subjectivities of people who cannot easily be absorbed into capitalist structures, lacking recourse to family or community structures (Fairbanks, 2009).

The dismissive perspective: the voluntary sector as dupe of roll-back/roll-out neoliberalism

From this perspective, national welfare state retrenchment, privatisation and devolution have produced a neoliberalised governance mode of welfare delivery in which multiple collaborations connect public, private and civil society institutions (Warshawsky, 2010; DeVerteuil, 2011c). This welfare pluralism is an obvious outcome of neoliberalisation (Williams et al, 2012), both its 'roll-back' and 'roll-out' manifestations and circumlocutions. The importance of the voluntary sector as a vehicle of service delivery and citizenship has grown unabated since the 1980s, 'under the guise of "third way" approaches to domestic social policy that have taken firm root in many countries' (Wolch, 2006: xii). In effect, the (welfare) state and the voluntary sector are now co-dependent and co-productive. Voluntary-sector organisations increasingly supply collective and public consumption within the context of a receding welfare state (Wolch, 1990; DeVerteuil, 2012).

For the 'roll-back' phase, we can detect a co-optation of the voluntary sector to align with neoliberal goals of leaner governance, a corporatist and hierarchical model based on bureaucratisation, marketisation and professionalisation (Salamon, 1999; Fyfe, 2005; Milbourne, 2013), at best a 'junior partner' in the management of surplus populations (Wolch, 1990; Trudeau, 2008). In the early years of roll-back neoliberalism, the voluntary sector was seen as more of a self-serving, stop-gap measure, inadvertently plugging holes in the offloading welfare state (Evans, 2011). It was during this era that Wolch (1990) detected something more systematic at work – an emerging partnership model. Her highly influential *shadow state* thesis stated that the voluntary sector's scale and scope had increased significantly since the demise of Keynesianism, as a way for the (welfare) state to safely offload responsibilities and risk to non-state actors, and to fill in the missing gaps while eroding basic entitlements. More to the point, the shadow state constitutes (1990: xvi):

> a para-state apparatus comprise of multiple voluntary-sector organisations, administered outside of traditional democratic politics and charged with major collective service responsibilities previously shouldered by the public sector, yet remaining within the purview of state control.

The state is central in orchestrating the shadow state. As Wolch argued (1990: 29), 'only the state has the level and variety of resources to authoritatively intervene, direct, and suppress the use of voluntary group resources'. The shadow state was also fundamentally about the rolling back of the welfare state from its apotheosis – some would say excesses – of the Keynesian era. Although Wolch (1990) did not explicitly connect her theory with roll-back neoliberalism, the two accord reasonably well (see K. Mitchell, 2001; Peck, 2003). After a period of disengagement (Milligan & Conradson, 2006), critical attention is once more being directed towards the shadow state concept. Subsequent research (Fyfe & Milligan, 2003b; May et al, 2006) has extended Wolch's observations on how the shadow state is an essential component of the state's strategy of welfare pluralism, and by extension the roll-back neoliberal state. Yet Trudeau (2012) noted that even within this shadow state construct, voluntary-sector organisations still exercise a certain degree of latitude to engage communities in ways different than the neoliberal, the co-opted and the overbearing (Williams et al, 2012), a point I will emphasise in the more ambivalent to hopeful perspective.

For the 'roll-out' phase, I can detect the enlistment of the sector to do neoliberalism's dirty work, of micromanaging and punishing surplus populations – part and parcel of 'the criminalization of urban poverty' at the social/penal frontier (Peck, 2003: 230) and the emerging carceral-assistential state (Wacquant, 2009). As Corry stated (2010: 17), 'organizations are recruited to implement neoliberal policies of downsizing the state [and] disciplining the individual and family'. This perspective assumes that the state's funding and administrative rules leave the voluntary sector with little power to disassociate itself from such goals. The voluntary sector is therefore enrolled (either wittingly or unwittingly) in the punitive oversight of surplus populations. This punitive framework has become the dominant approach to understanding regulation of the urban poor in places like the US and the UK, and increasingly beyond (DeVerteuil, 2014). Its tenets are by now well known and well rehearsed (DeVerteuil, 2014: 877):

> … these frameworks all point to the emergence of a meaner city, the brunt of which has been born by the visibly poor and the homeless. A variety of well worn tactics are used – criminalization of survival tactics, street sweeps, restrictions to accessing public space – to ensure a pristine city image and thereby future growth. Despite their heavy reliance on discourse and desktop analysis, these frameworks have proven enormously popular and influential, dominating our understandings of the geographies of homelessness in US cities but also well beyond.

In this highly polemical trope, the voluntary sector can be conceived only as a partner with neoliberalism, using its resources to coerce surplus populations off the streets and away from gentrifying zones of affluence; the voluntary sector becomes threadbare and disciplinary, imposing workfarism rather than welfare (Wilson & Keil, 2008; Gowan, 2010; Johnsen & Fitzpatrick, 2010). The work of urban sociologist Teresa Gowan (2010) is useful here. She framed the voluntary sector in terms of abetting the state's desire to both warehouse and control the homeless and visibly poor, framed by what she calls sin-talk (homelessness as a consequence moral offence, requiring exclusion and punishment) and sick-talk (homelessness as a consequence of addiction and mental illness, requiring therapeutic treatment). These discourses frame voluntary-sector responses across what Gowan deemed the 'homeless archipelago'. Her views were reflected in other writings that employ Foucauldian approaches to street-level neoliberal governmentality and subjectivities. Examining recovery homes in Philadelphia, Fairbanks (2009) accounted for their emergence and proliferation as a site of local state re-regulation upon the everyday lives of addicts, deeming the recovery house a 'supporting boundary institution' (2009: 232) between workfarist and carceral impulses. Finally, Wilson and Keil (2008) underlined the controlling elements common to shelters and drop-ins run by the voluntary sector, where food, shelter and clothing are available only to those who strictly follow a narrow, frequently religious, code of behaviour.

Abeyance captures these motivations quite well (DeVerteuil & Wilton, 2009): it involves the 'generic problem of a mismatch between the available positions in a society (too few) and the supply of potential claimants to those positions (too many). A variety of mechanisms have been devised to "absorb" surplus populations and neutralize the potential mischief of idle hands' (Hopper & Baumohl, 1994: 530). To Smith (1996), Mitchell (1997) and Wacquant (1999), abeyance is structured by the state's interventions to contain, punish, criminalise and evict, essential to the escalating vengefulness of measures directed at surplus populations, leading to what Don Mitchell called the 'post-justice city' (2001) in which redistribution has been superseded by mass incarceration and vague threats of extermination. While I do not deny some of these tendencies, the dismissive perspective becomes a straitjacket of unreconstructed punitiveness that blinds us to the more supportive, perhaps even rogue, voluntary sector that follows.

The ambivalent to hopeful perspective: the voluntary sector as platform for poverty management

For those who adhere to the first perspective, the news has not been good so far – how can the voluntary sector possibly be anything other than constitutive (and perhaps the epitome) of neoliberalism and the uneven post-welfare city, tamed and co-opted to do their dirty work, its very existence (and spectacular growth since the 1980s) propped up by the neoliberalised state, a case of voluntary-sector resilience aligned with the neoliberal context? It would follow that the very resilience of the (subservient) voluntary sector in the service hub is due to the neoliberalised state, which needs and wills it. If this is the case, then how can neoliberalism possibly be seen as a threat to the service hub and to the voluntary sector? Two responses that frame my reconsideration of the voluntary sector in this subsection and in the rest of this chapter come to mind: (1) that the service hub is far too spatially concentrated and conspicuous to be co-opted into the current context, presenting instead a distinct barrier to the unevenly neoliberalising post-welfare city and its drive to *physically displace* Keynesian relics in the name of gentrification; and (2) that the voluntary sector, while certainly suffering from some degree of co-optation, remains quasi-independent of the current context, retaining an urge to care for its clientele that more than balances out the obscuring and controlling aspects of neoliberal co-optation (Wolch, 1999; Cloke et al, 2010; Evans, 2011; May & Cloke, 2014).

And so this perspective takes the complexity of the voluntary sector seriously – not dismissing it as a band aid or a minion, what Peck and Tickell (2002: 43) called the "'little platoons" in the shape of (local) voluntary and faith-based associations in the service of neoliberal goals' – but rather as a crucial and semi-autonomous (political) agent in the uneven post-welfare city, a manager of poverty and vulnerable populations, strategic sites that connect market, state and community, a hinge among tendencies of abeyance, care and sustenance, and holdovers of residualised, Keynesian and pre-neoliberal modes of governance (Amin et al, 2002; Williams et al, 2012). The sector is more than merely the building blocks of the service hub. It would be impossible – if not irresponsible – to approach crucial urban issues such as post-welfarism, concentrated poverty, surplus populations, inequality, citizenship, social movements, the secular and post-secular, contested urban space, governance and social inclusion/exclusion without at least some recourse to the voluntary sector and its multiple roles and directionalities (see Wolch, 2006). More than filling the gaps left behind by the receding welfare state (Fyfe, 2005), the voluntary sector also provides a vehicle for social movements, alternative citizenship and survival, despite its notoriously asymmetrical, uncoordinated and uneven nature, and its continued dependency on the state (Fyfe & Milligan, 2003; Mohan, 2003). As Amin et al (2002: vii) claimed,

> [the social economy, which includes the voluntary sector] is no longer seen as a residual and poor cousin to the state or the market, a sphere of charity and social or moral

repair. Instead, it is imagined as a mainstay of future social organization in both the developed and developing world, set to co-exist with the welfare state, meet social needs in hard-pressed communities ... empower the socially excluded by combining training and skills formation with capacity and confidence-building, and create a space for humane, co-operative, sustainable, and 'alternative' forms of social and economic organization.

The first step in dispelling the gloom and providing a more ambivalent, if hopeful, perspective of the voluntary sector is to embed it within a frame that incorporates (but also largely exceeds) the neoliberal one. I propose the poverty management framework as a promising alternative (Wolch & DeVerteuil, 2001). The poverty management framework embraces a wider range of impetuses that motivate voluntary-sector activity, impetuses that are sometimes punitive but also ambivalent or even supportive to surplus populations. This rebalancing also moves us away from any totalising accounts of welfare state restructuring that fail to appreciate the necessarily path-dependent, contingent nature of processes operating at local, regional and national scales, interacting with and emerging through inherited institutional landscapes (DeVerteuil & Wilton, 2009).

Drawing 'on concepts of the public city, urban managerialism, governmentality, abeyance theory and landscapes of care, poverty management refers to the creation of spatial and temporal structures designed to regulate and manage the spillover costs associated with so-called disruptive populations' (DeVerteuil et al, 2009a: 652). Within a management frame, the state – alongside other institutions and elites – articulates and employs poverty management techniques to maintain the social order, including the supportive (for example, affordable housing), the ambivalent (for example, ceding the homeless agenda to the voluntary sector) and the punitive (for example, anti-homeless laws). These techniques translate into sites of management over surplus populations and social marginality that vary over time – from 19th-century asylums to the contemporary homeless shelter (Wolch & DeVerteuil, 2001). Since the 1990s, poverty management has seemingly become more punitive. However, there remain other motivations at work, and the poverty management perspective implies that the precise balance between a more obviously punitive/neoliberal and more obviously ambivalent or accommodative response to social problems will vary significantly over space (and time). As such, the poverty management approach recognises the variability and lack of inevitability in techniques and sites – current poverty management can create sites that are co-functional and co-dependent but not necessarily coordinated, and not even attached to any extrinsic structure such as neoliberalism. This flexible approach contrasts strongly with the overstated (and fictional) regulatory stability and durability of neoliberal frameworks, both on the ground and more theoretically (Barnett, 2005).

A poverty management approach acknowledges that Bourdieu's left hand of the state – the social support provided by social, health and educational spending – and the right hand of the state involved in authoritarian/economic policies of penalisation, marketisation and privatisation – may well be complementary in the current neoliberal conjuncture (Wacquant, 2009; Peck, 2010). However, at the same time they may be opposing in the sense that the left hand (including the voluntary sector) persists in maintaining some basic independence through active resilience and incomplete regulation to continue its caring and sustaining path. As such, the exact nature of the left hand/right hand relationship is never predictable, neither coordinated nor conspiratorial (Cameron, 2007), such that assistential forms of poverty management have yet to be fully superseded by penal, workfarist forms – the very core of this book explores just such a (residual) scenario. The poverty management approach appreciates that the voluntary sector is so diffuse that it cannot possibly be always neatly and jointly organising with the state to punish (or conversely accommodate) surplus populations – one should rather assume uncoordination, disconnects, lags, and so forth. Indeed, the 'neoliberal city' and punitive tropes are essentially pessimistic constructions that see only neoliberalism and the responses to it, focusing precious little attention on the alternatives, whether real or imagined (May & Cloke, 2014).

If we seriously consider the poverty management framework as a conceptual counterbalance to neoliberalism and punitiveness, then the voluntary sector now fulfils a wider range of roles: not just abeyance and control (this lack of progressive empowerment cannot be denied), but also caring and sustenance, both of which can enable resilience. This counterbalancing valorises agency and multiple directionalities among the voluntary sector, suggesting instances of 'strategic decoupling' (Arvidson & Lyon, 2014) and 'boundary work' (Evans, 2011). Voluntary-sector organisations can now as much negotiate, inflect and deflect state intentions as absorb them (Brown, 1997; Trudeau, 2008). While the more totalising and punitive interpretations seem to dominate geographical understandings of current social policy – if you seek revanchism you will find it, yielding a very narrow story (for example, Swanson, 2007) – I wish to explore the more liminal and therapeutic aims of operators, aims that belie the seemingly pervasive urge to control and contain clients (DeVerteuil & Wilton, 2009). Indeed, since the mid-2000s, numerous works critical of the punitive/neoliberal trope have emerged (for example, DeVerteuil 2006; Laurenson & Collins 2007; DeVerteuil et al, 2009a; Murphy 2009; Aalbers 2010; Cloke et al, 2010; Johnsen & Fitzpatrick 2010; Van Eijk 2010; DeVerteuil, 2014; MacKie et al, 2014). Consistent across all of this work is the need to acknowledge the co-existence of more supportive currents alongside the punitive/neoliberal (DeVerteuil, 2014). As Cloke et al (2010: 209) argued, in reference to homelessness:

> … to explain homeless cities simply in these terms [of punitiveness] is to ignore and disempower both the ability of homeless people as tactical authors of at least some of their own life experiences, and the extraordinary acts of generosity and care being exercised by the staff, volunteers and charitable donors who ensure a network of non-statutory services in the homeless city.

It is understandable that critical geographers salivate when they see how well homelessness and punitiveness mesh, but this tells but a partial story. Indeed, the second point of the quote emphasised the voluntary sector as a potential *space of care*, a platform for tolerance but sometimes contradictory and incoherent. Conradson (2003: 507) defined spaces of care as 'a sociospatial field disclosed through the practices of care that take place between individuals'. Feminist geographers have long underlined the centrality of care in everyday life, individual and collective survival and responsibility for social reproduction (Katz, 2001; McDowell, 2004; Lawson, 2007; Lawson, 2009; Jarvis et al, 2001), and have bemoaned the 'scarcity of work on care [which] represents a conspicuous silence on this topic' (Till, 2012: 8). Spaces of care are relational therapeutic environments designed to promote the well-being of the client. Voluntary-sector organisations care about (for example, advocacy) and give (formal) care, and their clients receive it. Care need not be selfish or with strings attached: many organisations are committed to the concept of *agape*, 'a genuine openness to, and outpouring of, unconditional love towards and acceptance of the other' (May & Cloke, 2014: 896). This idea of unconditional generosity and goodwill contradicts the idea of self-serving charity within a neoliberalised voluntary sector, and constitutes an alternative path at odds with neoliberalism entirely (Williams et al, 2014). In turn, care ethics 'questions (neo)liberal principles of individualism, egalitarianism, universalism, and of society organised around principles of efficiency, competition, and a "right" price for everything' (Lawson, 2007: 3).

Urban social geographers have recently begun to consider spaces of care, an ethos of solidarity, and collective welfare as a worthwhile line of inquiry, as well as a bulwark against the rising tide of individualistic and neoliberalised competition (McDowell, 2004; Lawson, 2007; Evans, 2011; Staeheli, 2013). Along these lines, Evans (2011) made the point that spaces of care are political, in that they help distinguish citizens deserving of help. This insight has also helped generate academic interest in faith-based organisations, some of which clearly fall within the umbrella of the voluntary sector and whose ethos usually intersects with care (Conradson, 2006; Cloke et al, 2010; May & Cloke, 2014). Once ignored, ideas of faith and the post-secular are attracting increasing academic scrutiny. Interestingly, some faith-based (and other) organisations extend beyond care, which is fundamental to the survival of their clientele, to include more progressive aims such as intervening in the 'political and social processes that contribute to disadvantage' (Conradson, 2008: 2117). In this way, the faith-based component of the voluntary sector contributes a distinctly social justice perspective (and potential remaking) to the more mundane concerns of survival, a point picked up in Chapters Eleven and Twelve.

This groundswell of care in the voluntary sector can be explained by a variety of factors. Cloke et al (2010) contended that heavy-handed punitive responses actually created an upsurge of supportive responses, effectively countering the view of a controlling voluntary sector that acts as a punitive dupe. Along these lines, I have argued (DeVerteuil, 2014) that care not only co-exists with a more punitive bent, but that the latter has come to *depend* on the former. The need to remove and contain (surplus) populations deemed disruptive certainly involves the voluntary sector, but in turn these same agencies also provide offsetting and crucial elements of caring (DeVerteuil & Wilton 2009). This means that abeyance is tempered by care, but that the latter may not always be offered without at least a recognition of the former – what Johnsen and Fitzpatrick called 'coercive care', or forcing people to seek care against their will, ostensibly for their own good (2010: 1712). Cloke et al (2010) recognised that care and compassion have limits, usually stemming from the need to obscure and control the sometimes abrasive presence of surplus populations.

Alongside care, the voluntary sector can further act as a *space of sustenance*, ensuring the survival of clients through their own actions. Social reproduction for surplus populations is highly challenging: since there is little guarantee of securing housing, health, food, clothing and the like through the market (and sometimes the state), support must be sought from, and absorbed by, the informal community and the voluntary sector. This is a homegrown resilience that capitalism depends upon, but also abuses (Katz, 2001). Dear and Wolch (1987) and Takahashi (1998) both suggested that the concentration of helping agencies in service hubs facilitate and largely structure the geographies of survival among surplus populations. From the point of view of the client – one that will not be taken up in this book (but see DeVerteuil, 2003b; DeVerteuil & Wilton, 2009) – the tension between spaces of abeyance and spaces of care overlaps with the demands of everyday survival across an increasingly diverse array of nodes, including day and drop-in centres, shelters, recovery homes, public feedings, employment centres, clinics and so forth (DeVerteuil & Wilton, 2009). Evans (2011: 31) talked about how the voluntary sector can provide respite from highly exclusionary urban landscapes marked by punitiveness and displacement, challenging 'the prevailing neoliberal citizenship regime by providing sustenance to individuals who are beyond being included because of their inability to meet social obligations'. We can also detect in this process the strong presence of client agency. Using street-level ethnography, Wiseman (1970) was one of the first social scientists to recognise that clients redefined the system for purposes other than those intended by service providers. So sometimes sustenance makes a mockery of care; clients abuse and waste the care given to them so that they can survive from day to day.

Resilience and voluntary sector geography

Now that both perspectives on the voluntary sector have been unveiled – with the second perspective largely (but not exclusively) structuring and informing the remainder of the book – it is time to unpack its geography and links to the production of spatial resilience, themselves the product of specific voluntary-sector agency that purposefully seek and preserve both centrality and accessibility. Geographers have long recognised that the spatial imprint of the voluntary sector is highly uneven (Wolch & Geiger 1983; Wolch, 1990; Fyfe & Milligan, 2003; Cloke et al, 2010; Milbourne, 2013). This should not be surprising, given that voluntary-sector geographies are largely unplanned, uncoordinated and unregulated by the state; indeed, most service hubs have emerged organically and haphazardly, sometimes a century ago. So if the state has little to do with this unevenness, what else may explain it? There are constraints, of course: voluntary-sector organisations that serve the most stigmatised surplus populations (for example, those who are substance abusers, homeless people, those on parole, people with a mental illness) are systematically excluded from middle-class areas through community opposition (Dear & Wolch, 1987). This builds on the understanding that NIMBY is a key determinant of voluntary-sector geographies (for more on gentrification and NIMBY, see Takahashi, 1998; DeVerteuil, 2013). The service hub itself is a product of these forces, while also seeking to maximise access to services by minimising distance to most clients (DeVerteuil, 2000). In this regard, service-dependent ghettoes (Dear & Wolch, 1987) represented the strategic co-location of services and the populations dependent on them. The ghettoes were coping mechanisms for deinstitutionalised people but, given pervasive community opposition, burdened by saturation effects that made it virtually impossible for clients to engage with larger society. Less dramatically, services for other surplus populations, such as elderly people or those seeking asylum, tend to centralise as much as possible. Advocacy organisations require highly visible and symbolic locations to promote their causes, which usually means highly central. Finally, for certain non-emergency organisations, the spatial pattern reflects less on need and more on the local ability to fund them, thus favouring locally well-off areas; the organisations serving the most disadvantaged groups tend to be those most reliant on state funding (Wolch, 1999; Clifford, 2012; Milbourne, 2013).

Within these contexts, I am interested in using resilience to move beyond the recognition of the voluntary sector's obviously place-based and uneven nature to consider the *spatial tension* between (gentrification-induced) physical displacement and resilience, critically evaluating the dis/advantages of spatial resilience (Chapter Eleven), directly comparing Australian, UK and US voluntary-sector regimes (Chapters Four and Five), and drawing upon the rich legacy of public facility location theory and welfare geography to say something about the voluntary sector in 2014 (Chapter Twelve). The extension will necessitate a wider array of spatial and place-based approaches across these chapters. Here I wish to return to concepts of *centrality* and *accessibility*. In a Lefebvrian sense, the city is understood as 'a potent battleground for struggles seeking greater democracy, equality, and justice' (Soja, 2010: 96). One of those battlegrounds is necessarily spatial and symbolic – not just the right to the city, but the right to access the city and prime urban spaces in particular. Taking Paris as the proverbial case, Haussmann's renewal in the 19th century was all about increasing access and consolidating centrality while dispersing the working classes; access to the city in the 1960s was all about the right to centrality within a context of enforced dispersion to the *banlieues* (from the French *banir*, literally to banish).

Nonetheless, most surviving voluntary-sector and service-hub geographies have remained adamantly centralised. Why? Again, the combined effects of NIMBY with voluntary-sector proximity-seeking and access-maximising, together with adaptive resilience and (less so) persistence. Inner-city locations are attractive to voluntary-sector facilities because of their high accessibility (for direct services, 'caring for') and visibility (for advocacy services, 'caring about'). And so inner-city locations are ideal sites for the service hub as well. Various mappings of voluntary-sector geographies across metropolitan areas as diverse as Glasgow, Manchester and Los Angeles (Wolch & Dear, 1993; Ruddick, 1996; Fyfe & Milligan, 2003; Marr et al, 2009; Clifford, 2013) revealed that these service hubs remain steadfastly inner city, and positively correlated with areas of high deprivation. This obstinate attachment to the inner city matters more than ever in an era of polycentric urbanism where residual centrality and accessibility are under threat by forces of de-concentration (for example, suburbanisation) and especially re-concentration (for example, gentrification). Anachronistic as it might be, service hubs anchor the survival patterns of surplus population who themselves favour centrality because they suffer limited ability to access all but the most publicly connected urban areas. Returning to Paris, Clerval (2013) noted that the working classes, immigrants and surplus populations all value accessibility not only to jobs and social solidarity but social services, the loci of which all remain in the centre of Paris. Yet this centrality is never a given; it must be constructed and reinforced by powerful actors in the form of regional development, infrastructure and zoning, and more recently through gentrification.

Residual centrality and accessibility for poor people are threatened by neoliberalism in many forms; my interest lies in the gentrification-induced physical displacement of voluntary-sector organisations arranged in service hubs. With gentrification, the pre-existing (and relatively untouched) centrality of the service hub (and the surplus population who depend on it) now increasingly overlaps with a centrality favoured by gentrifiers – urban spaces once forsaken are now revalorised, urban spaces once benignly ignored or neglected become intensely contested. To Clerval (2013: 15), '*la centralité, en tant que pouvoir attractif (et prestige) du centre urbain, est au cœur du processus de gentrification dans les grandes villes*' (centrality, in terms of the powerful attractiveness and prestige of the urban centre, is at the heart of the process of gentrification in large cities). For gentrifiers, this centrality is non-negotiable (Ley, 1986), and so the very centrality, accessibility and visibility of service hubs intuitively render them vulnerable to being displaced as gentrification may induce rents too high for voluntary-sector organisations, generate greater community opposition to existing (or expanding) services, as well as shrink the service-dependent population (DeVerteuil, 2011a). Moreover, the very conspicuousness of the service hub makes it antagonistic to an image of control, order and spectacular progress that global city-regions are desperate to project, and are akin to the highly visible (and concentrated) poverty of social housing (Reese et al, 2010).

I wish to follow up on the uneven, asymmetrical, uncoordinated and sometimes unfair distribution of voluntary-sector resources across urban space in Part Two. The service hub is indeed an anachronistic and residual spatial arrangement, a relic of the pre-Keynesian and Keynesian welfare state, and thus pre-dates the displacing logics of neoliberalism. The value of the service hub as a spatial arrangement is exactly its beneficial clustering, increasingly under threat in a world of displaced, dispersed, placeless and personalised care (Power, 2013). However, the service hub is only as resilient as its constitutive parts. As the subject of this chapter, I have shown the voluntary sector to be both co-opted and resistant, controlling, caring and sustaining, partially neoliberalised and partially Keynesian, and above all adaptive. In Part Two, I shall empirically examine the practice and promise of resilience, using the case studies of inner-city London, Los Angeles and Sydney. In the next chapter, I will outline my methodological approach to comparatively detect the threat of gentrification-induced displacement and the resilience arrayed against it within and among inner-city service hubs.

FOUR

Methodological approaches

In this chapter, I outline my methodological approach to the multi-site, comparative project at hand. Strictly with regards to the literature on surplus populations and the voluntary sector, it is my opinion that a comprehensively laid-out, on-the-ground approach has frequently *yielded more nuanced, fine-grained and systematic* understandings than approaches that are more high altitude and cursory. With reference to the debates over urban punitiveness in Chapter Three, those studies that took a more grounded approach (for example, Cloke et al, 2010) presented a more ambivalent and supportive response to homelessness than the more desktop work by Davis (1990), Smith (1996) and Mitchell (2001), which presented an unacceptably clearcut and negative representation of street-level reality. This parallels how the voluntary sector was represented: while the more high-altitude work tended to denigrate and dismiss the voluntary sector as a neoliberal stooge, the more grounded work tended to provide a far more nuanced, if alternatively positive, portrayal of the sector. And so it is in this fine-grained and nuanced spirit that I proceed with my methodological outline. The chapter is divided into three sections: (1) the sample frame for the three global city-regions, the 10 inner-city areas and the 100 voluntary-sector organisations, referencing global cities theory; (2) an operationalisation of resilience and the threats to it, in the form of proxies and metrics of social and spatial resilience to the displacing logics of gentrification in the uneven post-welfare city; and (3) an exposition on the comparative methods, referencing the burgeoning literature on comparative urbanism and how it may inform (comparative) resilience among the voluntary sector.

Sampling frames

My sampling frame for voluntary-sector organisations within service hubs was limited to the 1998–2011 period, which overlapped with a consolidation of neoliberalism in Global North cities, state-sponsored gentrification and the fallout of significant welfare state restructuring in Australia, the UK and US, as well as the incipient impacts of the 2008 financial crisis and subsequent austerity. The study period also overlapped with the rebound in gentrification after the early 1990s recession and its intensification with the housing bubble of the mid-2000s. Moreover, 2007 can be seen as the high water mark of the last round/phase of upgrading in London and Los Angeles, the peak of third-wave gentrification, but now with hints of an emerging bubble in the post-2011 period; Sydney did not see a real estate lull in the post-2007 period at all, and has enjoyed consistently rising prices since the mid-2000s.

As mentioned in Chapter One, London, Los Angeles and Sydney share relatively few obvious commonalities. But the commonalities they do share – especially global city-region status[1] – go some way in making up for these differences. Although the global city concept has come under severe criticism for its narrow, primarily financial and economistic criteria, exclusionary and parochial outcomes that ignore most (ordinary) cities in the Global South and the Global North, a mania for rankings and hierarchical ontology, a prescriptive-emulative approach to urban policy, and the shortcomings associated with paradigmatic thinking more generally (for example, Robinson, 2002; McCann, 2004; McNeill et al, 2005), it does provide a robust conceptual scaffolding for examining the more intense social, spatial, housing, income, social welfare, immigrant status and employment *polarisations*[2] found in the most globalised cities – in other words, all cities are globalising, but global city theory makes a certain amount of sense for those cities at the top of the urban hierarchy, and makes a certain amount of sense in terms of a (global) city-region's polarised social geography (Keil, 1998; Sassen, 2001; Wills et al, 2010). This suggests that service hubs are qualitatively and quantitatively different in global city-regions than in ordinary cities – more clientele with more complex needs, more pressure to hide them, more land inflation (and gentrification?) and thus more displacement pressure – such that service hubs are always *in* and *of* the global city-region. John Friedmann (1986) recognised that being at the top of the urban hierarchy generates social costs – especially related to the burgeoning numbers of working poor people and their need for housing, health, transportation and welfare – that tended to exceed the fiscal capacity of the local state, inevitably generating greater pressure on the voluntary sector. Certainly all three global city-regions suffered from high and low earners (or job quality) growing at the expense of the middle, and these conditions were largely a function of their shared status as immigrant magnets. To Sassen (2001) and Massey (2007), global city status and immigrant magnet go hand in hand with polarisation, with evidence in London (May et al, 2007; Wills et al, 2010), Los Angeles (Sassen, 2001; Soja, 2010) and Sydney (Baum, 1997; O'Neill & McGuirk, 2002; Randolph

& Holloway, 2005). And like all global city-regions, social polarisation was reflected through deep spatial divisions – Zukin's (1992) landscapes of power (and gentrification) versus the residual vernacular (such as service hubs) – set within increasingly polycentric built environments (Connell & Thom, 2000; Soja, 2000). The challenge for all three global city-regions necessarily involves managing this heightened polarisation, which in turn crucially implicates the local welfare state settlement and the voluntary sector (Keil, 1998).

The sample of the ten inner-city areas across the three global city-regions was undertaken with two criteria in mind: that each area featured evidence of the displacing logics of neoliberalism via gentrification, and evidence of resilient service hubs – capturing the balance between Zukin's (1992) landscapes of power and vernacular. But to get to this point, an overall mapping of the inner city for London, Los Angeles and Sydney was necessary, itself dependent on finding a centre, or centres, to each global city-region. Inner-city London is composed of the 13 boroughs found in Inner London, demarcating Victorian London (and, roughly, the old County of London) from its 20th-century suburbs: the wealthier inner-west boroughs of Camden, Hammersmith and Fulham, Kensington and Chelsea, Wandsworth, Westminster; and the poorer inner-east and south boroughs of Hackney, Haringey, Islington, Lambeth, Lewisham, Newham, Southwark and Tower Hamlets (Jarvis et al, 2001; MacInnes et al, 2011). Inner London had a population in 2011 of 3.2 million people, some 38% of Greater London's population (see Figure 4.1). Most of the built environment is from the Victorian era, punctuated by mid-20th-century council estates and late 20th-century new-build gentrification and skyscrapers (Hamnett, 2003). While London's centre is quite clear and has been established for centuries, it is increasingly marked by polycentrism, both within (Canary Wharf, the City, West End) and beyond (Chiswick, Croydon, Hammersmith, Heathrow, Stratford) (Hutton, 2010).

Sydney is equally polycentric and far more suburbanised, yet also features a dominant centre: the CBD found in the Local Government Area (LGA)[3] of Sydney (Connell, 2000; Raskall, 2002). The inner city is the Sydney LGA combined with what Aplin (2000: 69) deemed inner-core LGAs: Leichhardt; Marrickville; Mosman; North Sydney; Woollahra. Together, Inner Sydney's population in 2011 was 440,102, which was slightly more than 10% of Metropolitan Sydney (see Figure 4.2). Most of these areas were developed in the late 19th century, and have recently become gentrified and densified, accompanied by important population growth after many decades of decline (Engels, 1999; Aplin, 2000; Shaw, 2007).

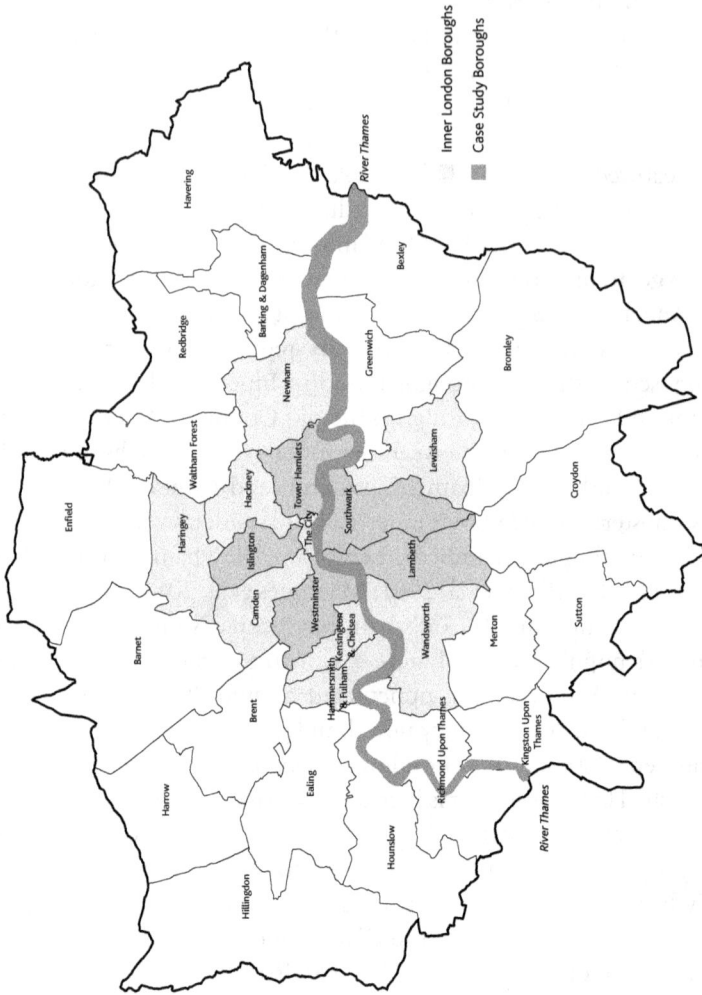

Figure 4.1 Inner London and case study boroughs

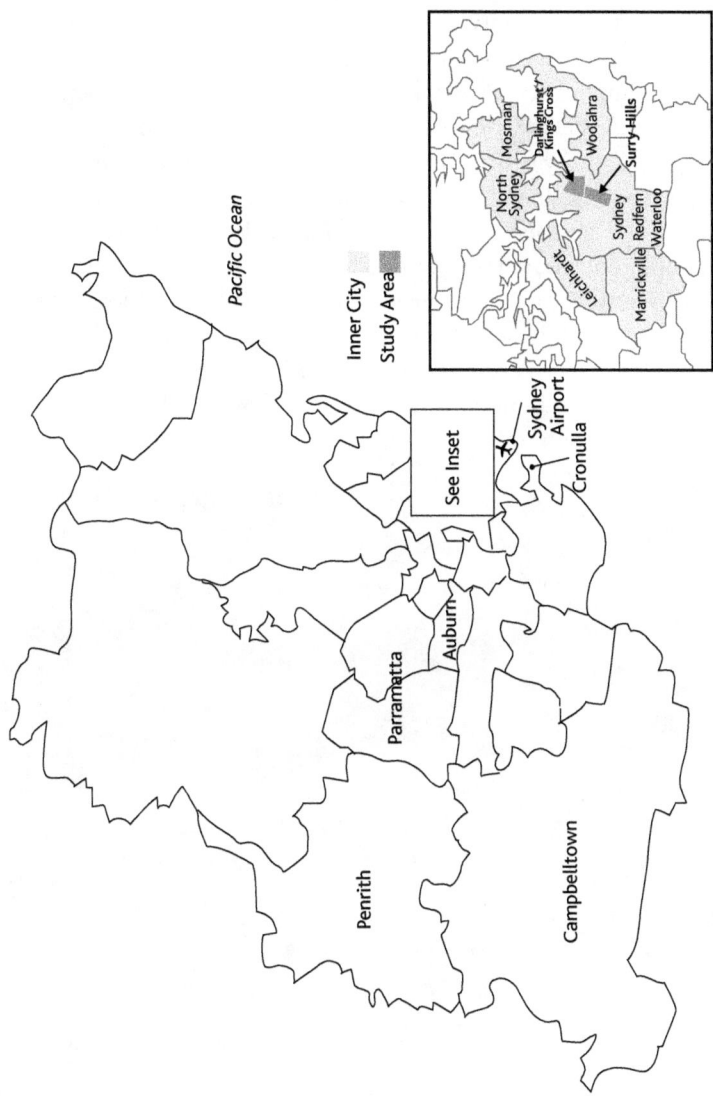

Figure 4.2 Inner Sydney and case study areas

Defining inner-city Los Angeles could not be undertaken using administrative boundaries, since none exist – and in any case, the polycentric nature of Southern California precludes an easy identification of a dominant centre, which also does not exist. In this case, I have updated the Marr et al (2009) place-typology of Los Angeles County with 2010 census data, replacing the 'marginal' census tracts with 'inner city' ones – those with built environments older *and* denser than County median values (see also DeVerteuil et al, 2007, for an application to Winnipeg in Canada). These denser, older parts of Los Angeles County were largely found in the central portions of the County – including South and East Los Angeles, Downtown Los Angeles, and areas directly west of it – but also established nodes such as Long Beach and Venice. The 2010 population of 1.9 million people constituted 19.4% of Los Angeles County's total population (see Figure 4.3), a lower proportion than Inner London but still much greater than Sydney's. Surprisingly, population density levels in inner-city Los Angeles were higher than in Inner Sydney, and not far below those of Inner London, suggesting that Los Angeles is more than some overgrown suburb!

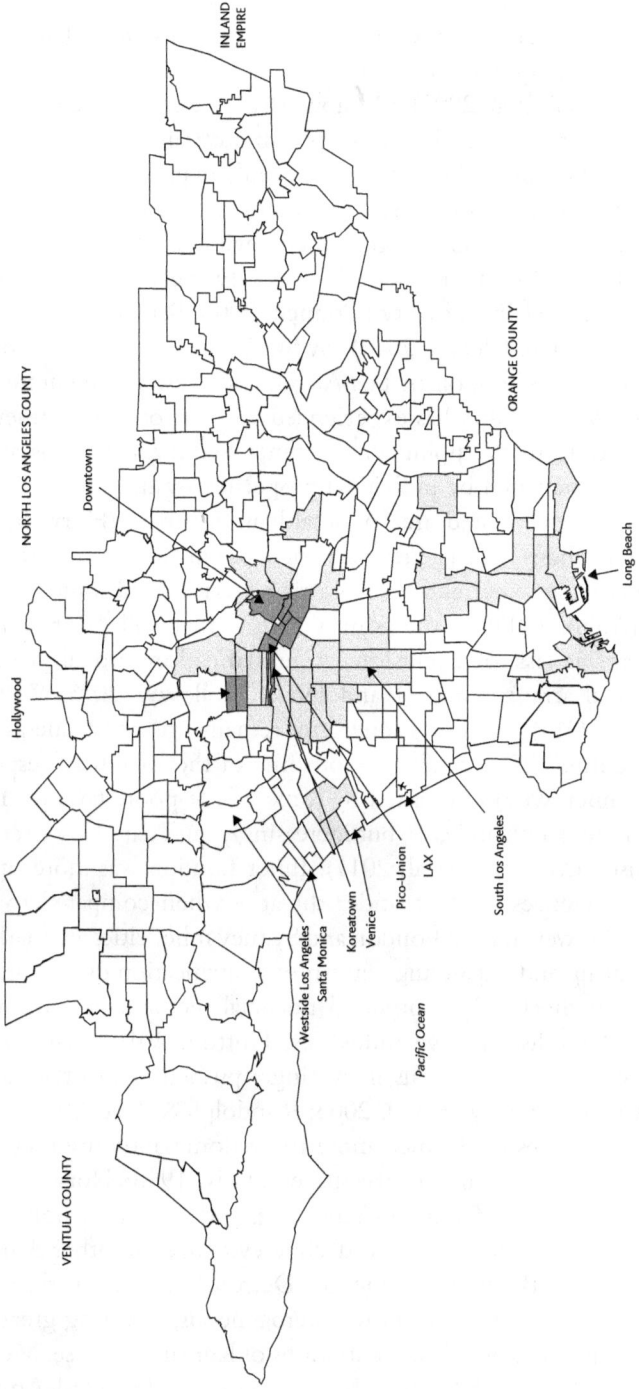

Figure 4.3 Inner-city Los Angeles and case study zip codes

Inner-city areas in global city-regions usually bear the brunt of the most intense globalised pressures and polarisations on land, people and capital, and frequently act as synecdoches for the global city-region itself (McNeill et al, 2005). It follows that all areas featured tendencies towards polarisation, globalisation, post-industrialism and gentrification rather than decline – but this was unevenly expressed across the three global city-regions. Inner Sydney conformed most to the dominant image of the repopulated, gentrified/revitalised (global) inner city, set within a Parisian model of inner-city wealth versus suburban diversity and relative poverty (Connell, 2000; Raskall, 2002; Bounds & Morris, 2006; Clerval, 2013). Sydney's inner city is quite compact compared with London or Los Angeles, and used to be quite slum-like (Shaw, 2007), but has experienced 40 years of re-investment and densification, to the point where 'inner Sydney appears as a sea of renewal punctuated by individual properties awaiting rehabilitation', the most concentrated area of wealth in Australia (Horvath, 2004: 102). This aligns with a general lack of depopulation and disinvestment of the core, as experienced in North American and some European cities (Aplin, 2000), to the point where virtually all Australian inner cities are at risk of exclusionary gentrification and displacement of residual arrangements (Randolph & Holloway, 2005; Walters & McCrea, 2014). London's inner city remains the most unequal area in the entire UK, a patchwork of some of the wealthiest (especially in the Inner West) contrasted by some of the poorest wards, mostly in the inner south and east, but increasingly (and dare I say decisively) revitalised (MacInnes et al, 2011). Inner London was more open to social differences – albeit under threat – when compared to Inner Sydney. However, both London and Sydney inner cities are marked by an enduring and expanding pattern of gentrification due to dramatic growth in the highly centralised financial sector (and some inner-city post-Fordist creative industries; Hutton, 2010), with poverty and immigrant populations increasingly pushed out to the suburbs, especially for Sydney (Flood, 2003; Randolph & Tice, 2014). Inner-city Los Angeles conformed more to predominantly disorderly (and possibly dystopian) inner-city space (Davis, 1998; Horvath, 2004) – but slowly gentrifying and renewing, and displaying none of the catastrophic abandonment and decline evidenced in other American cities such as Baltimore, Chicago, Detroit and New Orleans. Los Angeles' inner city is also more heterogeneous, featuring great racial diversity and substantial concentrations of Korean, Chinese, Mexican, African-American, Filipino, Thai, Armenian and Central-American people (Keil, 1998). Soja (2010: 124) emphasised how the pouring in of some 5 million immigrants since the 1960s, mostly to LA's inner city, has created 'densities ... at levels comparable to Manhattan', and has contributed mightily to a 'remarkable refilling of the Los Angeles urban core [which] has resulted in an unusually large geographical concentration ... of the working poor'. Presumably such a density of working poor immigrant people also posed a distinct barrier to inner-city gentrification – a topic picked up in Chapters Eight and Nine.

Of the 10 study areas, five were in London (the boroughs of Islington, Lambeth, Southwark, Tower Hamlets and Westminster); three areas were in Los Angeles (Downtown zip codes 90012, 90013, 90014, 90015, 90017 and 90021, Hollywood zip codes 90028 and 90038, and Pico-Union zip code 90057); and the Sydney census communities of Surry Hills and the combined census communities of Darlinghurst/Kings Cross (which is in Potts Point). These were chosen due to gentrification-induced displacement threatening well-established service hubs – as of 2013, all had per capita measures of voluntary-sector organisations that were above the global city-region and inner-city rates. Table 4.1 gives a regional breakdown of voluntary-sector[4] totals and concentrations for the entire global city-region and the designated inner city.

While organisations were not weighed by budget or total clientele, Table 4.1 clearly shows a consistently greater proportion and concentration of voluntary-sector organisations in the inner city, underlining its importance for service hubs more generally.[5] While

Table 4.1: Totals and concentrations of voluntary-sector organisations in 2013

	Greater London	Inner London	Los Angeles County	Los Angeles inner city	Metropolitan Sydney	Inner Sydney
2013 totals	18,958 registered charities	9,137 registered charities	36,186 registered non-profits	7,273 registered non-profits	3,435 registered not-for-profits	1,638 registered not-for-profits
2013 per capita	2.34 organisations per 1,000 persons	2.85 organisations per 1,000 persons	3.61 organisations per 1,000 persons	3.8 organisations per 1,000 persons	0.79 organisations per 1,000 persons	3.73 organisations per 1,000 persons

London sources: 2011 UK Census Data; 2013 UK Registered Charity Database. Registered charities are defined as 'registered with the Charity Commission ... a charity must register if it has a permanent endowment, a total income of more than 5000 Pounds a year or a rateable occupation of any land, including buildings' (Hopkins, 2010: 8). Los Angeles sources: 2010 US Census Data; 2013 National Center for Charitable Statistics website by geography (www.nccs.urban.org). Registered non-profits are those registered with the Internal Revenue Service, including public charities and private foundations. Sydney sources: 2011 Australian Census Data; Australian Charities and Not-for-profits Commission (ACNC) website (2013, www.acnc.gov.au). Registered not-for-profit charities were defined by the Australian Taxation Office as 'not operating for the profit or gain of its individual members' (www.ato.gov.au/Non-profit/) and registered with the ACNC.

the service hub concept, like the service-dependent ghetto, might be considered a North American invention (Milligan, 1996), the proportion (48.2% and 47.7%) and concentration of organisations (2.85 and 3.73 per 1,000 persons) were actually higher in Inner London and Inner Sydney when compared to their respective global city-regions, and at a higher proportion than in inner-city Los Angeles (20.1%), although the latter still featured the highest concentration overall at 3.8 per 1,000 persons. I should note that the data presented in Table 4.1 covered a wide range of voluntary-sector agents and activities; if the voluntary sector had been broken down to those directly serving surplus populations, the inner cities would have featured even higher per capita figures (Marr et al, 2009). As such, the relationship between poverty and voluntary-sector concentration was mixed: in inner-city Los Angeles, there was a clear and positive overlap; in Inner London it was more varied, with wealthy boroughs like Westminster featuring concentrations at least as high as poorer boroughs like Tower Hamlets; and in Sydney, where poverty had decidedly suburbanised (Randolph & Tice, 2014), there was a clear lack of overlap as most services remained inner city in nature.

Gentrification became a pervasive, on-the-ground threat when it moved from a quaint, localised phenomenon to a systematic private–public urban strategy at the forefront of a globalised neoliberal urbanism (Smith, 2002). Gentrification was present in different degrees and at different stages across all of the 10 inner-city areas during the period under consideration (1998–2011). Both London and Sydney were further along than Los Angeles in the stage model of devalorisation followed by reinvestment and institutional financial input (Carpenter & Lees, 1995). More to the point, few cities in the world have been so extensively researched in terms of gentrification as London – the process was first identified there in 1964 by Ruth Glass. There is longstanding agreement that all Inner London boroughs have experienced upgrading since the 1960s (Hamnett, 2003; Butler et al, 2008). Westminster's gentrification is the most sedimented and intertwined with pre-existing enclaves of wealth. The other four boroughs were all once very working class and even poverty class. Islington is the most polarised, with Barnsbury as the epitome of a super-gentrified neighbourhood, yet the borough is also the fourth most deprived out of 32 (Butler & Robson, 2003a; Hamnett, 2003; Butler & Lees, 2006; Hamnett & Whitelegg, 2007). Lambeth and Southwark have seen (new-build) gentrification mostly along the River Thames, with spottier upgrading beyond (Short, 1989; Butler & Robson, 2001; Butler & Robson, 2003b; Davidson & Lees, 2005; Harris, 2008;

Hutton, 2010). Tower Hamlets has seen patchy gentrification anchored to new-build developments around Canary Wharf and the 2012 Olympics site, but also more robust spillover from the neighbouring City (Amin et al, 2002; Fainstein, 2010).

The task of identifying gentrified areas was more challenging in Los Angeles, since relatively little has been written about its pattern (but see Barney, 2007; Reese et al, 2010; DeVerteuil, 2011a; 2012; Deener, 2012). Using median sale price between 1998 and 2008 (per square foot), I was able to establish that both Downtown and Hollywood experienced significantly greater increases between 1998 and 2007 (the height of the market) than the County as a whole (DeVerteuil, 2011a). Both Hollywood and Downtown were once attractive areas that suffered massive disinvestment in the 1950s–1980s period and have only recently, through new mega-projects and loft conversion laws, become part of an arc of emergent upgrading from Downtown north-west and west through Koreatown, Silverlake and Los Feliz towards Hollywood and the Hollywood Hills. Gentrification in Pico-Union was more modest again, composed of spillover from Koreatown and Downtown. Unlike London, and despite incipient gentrification, wealth in inner-city Los Angeles remains more an island than a sea, with isolated but consolidating pockets of citadel, new-build and established regeneration in Downtown, Hollywood, West Adams and Koreatown.

As for Inner Sydney, gentrification has taken firm hold in all of the inner core LGAs, reinforcing areas of established wealth to the north and east of the CBD (Aplin, 2000; Connell, 2000; Raskall, 2002; Shaw, 2007). Stone (1988) chronicled the increasing stress on inner-city housing in the 1980s, as Sydney's CBD began to recover from its 1970s losses under conditions of deconcentration and suburbanisation. Moreover, certain large-scale city infrastructure projects were dropped or put underground (such as the Eastern Distributor), thereby sparing the inner-city housing stock from further demolition and blight. This parallels Horvath's (2004) focus on the 'Green Bans' in inner Sydney in the 1970s, which limited massive renewal and redevelopment (see also Iveson, 2014), and which ultimately paved the way for pervasive incumbent gentrification in the decades to follow. The CBD boom in the run-up to the 2000 Olympics, and its subsequent resource boom, fuelled prolongation, producing a well-remunerated workforce that increasingly chose to live in the (revitalising) inner city, further marooning islands of poverty such as urban Aboriginal Block in Redfern (Shaw, 2007) and high-rise social housing in Waterloo, further to the south.

The images presented here as Figures 4.4 to 4.12 are arranged in a photo essay to give a general portrayal of Inner London, inner-city Los Angeles and Inner Sydney, respectively.

Figure 4.4 London: Westminster, the Houses of Parliament, October 2006

Photograph taken by G DeVerteuil

Figure 4.5 London: rough sleeping in Vauxhall, Lambeth, June 2009

Photograph taken by G DeVerteuil

Figure 4.6 London: gentrification in Islington, June 2009

Photograph taken by G DeVerteuil

Figure 4.7 Los Angeles: aerial image of Downtown Los Angeles and Pico-Union, November 2004

Photograph taken by G DeVerteuil

Figure 4.8 Los Angeles: new-build condo tower in Downtown Los Angeles, November 2006

Photograph taken by G DeVerteuil

Figure 4.9 Los Angeles: Hollywood and Downtown Los Angeles, February 2012

Photograph taken by G DeVerteuil

Figure 4.10 Sydney: CBD, July 2014

Photograph taken by G DeVerteuil

Figure 4.11 Sydney: Darlinghurst gentrification, July 2014

Photograph taken by G DeVerteuil

Figure 4.12 Sydney: new-build gentrification in Surry Hills, March 2011

Photograph taken by G DeVerteuil

A total of 100 voluntary-sector organisation facilities were interviewed in-depth between 2008 and 2014 (London=42; Los Angeles=37; Sydney=21) alongside an additional eight 'big picture' interviews (planners, politicians) about local service hubs across London, Los Angeles and Sydney, for a grand total of 108 interviews, (Table 4.2) as well as significant documentary, photographic and census analysis.

Table 4.2: Interviews by inner-city area

	Number of facilities interviewed	'big picture' interviews
Islington (London)	8	1
Lambeth (London)	9	1
Southwark (London)	11	1
Tower Hamlets (London)	7	0
Westminster (London)	7	1
Downtown (Los Angeles)	17	1
Hollywood (Los Angeles)	11	1
Pico-Union (Los Angeles)	9	1
Surry Hills (Sydney)	10	1
Darlinghurst/ Kings Cross (Sydney)	11	0

For London and Los Angeles, facilities were purposively sampled from comprehensive service databases that spanned the 1998–2011 period to capture a wide range of voluntary-sector organisations (see DeVerteuil, 2011a, for more detail). The Sydney sampling frame followed the same logic, using a directory of community-sector organisations (City of Sydney, 2011). Following the need to capture a wide diversity of voluntary-sector organisations that may be subject to displacement, the samples were convenience rather than random or stratified. I relied on what Lofland et al (2006: 91–3) termed 'maximum variation sampling', in which the researcher seeks out the variability within the known universe (in this case, the service databases). More than 300 facilities were contacted through the service databases between November 2008 and June 2014, with roughly 30 in each inner-city area. Overall, the response rate was relatively low at 34%, but fairly typical for studies of the voluntary sector (Trudeau, 2008). Those who did respond tended to be interested in the topic, had themselves experienced displacement, wanted to draw attention to their services or were simply accommodating. Crucially, responses were more likely from organisations directly serving surplus populations, although a significant minority were organisations focused on advocacy, research and fundraising; such was the nature of service hubs in many inner cities. Although it was easier to track voluntary-sector facilities than displaced residents – especially given these comprehensive service databases – challenges remained: disentangling gentrification effects from other locational pressures upon organisations; locating organisations that have been displaced well beyond the study area; and locating those organisations that have disbanded completely because of gentrification (DeVerteuil, 2011a). These challenges required mixed methods that included longitudinal numerical analysis with large enough samples, along with qualitative interview material to pinpoint actual displacement and the reasons behind it (Atkinson, 2003).

Operationalising displacement

As the building block of the service hub, the voluntary sector has also seen much growth since the 1980s (Wolch, 1990; Salamon, 1999; Milbourne, 2013). In the US, the number of legally recognised 501(c)3 non-profits grew by 87% between 1995 and 2012, to close to 1.6 million organisations (NCCS, 2013). In the UK, growth in numbers of registered charities has been essentially flat since 2000, but the number of large charities (over £10 million/year) tripled between 1999 and 2014, while aggregated annual gross income grew 610% between 1999 and 2014 (Charity Commission, 2014). In Australia, employment growth for the voluntary sector has been second only to the mining sector since 2000 (Lyons, 2009). This growth has certainly been abetted by direct state involvement – some of which has been surley enrolled into various neoliberal welfare reforms – but the geographical distribution was and is never guaranteed, always *provisional* and subject to the pressures of dynamic global city-regions. As an incomplete yet consolidating and potent structure, neoliberalism may tolerate and depend upon the voluntary sector, but may also directly threaten conspicuous spatial arrangements – such as the service hub – on the ground in the gentrifying inner city. By their very conspicuousness and centrality, as well as their ability to obscure the abrasive presence of surplus populations, service hubs are vulnerable to gentrification-induced displacement and outright dismantlement within an increasingly revalorised, antagonistic post-industrial city (Mair, 1986). Displacement potentially reduces accessibility for these same populations, many of whom have limited mobility and would find it difficult to access a more dispersed service configuration (DeVerteuil, 2011a).

I therefore highlight *physical displacement* as the direct threat to resilience (Wright, 1997). As Adger underlined, (spatial) displacement is 'frequently an indicator of the breakdown of social resilience' (2000: 357). My particular focus is on gentrification-induced displacement, and this phenomenon requires some unpacking. Gentrification is fuelled, accelerated and intensified through the substantial growth of globalised advanced services and the stupendous remunerations that accompany it (Sassen, 2001; Atkinson & Bridge, 2005; Butler & Lees, 2006). In global city-regions, gentrification may be seen as the driving wedge of the violence and dispossession inherent in property (Blomley, 2003), the stinging evidence that class antagonisms, inequality and polarisations have not gone away in the post-industrial (and so-called creative) city (Davidson & Wyly, 2012). From this critical perspective, gentrification is 'nothing more and nothing less than the neighborhood expression of class inequality' (Lees et al, 2008: 80). A wide array of research has shown gentrification to be harmful, including increased cost of housing, depletion of neighbourhood place-identity, homelessness, community conflict and, crucially, the direct and indirect displacement of low-income groups and their attendant landscapes (Atkinson, 2000; Shaw, 2005; Davidson, 2008). Hackworth (2007: 98) underlined that 'gentrification can be seen as the material and symbolic knife-edge of neoliberal urbanism, representing the erosion of the physical and symbolic embodiment of neoliberal's putative other – the Keynesian activist state'. So I see gentrification as more than just replacement – it potentially sweeps aside residuals, and reconfigures centrality and accessibility. Yet while I recognise gentrification and its displacements as mired in class antagonisms as well as threatening to service hubs, the result is not always naked revanchism à la Smith (1996), but rather a more complex interplay between displacement and resilience, punitiveness and support (DeVerteuil, 2014). This suggests that we must be open to *other consequences* of gentrification *beyond* displacement, developed more fully in the next paragraph. The recognition of other consequences also aligns with poverty management's ambivalence and support offsetting naked punitiveness.

Gentrification-induced displacement generally involves involuntary movement, 'changes of residence which are hoisted on people, which they did not seek out on purpose, for which they may lack the social and economic coping resources … are detrimental to the individuals and families involved, and produce social costs as well' (Hartman, 1984: 302). Of course, there are other types of displacement that are more indirect, in the form of symbolic, psychic and social displacement, as well as a lowering of tolerance to diversity of which the service hub may present the sternest test. Indirect displacement captures the pressure in terms of negative neighbourhood change, rising NIMBY and clientele displacement that serve to protect class and racial entitlements (Shaw, 2007; Harvey, 2012; DeVerteuil, 2013). According to Atkinson (2000: 163), there is a 'social evacuation effect' with gentrification–induced displacement, producing 'impaired social networks and reduced service provision [and] adversely affect[ing] groups less able to cope with the psychological and financial costs of such shocks. Displacement removes social problems and rearranges rather than ameliorates the causes of poverty ... problems are moved rather than solved.' My focus on displacement as the harmful *sine qua non* of gentrification accords with Slater's (2006) castigation that geographers have spent too much energy defining gentrification, pinpointing its causes and describing the constitution and practices of gentrifiers themselves, rather than examining its potentially deleterious *consequences* on the worst-off, of (re)joining gentrification to marginality. It is to these consequences of gentrification, in the form of displacement to service hubs, that forms the empirical basis of this book. But, while agreeing with Slater, I see the consequences of gentrification as more than just physical displacement – they must also include the collateral costs of staying put, what I will deem entrapment, alongside deep-seated resilience (DeVerteuil, 2012). Together with Slater's admonitions, there has been a recent resurgence of studying the gentrification–displacement relationship (for example, Freeman, 2006; Newman & Wyly, 2006; DeVerteuil, 2011a; DeVerteuil, 2012) but, with the exception of Newman and Wyly (2006) and DeVerteuil (2012), relatively little on resilience against it. So while displacement has been (more or less) adequately addressed of late, considering the resilience against displacement doubtlessly represents a missed opportunity.

Now that the threat has been clearly identified, I propose some measures of social and spatial resilience along the lines of Adger (2000), who emphasised key properties such as stability, distribution and growth. In particular, I wish to underline stability, both spatial and social, as a key indicator of resilience. While stability may imply rigidity and a lack of creativity/proactivity, it is actually far from the case; just staying put frequently requires an enormous amount of energy, strategy and adaptability (see Chapter Two). This adaptive production of resilience will be approached (1) retrospectively and post-rupture, as Klinenberg (2002) did in his social autopsy approach, and Yoon and Currid-Halkett (forthcoming) in their discrete-time survival approach, and (2) as a process, the 'how' rather than the 'whether', both measured through interviews. Face-to-face interviewing was essential in order to determine that resilience was actually present, and due to gentrification and not other circumstances such as changes in funding, need for expansion, and so forth. I administered a semi-structured interview to one key informant for each facility, preferably a longstanding staff member. All facilities were asked to provide their aims, a basic profile of their clients, a brief history, funding streams and their rationale for their current location. The final set of questions focused on their locational history since 1998, including reasons for any movements and whether they were voluntary or involuntary in nature, and whether there were gentrification effects (and to validate whether gentrification was indeed occurring 'on the ground'). This information was supplemented by official documents. All facilities remained anonymous. Finally, I was able to undertake eight key informant interviews, usually a community spokesperson for each borough or area, in order to get a 'big picture' of gentrification, social change and social service dynamics within each study area (Newman and Wyly, 2006). These key informant interviews included speaking to voluntary-sector umbrella organisations, local politicians or planners.

I developed a fivefold typology of spatial outcomes for voluntary organisations in order to differentiate gentrification-induced displacement from spatial resilience (for more details, see DeVerteuil, 2011a: 1569): (1) voluntary immobility (resilience); (2) involuntary immobility (resilience but also entrapment); (3) voluntary mobility; (4) involuntary mobility (displacement); and (5) indirect displacement pressure. As Table 4.3 makes obvious, spatial resilience (voluntary and involuntary) is clearly measured by (1) and (2), and displacement by (4) and, to a lesser extent, (5). Spatial resilience involved a series of strategies in response not just to displacement but also to immobility when the upgrading of surrounding (central-city) areas and its attendant rise in NIMBY make it impossible to move and/or expand in situ.

Any of the 100 facilities could have experienced more than one of these processes and outcomes during the retrospective period, and in a myriad of sequences. However, my analysis measured displacement only on the likelihood of at least one instance of it (0 or 1); displacement rates are found in Table 5.1 in the next chapter. Displacement pressure may be experienced by any facility, whether there was movement or not.

While I give less attention to matters of social resilience, save for Chapter Nine, it remains essential for understanding how voluntary-sector organisations enabled resilience through care and sustenance to their clientele. The threat here was directly related to everyday survival, on the strategies for securing material security among surplus populations. For instance, there was an omnipresent threat of

Table 4.3: Resilience and displacement outcomes

Process	Movement 1998–2011	Voluntary or involuntary	Concept	Outcome
(1) Voluntary immobility	No	Voluntary	Hartman's (1984) 'staying put'	Spatial resilience, positive
(2) Involuntary immobility (entrapment – see DeVerteuil, 2011a)	No	Involuntary, and due to gentrification	Entrapment, where gentrification has effectively excluded any opportunity to relocate or expand in situ; precursor to Marcuse's (1985) concept of exclusionary displacement	Spatial resilience, negative
(3) Voluntary mobility	Yes	Voluntary	Captures voluntary movement within, into or beyond the study areas	
(4) Involuntary mobility (displacement)	Yes	Involuntary, and due to gentrification	Captures Marcuse's (1985) concept of 'direct last-resident displacement' within, into or beyond the study areas	Displacement
(5) Indirect displacement pressure	Not applicable	Due to gentrification	Captures indirect pressure in terms of negative neighbourhood change, rising NIMBY and clientele displacement	Displacement

homelessness among surplus populations, particularly in places like Los Angeles where social housing is a very scarce resource and where welfare is threadbare (Marr et al, 2009; DeVerteuil, 2011b). But, once homeless, Marr et al (2009) underscored the importance of the voluntary sector and the service hub in structuring the geographies of everyday survival, in terms of acting as crucial nodes of caring and sustenance (see also Takahashi, 1998; Duneier's 'sustaining habitats', 1999). Since I did not interview any clients for this book, the enabling of resilience was exclusively interpreted through interviews with voluntary-sector organisations. The perspective and role of these organisations was useful to obtain an overall picture of community survival, one that complemented the extensive research on how surplus populations themselves deploy a variety of survival techniques to 'get by' and socially reproduce on an everyday basis, absorbing the increased social burden left in the wake of welfare retrenchment, low wages and racial exclusion (for example, DeVerteuil, 2010; Martin, 2010).

Comparative methods

My study is more than just multi-site, multi-city and multinational – this wide-ranging case-study approach is common enough, from Castells (1983) to Hackworth (2007), Hutton (2010) and Cloke et al (2010). What distinguishes my study is its explicitly comparative approach of (1) inner-city space in London, Los Angeles and Sydney and, most importantly, (2) displacement and resilience among voluntary-sector organisations arranged in inner-city service hubs. While urban comparison has burgeoned of late, yielding important conceptual and methodological advances and interventions (for example, Abu-Lughod, 2007; Boudreau et al, 2007; Nijman, 2007a; 2007b; Ward, 2008; 2010; 2012; Bollens, 2009; McFarlane, 2010; Robinson 2011a; 2011b; Jacobs, 2012; McFarlane & Robinson, 2012; Till, 2012), these advances have yet to connect to cross-national comparisons of the voluntary sector (Wolch, 1990; Hasson & Ley 1997; Salamon & Anheier, 1998; Trudeau & Veronis, 2009; Von Mahs, 2013) and to comparative work on resilience (Adger, 2000; Hall & Lamont, 2013). The work that my comparative approach does is therefore more in its application *to* the voluntary sector and resilience, rather than developing my own methodological innovations. These innovations are certainly welcome, coming after many decades of theoretical lassitude (Ward, 2008), but have been accompanied by a sort of conceptual haste that would do well to catch its breath and take some (conceptual and methodological) stock – this is essentially my own contribution.

My overall comparative approach was informed by three specific methodological and conceptual hallmarks. In Chapter Ten, I will apply these hallmarks to the task of comparing voluntary-sector displacement and resilience across the 10 inner-city neighbourhoods –arranged in Chapter Five by four place-based typological categories – and the three global city-regions. First, my overall approach aligned with Nijman's insights on balancing difference and similarity and the associated task of selecting case studies. He contended that 'comparative urbanism … aims at developing knowledge, understanding, and generalization at a level between what is true of all cities and what is true of one city at a given point in time' (2007a: 1). Despite the fact that every city is different and even unique (widespread and singular processes such as post-Fordism, post-industrialism, marginalisation, globalisation and neoliberalism are uniquely filtered across different cities), part of his emphasis was on why cities can also display crosscutting similarities, but without the seeking of model or paradigmatic urbanisms that has plagued urban studies for 25 years. This insight forms the basis for debates around globalisation and global cities, in that some cities are more global than others, some rank higher than others, and some are putatively converging in their experiences (Sassen, 2001; Nijman, 2007b). There is very little analytical insight in saying that all cities are different and particular, and leaving it at that – it is the additional seeking of similarities, regularities and synthesis that becomes analytically more interesting, alongside (but never ignoring) the inevitable differences (Boudreau et al, 2007; Scott & Storper, forthcoming). Comparison is about learning from other cities, a willingness that implies a rejection of the clamorous yet theoretically limited particularism pervading certain post-structuralist/ colonialist approaches. According to the case-orientated comparative approach, which combines both historical interpretation and causal analysis (and so the idiographic with the nomothetic), the selection of case studies is absolutely crucial. Following on from my previous argument, the selection of case studies must be carefully considered, but *need not* involve comparing very similar cities to find similarities, and can (should?) now involve comparing somewhat unlike cities (since they are all in some ways unique) and search for both cross-cutting similarities and distinguishing differences, the product of the *general* roles that global city-regions have come to play in the contemporary world economy but also their *distinctive* histories, geographies, political economies and path-dependent developmental trajectories that produce different place particularities (Brenner & Keil, 2006). This aligns with Robinson's (2011b: 5) critique that much previous research never strayed from comparing similar cities, victim of the pervasive fear of 'incommensurability'.

So, from an epistemological viewpoint, I argue that it is at least as interesting to compare somewhat unlike cities (for example, Jerusalem and Vancouver in Hasson & Ley, 1997) to find similarities than to compare very similar cities to find similarities. The similarity approach has too long circumscribed the scope of comparative studies; difference and diversity should no longer be seen as methodological barriers but increasingly as the generators of insight and further conceptualisation (Robinson, 2011b; McFarlane & Robinson, 2012). It follows that studying relatively unlike cities can be bolstered if the focus is on the localised permutations of crosscutting, recurring and ubiquitous patterns and phenomena. This is precisely what Wacquant (2008) sought to do in his comparison of advanced marginality found in both Chicago's inner city and Paris's *banlieues* (Abu-Lughod, 2007). This approach also resembled Nijman's (2007b: 94) deployment of 'deep analogies' – that is, 'particular processes that are at work in places that are widely separated in space and/or time', in his comparisons of Miami to other global cities. While some of these deep analogies are globally applicable (Robinson, 2011b), especially neoliberalism and resilience, in my case, the extralocal contexts also included gentrification-induced displacement and service hub resilience that variously pervaded the inner cities of Global North global city-regions like London, Los Angeles and Sydney.

Second, the seeking of similarities, differences and deep analogies raises the epistemological question of how? Here I wade in to the more specific techniques of comparison, with the full knowledge that my choices will have important methodological and representational consequences (Robinson, 2011b). In particular, I employed what Robinson deemed the 'encompassing' approach, 'in which different cases are assumed to be part of overarching, systemic processes, such as capitalism or globalisation. In this case they can be analysed as instances or units, albeit systematically differentiated, within the broader system' (2011b: 5). The system here was neoliberalism and post-welfarism, and their relationship to resilient residuals, and the instances or units were global city-regions connected to and part of an encompassing whole. Given its wide scope, it is not surprising that comparisons among global cities tend to use the encompassing approach (Brenner & Keil, 2006). But I also imposed some stipulations to this approach: first, I was unconvinced of the convergence thesis among global city-regions, and thus did not use it as the basis for my comparison. Rather, I saw global city-regions as assemblages of the general and the particular that preclude uni-directionality. Second, while sampling from a relatively narrow band of (global) cities – the 'usual suspects' in globalisation/urbanisation research (McFarlane, 2010) – I again rejected the assumption that they need be very similar and thus pursued more of a 'variation finding' exercise based on difference and plural causality (Robinson, 2011b), as well as seeking similarities from difference places. Third, I did not make claims that Global North experiences were models or universal, but was certainly aware that 'there are many aspects of cities that are reproduced serially across the world of cities' (Robinson, 2011b: 14). Fourth and finally, my unit of comparison was fixed, place-based (the service hub) and territorial (the inner city of the global city-region), which was rather conventional but entirely suitable given my aims of studying the production of resilience among service hubs across a wide range of somewhat similar territories. Yet I also realised that this territorial rigidity falls into the trap of seeing the inner city, as well as the global city-region itself, as ontologically 'discrete, self-enclosed and analytically separate objects' (Ward, 2008; Ward, 2010: 479). In response, I remained open to flows and connections, not by following specific policy trajectories but through the more pervasive and indirect emulations and imitations that span the globe, including neoliberalism, gentrification (Harris, 2008), welfare models, displacement and the defence of residuals. As highlighted in Chapter One, I saw the inner city as heterogeneous, not monolithic, and as an arena of contestation, not a predetermined outcome.

Third, and moving beyond practicalities, I saw comparative methods as a *political opportunity* and as a *strategy*. McFarlane (2010: 726) argued persuasively that 'comparative thinking can be a strategy firstly for revealing the assumptions, limits and distinctiveness of particular theoretical or empirical claims, and secondly for formulating new lines of inquiry and more situated accounts'. I used my comparative approach as a strategy to query the received wisdom of certain taken-for-granted depictions and representations within the Global North, what Wacquant (2008) deemed 'folk concepts', stereotypical and pernicious designations (for example, the 'underclass') that pass for common sense among policy makers and local residents alike, and sometimes circulate across national lines. It is this latter transnational circulation of folk concepts that I was most interested in interrogating. Indeed, there is purported transatlantic convergence between the UK and US, and transpacific convergence between Australia and the US within the world of Anglo-American welfarism, propped up by rapid policy transfers originating in and exported from the US (Peck, 2001). But is this Anglo-American welfare model really circulating, or at least being imitated? Only a detailed comparative approach that takes national contexts seriously (in conjunction with the global city-region scale) can begin to unpack and challenge transoceanic convergence, a convergence about which I am sceptical given my pointed critiques of an all-encompassing, essentialist neoliberalism in Chapter One. A second folk concept is the purported spread and convergence of an Anglo-American gentrification (Harris, 2008), a blueprint emanating from London and New York City in the 1980s (Carpenter & Lees, 1995), emulated later in places like Sydney (Shaw, 2007), Vancouver, Toronto, San Francisco and the like, but perhaps not particularly applicable to Los Angeles, with its polyglot polycentrism run amok?

In terms of the mechanics of comparison, my approach was multi-staged. I first categorised the 10 inner-city areas into four place-types: established gentrified; mixed; pioneer gentrified; immigrant enclaves. More on this exercise will be outlined in the next chapter. In Chapter Ten, I will apply the lessons of comparative urbanism to the nascent field of 'comparative resilience' (Vale & Campanella, 2005; Hall & Lamont, 2013), developing a tripartite set of resilience strategies:

private; voluntary sector; and political. More on comparing resilience among the voluntary sector will be covered in Chapter Ten.

Notes

[1] According to the most-cited ranking (Beaverstock et al, 1999), London is a first-tier global city, particularly given its globe-spanning financial, insurance and banking cluster (Hamnett, 2003). Los Angeles' global city-ness is also first tier, but is less due to financial prowess and more aligned to its leading role in terms of logistics, entertainment and as a key immigrant destination (Alpha ranking of 10 out of 12 for world city-ness) (Soja, 2000). Sydney is clearly Australia's gateway city, and a second-tier global city (Baum, 1997; Fagan, 2000; Flood, 2003; but see McNeill et al, 2005). Using a wider range of variables that went beyond Sassen's (2001) focus on advanced services, the *Kearney Global City Report* (2014) put London at second, Los Angeles sixth and Sydney fourteenth.

[2] Indeed, many critiques of global city theory ignore the heartfelt emphasis placed by Friedmann (1986) and especially Sassen (2001) on the social order and consequences of global city status. Sassen's new book, *Expulsions* (2014), emphasises exactly the detrimental consequences of globalisation upon urban space.

[3] Local Government Areas are the lowest tier of government, under the national and state levels; there is no explicit regional government in Australia. Local governments are created through acts of state parliament and have historically been tasked with 'rates, roads and rubbish'. This is not as accurate these days, with local government roles having incrementally expanded, and it is more likely now to see local governments involved in the operation or funding of community services. Local governments in inner metro areas such as Inner Sydney are likely to be involved in welfare/community services to a greater extent because their revenues are high in relative terms.

[4] The term 'voluntary sector' is not only more capacious theoretically; it is also more amenable empirically (rather than 'NGO', 'third sector' or 'non-profit sector') due to its portability across national boundaries (the third sector in particular is a very UK term, and the non-profit sector rather American, and NGO and not-for-profit more Australian).

[5] Although data were not freely available for 1998 for Greater London and Metropolitan Sydney, inner-city Los Angeles in 1998 again featured higher per capita figures than Los Angeles County, suggesting a durable pattern of inner-city concentration.

Part Two
Case studies: spatial and social resilience in London, Los Angeles and Sydney

Part Two presents the empirical material of the comparative study, as well as its analysis. Chapter Five begins the comparative analysis by proposing four place-types across the 10 case studies. Each of the ensuring chapters (Chapters Six to Nine) then focuses on one of the four place-types, in terms of profiling both spatial and social resilience. The results suggested a wide range of resilience strategies adapting to the differing level of threat across the case studies. Chapter Ten compares the four place-types, alongside the three global city-regions themselves.

But before broaching the material on resilience in Chapters Five to Ten, I will briefly consider the pattern and profile of *displacement* across the sample – that is, to consider the on-the-ground nature of the threat itself before the response.

Table 5.1: Displacement rates by city, 1998–2011

	Displacement rate	Displacement pressure
London	21.4%	54.7%
Los Angeles	18.9%	75.6%
Sydney	16.2%	52.3%

Close to 20% of all facilities experienced at least one episode of displacement during the study period. This proportion may well be underestimated, given the difficulty in identifying services whose gentrification-induced displacement led to disbandment, as well as limitations of the service databases themselves, which do not pick up smaller, potentially more vulnerable organisations nor exits from the study areas. Yet the proportions may also be overestimated, given that responses may have been biased towards displaced organisations wanting to tell their story. Nevertheless, the proportions, if annualised, were not entirely dissimilar from residential displacement estimates by Marcuse (1985) and Atkinson (2000) in London and New York City, and Atkinson et al (2011) in Sydney and Melbourne. And even if the proportions seemed low, gentrification-induced displacement was greatly significant to the 19 facilities. These included disruption and loss of clientele base, smaller premises, higher and more precarious rental agreements, and lengthy efforts to find new premises within gentrifying neighbourhoods. The rate of displacement pressure was 62%, or three times more likely than the actual displacement rate.

Crucially, the profile of displaced facilities differed from those who were resilient (DeVerteuil, 2011a). Most displaced services were renting from the private market at the time of displacement, and found themselves involuntarily moving because of eviction and/or rent increases brought on by neighbourhood gentrification. Second, a majority were smaller than the average-sized facility in terms of client intake. Third, they relied more on (erratic) donations and client fees than on government funding. Fourth, advocacy services were more vulnerable to displacement than those providing direct services, possibly related to having less (or less consistent) government support given that advocacy may not be accorded equal importance. Fifth, the majority served the most stigmatised clientele – namely, homeless individuals and persons with substance abuse issues and/or mental health problems. All told, I can suggest that displaced services tended to not be 'trendy' (for an example, see Figure 5.1), to not fit in with gentrifying landscapes and the exchange (and use) values of gentrifiers, who would rather have a cafe or restaurant.

Figure 5.1 Displaced facility from Inner Sydney, July 2014

Photograph taken by G DeVerteuil

While displacement rates were similar for London, Los Angeles and Sydney, displacement pressure were not. There was much greater indirect displacement pressure in Los Angeles overall, due to the more established nature of gentrification in London and Sydney, where facilities were more adapted to their environments (DeVerteuil, 2011a). In Los Angeles, gentrification was still novel and facilities had little previous experience, suggesting that London and Sydney were in a more advanced stage of resilience, thereby rebuking the sense that it is ephemeral, doomed to eventual displacement. Greater displacement pressure also arose because of the much larger scale of homelessness in Los Angeles, which engendered more community opposition and NIMBY due to the higher visibility of clientele. The differing roles of the national welfare state, local welfare state, voluntary-sector regime and local governance structures also played crucial roles in deflecting displacement and displacement pressure – and thus in/directly abetting resilience. It is these crucial differences in governance structures that I examine in the ensuing chapter, which firmly politicises the study of resilience and calls attention to the key role of the extralocal in structuring patterns of resilience.

FIVE

National and local settlements: London, UK; Los Angeles, US; Sydney, Australia

The global city-regions under study have been thoroughly examined for decades (though rarely compared), particularly London and Los Angeles; so much so that they have become touchstones for global city-region theorisation, to the detriment of knowing and comparing other, more 'ordinary cities', especially in the Global South (Robinson, 2002). However, this does not mean that we know everything about London, Los Angeles and Sydney, especially with regard to overlooked service hubs in backwater inner-city space (but see Wolch & Dear, 1993, on Los Angeles). My overall aim in this chapter is to flesh out the critical exogenous dimensions of resilience. I first do this by embedding the global city-regions within their larger national political context. Second, I trace the local welfare and voluntary sector settlements in each global city-region, which also involved tracking the dramatic reinventions from the 1980s onwards, when London, Los Angeles and Sydney all attained a certain global city status. With reference to Sydney, but certainly applicable to London and Los Angeles, McGuirk and O'Neill (2002: 303) contended that the rise to global city status entails a 'deepening insertion into global circuits of capital [that] has coincided with the consolidation of neoliberalism, and an associated fiscal austerity as the dominant Western political ideology'. Third and finally, I will offer a place typology for the ten inner-city areas that will structure the empirical analysis from Chapter Six onwards.

Politicising the case studies: national welfare states and voluntary-sector regimes

An unintentional drawback to the global cities literature – and perhaps even the policy mobilities one – is that the primary emphasis on a relational yet emphatically autonomous urban scale downplays the premise that global city-regions are unavoidably and inextricably moored to and entangled with their national contexts (Jones, 2012; Marr, 2012). While global city-regions may well have economically detached themselves from their national space-economies to command

and control the global economy, the same autonomy cannot be assumed for certain political and social policies (McGuirk, 2007). This is only natural, given that cities do not have the fiscal capacity to escape the orbit of national social policies, taxation policies and currency controls (Peterson, 1981). Wacquant (2008) was well aware of these macro-level contexts when he compared Chicago and Paris: the withered American welfare state produced very different results on the ground in inner-city Chicago than the more robust French one did in the Parisian *banlieues*. While not denying the agency of urban governance and the endemic nature of policy flows (Peck, 2011), alongside the notion of path-dependency (Leiter, 2008), there is no doubt that national territorial contexts and trajectories continue to strongly mediate the circulation of policies that permeate the globe, if not block them entirely.

An approach that emphasised the mediating nature of national contexts was famously espoused by Esping-Andersen (1990; 1996), whose concept of *national welfare state regimes* has been used to compare the levels of universalism, stratification and de-commodification in Western nations. Esping-Andersen (1990) lumped Australia, the UK and the US as residual liberal welfare states, with modest attempts at de-commodification, modest levels of benefits, prone to retrenchment and strict entitlements for residualised poor people (DeVerteuil, 2011c). Yet I will use the comparative results to unpack this isomorphic 'Anglo-Saxon' liberal welfare state regime that might cloud some important national path-dependencies, mediations and differences. More specifically, I propose *four hypothetical points* of convergence and divergence derived from Esping-Andersen's original formulations, points that I propose with some scepticism and to which I will return in Chapters Ten and Twelve as part of the overall comparison of the results. First, I propose that the US welfare state could be understood as the most residual of the three, lacking not only foundational benefits such as universal health care but also featuring a patchwork of 50 states filtering, or self-providing, an uneven raft of benefits that appear, at least in comparison to other OECD countries, ragged. The American welfare state has also been prone to radical shifts. While the 1935 and 1965 welfare acts fundamentally established the modern American welfare state, the 1996 welfare reform – the Personal Responsibility and Work Opportunity Reconciliation Act (PRWORA) – fundamentally diminished it. Its hallmarks included devolution to the state, local and voluntary sector level, lifetime restrictions on eligibility, non-eligibility for legal immigrants, and entrenched a moral rather than structural understanding of poverty (Henriksen et al, 2012). It also cemented a two-tier system, between the deserving (the job ready, elderly) and the non-deserving (long-term unemployed, single mothers, immigrants) (DeVerteuil, 2003a; 2003b).

Second, I propose that influence and convergence (if any) could be unidirectional from the US model to Australia and the UK, but with the understanding that the receiving nations might only partially emulate and implement it (Castles, 1996; Peck, 2001; Mendes, 2009). Of the four hypothetical points, I am most sceptical about this one, as it undermines my own de-essentialised understanding of an incomplete neoliberalism set out in Chapters One and Three. To give but one example, both Australia and the UK have resisted the attraction of setting time limits to welfare recipiency, at least for the time being (Mendes, 2009). Conversely, Australia and the UK have certainly adopted the rhetoric around an American blueprint of residualism, responsiveness to neoliberalism and globalisation, and to a lesser extent devolution. Policy discourse around the welfare state has seen a remarkable convergence over the past decade,

> draw[ing] on the same vocabulary to a significant degree and also in the sense that similar institutional solutions to a large extent have been promoted across welfare regimes … this means that the ways in which welfare policies are being legitimised become more similar – cost efficiency, individual choice, competition, and accountability. (Henriksen et al, 2012: 497)

Third, and contradicting the second hypothesis, I propose that the UK welfare state could have remained open to, and uniquely influenced by, both US and European ideals, resisting the intense roll-back and roll-out as well as stinginess and near collapse of the former, while lacking the ambitious de-commodification of the latter (Peck, 2001; Wacquant, 2008; DeVerteuil, 2011a; 2011b). The UK welfare state has traditionally been highly centralised and rather resistant to wholesale devolution and retrenchment (at least until 2010). Nonetheless, there is now evidence of a harsher, more American-style approach to welfare, in the form of workfare introduced under the auspices of New Labour's Third Way in 1997 and further reinforced by the 2010 Coalition government, although again selectively titrated by particular UK tendencies of centralisation, incrementalism and concern for social exclusion (Peck, 2001; Amin et al, 2002). More on this apparent shift will be considered in Chapter Twelve.

Last, I propose that the Australian experience might be somewhere in between that of the US and UK, displaying its own uniqueness born of isolation and inertia. Mendes (2009) contended that, despite the Howard government's mid-2000s American-leaning rhetoric on a welfare state 'crisis', the embrace of neoliberal solutions and the supposed urgent need for retrenchment, the Australian welfare state remained rather robust in comparison to that of the US – after all, this was 'the first country to introduce a social service safety net through universal age and other pensions' (Flood, 2003: 1). Like the UK, Australia maintains universal health care (with threats of co-payment for 2015, however), but has certainly tightened eligibility and cut back on provisions to people with disabilities and lone parents (the truly vulnerable but increasingly labelled as the 'undeserving poor'), while paradoxically increasing spending on family payments and the voluntary sector. It has also introduced greater moral conditions – a trend whereby the welfare state increasingly (and narrowly) supports a 'deserving' middle class, which is also an issue in the US. Welfare is also somewhat more decentralised compared to the case in the UK, with six states and two territories (Hall & Taplin, 2007). In Chapter Twelve, I will consider in more depth the impending reforms that may nudge the Australian model towards the American one.

Inspired by Esping-Andersen, Salamon and Anheier (1998) outlined a series of voluntary sector regimes along two axes: government social welfare spending and the scale of the voluntary sector. The authors again grouped the US and the UK into a similar non-profit (voluntary) sector regime ('liberal model') characterised by low and retrenching levels of government social welfare spending absorbed by relatively large, growing and interventionist non-profit sectors. Although not part of the original study, presumably Australia also fitted in to this regime. Along these lines, all three nations have seen spectacular growth in the voluntary sector since the 1980s, including significant increases in governmental funding (Nevile, 2009; Clifford, 2012; Phillips & Goodwin, 2013). As for the welfare state regime framework, I would like to again propose points of convergence and divergence from Salamon and Anheier's (1998) voluntary-sector regime framework, which I will revisit in Chapter Ten armed with the results. Foremost has been the disagreement over the degree to which the voluntary sector provides a robust substitute to the receding welfare state, or merely plays second fiddle to a centralised national welfare state. In comparing the US and UK voluntary sectors, Wolch (1990) and Peck (2001) both argued that the American voluntary sector is larger, more developed and supported with private donations, and given more freedom owing to a far more decentralised federal welfare state. While the American voluntary sector is more substitute for direct governmental action, the

UK voluntary sector remains constrained by a far more interventionist (and highly centralised) national welfare state, and is seen more to be modestly filling unmet needs. A clear contrast may be provided between the 1996 American welfare reform, which greatly expanded the role and funding of the voluntary sector, and the post-2010 UK welfare reform, which has actually involved severe governmental cuts to voluntary-sector funding (Milbourne, 2013). The Australian voluntary sector again falls in between: smaller on average, less essential and less reliant on donations than the American sector (Leiter, 2008). As in the American case, Australia's voluntary sector stretches beyond service provision to take an active role in shaping policy (Phillips & Goodwin, 2013) – something that in the UK has been long denied, even with the emergence of the self-proclaimed 'Big Society' post-2010. In fact, welfare reforms proposed by the new Liberal government under Abbott in 2014 (see Chapter Twelve) are being overseen by Patrick McClure, former head of Mission Australia, one of the nation's largest charities.

Local welfare state and voluntary sector settlements

Despite the mediating influence of the national welfare and voluntary regime, each global city-region retained at least some autonomy to partially fashion its own local welfare settlement (DeVerteuil et al, 2003). Cities, as Castells (1983) and Fainstein (2010) argued, are the locus of collective consumption and justice respectively, and as Wolch (1990: 33) contended, welfare and voluntarism can be understood only with reference to local settlements:

> The locale is a complex condensate of historical, current, and evolving patterns originating at various scales. Interpreting local voluntarism requires a deconstruction of local structure, institutional process, and individual routines, and also the ways in which social structures, institutions and agents operating at higher spatial scale simultaneously impact local situations.

Since polarisation was a shared feature across all three global city-regions, a common challenge invariably involved its management through collective consumption, the local welfare state settlement and the voluntary sector (Keil, 1998).

Since its mid-century stagnation, London's upward trajectory has been dramatic and decidedly contradictory. According to Massey (2007; 2011), from the 1980s onwards, London reinvented itself as a wildly successful global node of finance and a purveyor of financial neoliberalism, becoming a top-tier global city with New York and Tokyo (Sassen, 2001). The Thatcher years (1979–90) saw London become more glamorous and wealthier, with robust job growth, but less egalitarian and more diverse (see also Hamnett, 2003). Massey did note, however, a certain contradiction with London's previous, and perhaps now residual, claim to openness and generosity, products of the Keynesian era: 'this is a city at the very center of the reassertion of marketization, profit, and privatization, which yet imagines itself (and not incorrectly) as open, as hospitable, indeed, in a certain sense, as generous to the outside world' (2011: 6). In her 2007 book *World City*, she reinforced the notion that London 'is a unique articulation: a place where market capitalism is in part produced and propagated, yet where it is also still embedded in (the remains of) a social democratic settlement' (Massey, 2007: 58). Fainstein appreciated that, while London lagged behind the more redistributive cities of Western and Northern Europe, it still 'has had a more activist and redistributional public sector than New York' (Fainstein, 2010: 113). This implied that London was more equal than other large American cities, the majority of which are less egalitarian than New York: London is less segregated, with higher proportions of social housing (but decreasing since the early 1980s), and a robust national health system and public sector (Massey, 2007). London's welfare settlement is administered on the ground in decentralised and uneven ways through 32 boroughs (and the City) that use national funds to provide local services such as health, education, and especially housing subsidies for local authority and private housing. This is generally done independently of the Greater London Authority (the replacement for the defunct Greater London Council, 1965–86), which currently focuses on London's strategic directions and certain city-wide services such as transportation (Pilgrim, 2006; Hamnett, 2009; Ancien, 2011). As such, 'the metropolis remains decentralised to the 33 local authorities … the borough authorities continue to be the most important decision makers regarding services and the specific forms that development takes; although they must work within the guidelines stipulated by the mayor, they have substantial discretion' (Fainstein, 2010: 136). Inner London boroughs have, for the most part, been considered more generous (particularly for social housing) than their Outer London counterparts, albeit responding to more need, and hold greater concentrations of voluntary-sector organisations, as Table 4.1 suggested.

The dramatic rise of Los Angeles to global city-region status in the 1980s would itself influence the emergence of world city and global city theory, with key works by Friedmann (1986), Sassen (2001) and Soja (2000). While the LA School would in turn exaggerate the global city-region's importance in theoretical terms while neglecting its actual comparative positioning, this does not mean that Los Angeles is insignificant empirically – it remains a fascinating and instructive, though certainly not paradigmatic or prototypical, place to study post-Fordism, polarisation, polycentrism, immigration and the relationship between globalisation and cities (Soja, 2000; 2010). Los Angeles is more representative of the typically car-dependent, decentralised American metropolis than its global city-region rival New York. Some of the signature concerns of the LA School – particularly the fascination with dystopian urbanism (for example, Davis, 1990) and exclusionary suburbanism – are slowly shifting to a more balanced and even upbeat representation, reflecting a steady rise in activism and concern for social justice that belies its traditionally conservative governance (Pastor, 2001; Soja, 2010). The local welfare settlement very much reflects this tension and fragmentation between conservative and liberal approaches. Table 4.1 indicated that Los Angeles County had the largest voluntary sector (in absolute and per capita numbers) when compared to London or Sydney, framed within a decentralised, highly localised set of 88 unique local welfare state settlements that ranged from the highly generous, mostly in the inner parts of the County (for example, City of Los Angeles, Santa Monica, West Hollywood) to the completely neglectful (mostly the newer suburban communities to the east and south of the City of Los Angeles), atop a woefully threadbare County system of benefits (Wolch, 1990; Keil, 1998; Law, 2001; DeVerteuil et al, 2002). As such, parts of Los Angeles County encompassed the more established urban welfarism of places such as New York, Philadelphia and Chicago, while other embraced a more Sunbelt laissez-faire approach. The 88 municipalities in the County enjoy substantial autonomy, but set within a 'dog-eat-dog' American system of inter-urban competition, the race to the bottom and the fear of the magnet effect, with relatively little state or federal assistance.

Sydney became Australia's undisputed global city-region, migrant magnet and Pacific Rim gateway from the 1980s onwards, the product of financial deregulation (Daly & Pritchard, 2000) similar to that in London, deepening global integration as well as economic mimicry of the US (O'Neill & McGuirk, 2002). The 1990s and 2000s booms both consolidated Sydney's global city status but also further grew the divide between 'global Sydney' (the globalising CBD, Inner Sydney and suburban areas along the coast) and the far-flung and somewhat economically isolated western suburbs (Connell & Thom, 2000; Daly

& Pritchard, 2000; O'Neill & McGuirk, 2002; Raskall, 2002; Baker & Ruming, forthcoming). The contrast between the 'dreary suburban sprawl' and the 'tinseltown precincts of the city and the wealth and privilege of the northern suburbs' was, according to Flood (2003: 2), inevitable given the strongly contrasting natural amenities between the coastline and the interior, reinforced by planning strategies 'heavily influenced by the quest to secure global city status' (Baker & Ruming, forthcoming: 9), articulated in detail within *Sydney 2030: Green/global/connected* (City of Sydney, 2008). In the favoured areas, gentrification and densification went hand in hand, with the City of Sydney LGA experiencing a quadrupling of population during the 1990s alone (Raskall, 2002), while its real estate prices outpaced those of the outer areas (Shaw, 2007). As in Los Angeles, wealth followed the coastline, while more inland areas suffered from the 'bedroom community' syndrome, and Sydney is similarly decentralised, car-dependent and spatially divided, yet also featuring a more consolidated and higher-density inner city (McGuirk & O'Neill, 2002). The concentration of wealth, however, had not yet pushed out the voluntary sector, as it remained disproportionately concentrated in Inner Sydney, at five times the rate per 1,000 persons found in Metropolitan Sydney (Table 4.1). Sydney's welfare settlement is mostly determined by the state government (social services) and federal government (income support), but the LGA level has a role to play as well, as key 'community-based vehicles providing access to the benefits of government services for all the people of New South Wales' (Forrest & Dunn, 2007: 710). All LGAs must come up with their own social plans, and have legislative responsibility to support community organisations under the Local Government Act of 1993 (City of Sydney, 2005). Like their Inner London borough and inner-city Los Angeles counterparts, Inner Sydney LGAs have similarly proven more generous, with long histories of assistance to people in need, especially Aboriginal, LGBT and homeless people, sex workers and public housing (12% of the housing stock in Sydney City LGA when compared to Metropolitan Sydney's rate of 5%; City of Sydney, 2005). While some of the welfare funding is localised, most of it also comes from federal taxes administered autonomously by the state government level (in this case, New South Wales); the federal government has relatively little constitutional power over welfare, but most of the financial levers set within a cooperative, rather than competitive, system (Jamrozik, 2009).

Comparing inner cities: place-based typology

The first comparison of the book is purely place based, and parallels typologies developed in DeVerteuil et al (2009b) and Marr et al (2009) for Los Angeles County. As categorising devices, typologies are complexity reducing but inevitably partial; they are also necessarily *contingent* on the time and places at which they are constructed, so cannot be construed as universal. I propose a fourfold place-based typology, providing an additional comparative 'cut' to supplement comparison of the three global city-regions, but also as a way to structure the remainder of the empirical results when comparison turns to the voluntary sector. To develop my typology, I used a series of variables that summarised key policy/social trends imposing themselves upon the inner city: (demand-side) gentrification, voluntary-sector presence, population diversity and punitive social policy (see DeVerteuil, 2014, for a similar analysis). The *gentrification index* was employed by Ley and Dobson (2008: 2478) as the 'change through time in the value of a social status index for census tracts, computed by averaging the percentage of professional-managerial employment and postsecondary education'. I subtracted the 1990s index from the 2010s index to give a measure of social status change in percentage. The *voluntary-sector organisations per capita* measure indicated the concentration of organisations per 1,000 people using the same data as that for Table 4.1. The diversity measures looked at the proportion of the population that is *minority*, which in Western global city-regions is an indicator of immigration and possibly polarisation, but usually not gentrification (see Chapter Nine). Finally, the *criminalisation index* measured the social policy of punitiveness towards homeless people, paralleling Wyly and Hammel's (2005) use of the raw number of laws, but this time combined with the number of business improvement districts (BIDs, where local businesses tax themselves more to provide private security and cleaning) or other equivalents. I categorised the 10 case-study neighbourhoods into four place-types: established gentrified; mixed; pioneer gentrified; immigrant enclaves (see Table 5.2).

Established gentrified areas featured the most concentrated and enduring levels of gentrification but a relatively less diverse population, medium-profile service hubs, and medium levels of criminalisation. The examples will be Westminster in London and Surry Hills in Sydney, with the former especially moving towards what Butler and Lees (2006) termed 'super gentrification', in which new layers of investment are superimposing earlier rounds of pioneer revitalisation. *Mixed* areas were more balanced in terms of gentrification, voluntary-

Table 5.2: Place typology of inner cities

	Gentrification index	Voluntary-sector organisations per capita	Minority population	Criminalisation index
Established gentrified	High	Medium	Low	Medium to high
Mixed	Medium	Medium	Medium	Medium
Pioneer gentrified	Low	High	High	High
Immigrant enclaves	Low to medium	Medium	Very high	Low

sector organisation presence, criminalisation, and diversity. The examples will be Islington, Lambeth and Southwark in London, and Darlinghurst/Kings Cross in Sydney. *Pioneer gentrified* areas featured relatively new instances of gentrification, with high-profile service hubs that have only just begun to feel the impacts, and strongly diverse populations. The examples will be Downtown and Hollywood in Los Angeles. Finally, *immigrant enclaves* were areas with low to medium levels of gentrification – never much higher than the pioneer areas – but scored very high on diversity through the dominant presence of immigrants (who are seen to be traditional barriers to gentrification), with modest service hubs and a relatively tolerant criminalisation index. The examples will be Pico-Union in Los Angeles and Tower Hamlets in London. Further, immigrant enclaves will be the only place-types with a strong focus on enabling (social) resilience.

How did these four categories crosscut the inner cities of London, Los Angeles and Sydney? At the bottom end of the range was Downtown Los Angeles, which conformed more to the sequence of inner-city punitiveness making (and taming) space for pioneer gentrification. It scored lowest on the gentrification index, but highest on the criminalisation index. Downtown Los Angeles was polarised between the redeveloped Bunker Hill and the older, denser Historic Core, which has seen pioneer gentrification but abuts Skid Row, a notorious service hub that caters to the most destitute of surplus populations, including a large concentration of homeless people (Reese et al, 2010). Yet Downtown Los Angeles also featured strong residues of support, with the highest levels of voluntary organisations per capita, protected by sheer numbers and concentration but also offset by the somewhat tentative gentrification (and punitiveness) of Downtown set within the polycentric, 'weak centre' nature of Los Angeles (Reese et al, 2010). In the middle of the spectrum are the immigrant enclaves and areas such as Hollywood and Darlinghurst/Kings Cross, where a rough balance existed between the more punitive and supportive logics, between gentrification-induced NIMBY and entrepreneurial politics on the one hand, and voluntary-sector solidarity, 'staying put', and neutral, if not occasionally beneficial, political support on the other (DeVerteuil, 2011a). Finally, the five London boroughs were all marked by a well-established pattern of gentrification, alongside Surry Hills in Sydney. All five London case study boroughs also featured low criminalisation scores and were the most supportive in terms of the concentration of social housing, a crucial Keynesian legacy that, despite the encouragement of private ownership since Thatcher in 1980, constituted an essential bulwark against displacement of poor people and an important buffer against gentrification (Campkin, 2013; Watt, 2013). Rates of social housing in Inner London were considerably higher than in Outer London. Yet the five boroughs also featured the lowest concentrations of voluntary-sector organisations overall, which may be explained by their large populations as well as the stronger role played by the local and national welfare state, obviating the need for pervasive voluntarism (DeVerteuil, 2011c).

I now draw on this comparative typology for my analysis of comparative resilience, which frames the next five chapters. Table 5.3 shows the range of resilience and displacement rates for each

Table 5.3: Actual resilience and displacement outcomes

	RESILIENCE: in/voluntary immobility	DISPLACEMENT: involuntary mobility, due to gentrification	Displacement pressure (due to gentrification)
ESTABLISHED GENTRIFIED	16 out of 18	4 out of 18	5 out of 18
Westminster	7 out of 8	3 out of 8	3 out of 8
Surry Hills	9 out of 10	1 out of 10	2 out of 10
MIXED	26 out of 38	7 out of 38	24 out of 38
Lambeth	5 out of 8	1 out of 8	5 out of 8
Southwark	8 out of 11	1 out of 11	5 out of 11
Islington	5 out of 8	3 out of 8	5 out of 8
Kings Cross/Darlinghurst	8 out of 11	2 out of 11	9 out of 11
PIONEER	25 out of 28	6 out of 28	26 out of 28
Downtown	15 out of 17	3 out of 17	16 out of 17
Hollywood	10 out of 11	3 out of 11	10 out of 11
IMMIGRANT ENCLAVE	14 out of 16	2 out of 16	7 out of 16
Tower Hamlets	6 out of 7	1 out of 7	5 out of 7
Pico-Union	8 out of 9	1 out of 9	2 out of 9
TOTALS (percentage)	81 out of 100	19 out of 100	62 out of 100

of the place-types. As outlined in Table 4.3, spatial resilience is the combination of voluntary (staying put) and involuntary immobility (entrapment). I have also included displacement and displacement pressure by place-type as a way to show how punitiveness was usually offset and rebalanced with supportive and resilient measures.

Resilience rates differed not just by place-type but also by global city-region, with London (74%) below Los Angeles at 89% and Sydney at 81%. The forces behind this difference will be explored in the next four empirically based chapters, but certainly related to diverging welfare-state and voluntary-sector settlements. For each of the case studies, the profiling necessitated giving a flavour of the service hub landscape, in terms of clientele, specialisations, locational arrangements and challenges. This is roughly akin to Cloke et al's (2010) 'homeless city', which emphasised the various localised layers of historical, political and organisational circumstances that mesh in to specific service provision landscapes. Each chapter will also feature different themes and facets of the relationships between displacement and resilience, punitiveness and support.

SIX

Established gentrified place-types

Here I consider voluntary-sector resilience within the two areas with the highest levels of gentrification and upgrading: London's Westminster Borough and the Surry Hills area in Sydney. Westminster is London's showcase borough – the most visited (for example, Buckingham Palace, Leicester Square, Oxford Street, Parliament Square, Piccadilly Circus) and the most entertainment-orientated (for example, Soho, the West End) with the second-highest housing prices (after Kensington and Chelsea), but also a well-known service hub in its own right, attracting dependent populations through Victoria Station and Victoria Coach Station, as well as Trafalgar Square and the Strand. Surry Hills epitomises the dramatic reversal of fortune for most of Inner Sydney: from a 70-year legacy of grinding poverty, deteriorated housing and light industry, transformed over the past 30 years into a gentrified landscape and colonised by the higher classes. However, and despite these pressures, a significant voluntary-sector presence has remained in Surry Hills as well. As Table 5.3 showed (see Chapter Five), these two established gentrified areas experienced somewhat similar evidence of resilience and displacement as the other areas; and, from Table 5.2, I know that both featured low minority populations and medium criminalisation index scores. High and sustained levels of gentrification engendered spatial resilience among voluntary-sector organisations that was more longstanding, embedded and strategic, but at a price, as these hubs were also thoroughly entrapped within the gentrified inner-city – in some ways, frozen by the forces of neoliberalism and NIMBYism but not mortally threatened.

The experience of these two established gentrified neighbourhoods suggested several themes. The first was indeed entrapment, which can be seen as involuntary immobility but equally as spatial resilience. Hartman's (1984) 'right to stay put' assumed voluntary immobility, but for many services, it is involuntary immobility that is more prevalent and perhaps more vexing, involving issues of NIMBY, image management and visibility (DeVerteuil, 2012). The second theme revolved around the notion of centrality itself, in which Westminster occupies a symbolically central (both geographically and politically) location within London, if not the UK, and one which is not, and never has been, in question. This centrality translated into a highly sought but highly fraught landscape for voluntary-sector organisations. For Surry Hills, however, the centrality it enjoyed during most of the 19th century – at least in terms of industry and housing – had faded considerably by the mid-20th-century era of mass suburbanisation, only to return as Inner Sydney became revalorised. Surry Hills has always been pivotal as a service hub, however, given its highly accessible location near Sydney Central Station as well as its proximity to areas of traditionally high poverty, including Redfern and Waterloo directly to the south. Given the centrality to the broader voluntary sector in their respective cities, both areas were showcase locations where voluntary-sector organisations stayed put (voluntarily or involuntarily) in order to be taken seriously, accompanied by fears of the magnet effect and service saturation (especially in Westminster) and the growing gap between facility location and a dispersing clientele (Surry Hills).

Westminster case study

In 2011, the City of Westminster had a population of 219,000, which represented a 21% increase since 2001 following a general trend of inner-city repopulation as well as overall growth in the Greater London population, which increased by 1 million (14%) during the same period (UK census, 2011). Westminster is the pre-eminent borough of London, containing the political power of the UK in the form of the Houses of Parliament and the majority of important governmental agencies. Westminster is job rich, with three times more employment than population, and reasonably diverse (half the population was born elsewhere), although not nearly as much as other Inner London boroughs like Tower Hamlets, where British-born white people are currently in the minority (UK census, 2011). The average home price in 2013 was £1.3 million, second only to Kensington and Chelsea, and an increase of almost 20% from 2012 (Land Registry, 2013). Despite these very high levels of wealth, there remain important residues of both social housing – 28.9% in 2001 and 26% in 2010, far higher than most Outer London boroughs but lower than the Inner London boroughs of Islington (44%), Lambeth (38%), Southwark (47%) and Tower Hamlets (42%) (Mayor of London, 2011) – and voluntary-sector organisations (3.1 organisations per 1,000 persons in 2013), which was the highest rate of all boroughs in London save the City and Hackney.

Westminster is the heartland of the west-central arc of postcodes (for example, W1, WC1, SW1) that display extremes of wealth. It sits alongside Inner London's other 'high-status boroughs of Kensington and Chelsea, Hammersmith, Camden, Wandsworth and the City of

London ... which suggests that gentrification is either on-going in terms of more properties being gentrified or else the re/displacement of lower-middle-class professionals by a super-gentrifying group ... is occurring' (Butler et al, 2008: 83). According to an interview with a local planning agency, Westminster regeneration and gentrification was already well established by 1990, moving out from Covent Garden and Soho in all directions. My own analysis found that Westminster had the highest gentrification index, at 17.35%, of all the ten study areas. Westminster typifies what Massey (2007: 91) deemed the 'unrelenting support ... for finance and the surrounding constellation of sectors as the centerpiece of economic strategy that effectively buttress the further gentrified takeover of the city'.

This process of gentrification also rubs shoulders with certain parts of Westminster (Figure 6.1) – such as Belgravia and Mayfair, but also Pimlico – that never knew the rent gap, and so one cannot speak there of supply-side gentrification or even super-gentrification, but rather well-established enclaves of wealth being consolidated by even wealthier, usually overseas investors and transnational elites, a process usually ignored by those who rail against gentrification and displacement per se (Beaverstock et al, 2004). This overseas super-rich group has flocked to wealthy enclaves in Westminster and

Figure 6.1 City of Westminster boundaries and key infrastructure

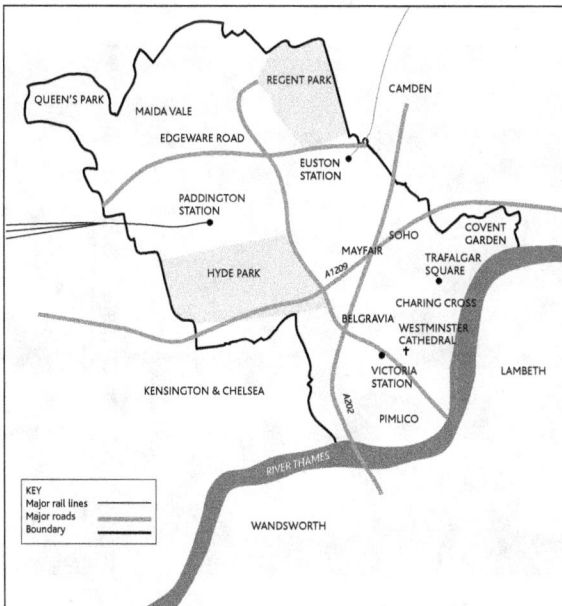

has superimposed a further layer of wealth. While not technically constituting gentrification, this pied-à-terre urbanism has precluded traditional, City-employed gentrifiers from such areas and pushed them elsewhere, thereby putting additional pressure on other gentrified and super-gentrified areas, part of what Harvey (2012) described as an increasingly inaccessible urban centre of London (Figure 6.2). In 2011, £5.2 billion was spent by overseas investors in London, with the lion's share going to the Boroughs of Westminster and Kensington and Chelsea (Heywood, 2012: 33), the nexus of what Davidson and Wyly (2012) dubbed the 'Rich Ricci index' of London. This transnational elite aligns remarkably well with what Ley (2004) cautiously dubbed the 'Masters of the Universe', treating Westminster as a safe-haven investment. Burrows et al (2013) deemed Westminster prime 'Alpha Territory' – using geodemographic data (for example, MOSAIC) to chart the disproportionate concentration of 'Global Power Brokers' as well as 'super-prime sales' of £10 million-plus sales in 2011 and 2012. Despite all of this wealth and its attendant valet industry, Westminster remained marked by pockets of poverty, invariably anchored to social housing or social landlords, and not surprisingly ranked among the four most unequal boroughs in London (MacInnes et al, 2011). Areas of poverty include Edgware Road, Westbourne, Queen's Park, Church Street and Maida Vale, and all these areas registered strongly in terms of voluntary-sector activity (VAW, 2009). But poverty in Westminster

Figure 6.2 Image of Belgravia, August 2007

Photograph taken by G DeVerteuil

is also of the transient sort, as its service-rich and tourist-heavy core attracts people who sleep rough and other precariously housed individuals from across London and beyond.

Within this context of pervasive wealth and gentrification juxtaposed with both entrenched and transient poverty, as well as its high degree of centrality and accessibility as the showcase borough of London, Westminster emerged as perhaps London's most contested service hub. In this regard, Westminster voluntary-sector organisations must tread a fine line between serving their clientele but also maintaining their spatial resilience. Massey (2007: 62) captured this risk by quoting the London Voluntary Council, which suggested that 'rising property prices have led to a detrimental effect on voluntary and community organisations, with many priced out of their local area'. Acknowledging these pressures, the 2008 Westminster Local Development Framework outlined a 'social infrastructure' policy that admitted to these pressures:

> Policy 3A.18 of the London Plan focuses on the protection and enhancement of social infrastructure and community facilities. It states that ... policies should assess the need for social infrastructure and community facilities in their area, and ensure that social infrastructure needs can be met ... Policies should ensures these facilities are provided within easy reach by walking and public transport for the population that use them. The net loss of such facilities must be resisted and increased provision be sought, both to deal with the increased population and to meet existing deficiencies. (Westminster Council, 2008: 215)

This was further outlined in the 2007 Unitary Development Plan (284):

> There is often pressure for buildings and sites used for community facilities to be developed for other, more profitable uses, such as commerce or housing. However, community facilities are important for the communities they serve, and are difficult to replace if their sites are developed for other uses.

In the same plan, there were also statements warning against the over-concentration of hostels and special needs housing: 'care must be taken over the location of hostels, to prevent over-concentration that might damage the character of the local environment' (2007:170). Westminster Council has long been sensitive to the potential risk of dumping, both of services and surplus populations. So the 2007 plan recognised two areas of special interest in Westminster: pressure on land, and the fear of saturation and the magnet effect. This caution has made the Council quite averse to creating special spaces for the voluntary sector, which in turn has led to a lack of overall space for organisations. In a survey of 268 voluntary-sector organisations in Westminster, those with annual incomes lower than £50,000 felt that 'access to space to operate' was far less than required (VAW, 2009). Westminster has also received more than its per capita share of social spending – an issue that causes some resentment among Outer London boroughs – but Inner London boroughs have always argued that poverty and need remain concentrated there, at least for the time being.

There is a longstanding sense that the largely Conservative-led Council only barely tolerates the poor, particularly after 1965 when less well-off parts of the borough, such as Paddington, were amalgamated into the wealthier southern portions; this also led to clashes over social housing in the 1980s (personal interview, Westminster Voluntary Action Council). From a key informant interview with Voluntary Action Westminster,[1] it was garnered that Westminster had always been a service hub for London's transient and destitute. A survey of 268 voluntary-sector organisations in Westminster in 2009 (VAC, 2009) found that fewer than half of clients were from Westminster itself, suggesting London-wide coverage and perhaps UK-wide as well.

As the local council most affected by homelessness in the UK, Westminster has tended to act as a springboard for tougher, more coercive actions (Johnsen & Fitzpatrick, 2010). This put Westminster somewhat at odds with broader national trends since the 1990s, when England embarked on greater support and services for homeless people, including (in chronological order) the 'Rough Sleepers Initiative', the 'Rough Sleepers Unit', the 'Homeless Programme Initiative' and the 'No One Left Out' policies (Cloke et al, 2010; Johnsen & Fitzpatrick, 2010). At the very same time that Neil Smith (1996) was putting forth revanchism as the dominant response to homelessness on the streets of American cities – or at least New York – these policies shifted England towards a more supportive, if occasionally coercive and devolved, landscape for homeless people (May et al, 2006). Under the New Labour government (1997–2010), local councils were given statutory responsibility for homeless individuals in their borough. Throughout this time, Westminster Council sought to reduce the visibility of the homeless through anti-begging campaigns designed to coerce individuals into services. Moreover, they stuck fast to the 'Local Connection' criteria, which ensured that only those homeless people from Westminster could receive services; this became formalised in the 2011 'No Second Night Out' policy. The Local Connection criteria could also be seen as a reaction on the part of Inner London boroughs – and, above all, Westminster – to being swamped by transient populations from across London, counterbalanced by pressure for London-wide solutions that went beyond 'passing the buck' (Mayor of London, Rough Sleeping Group, 2013). Additionally, it should be noted that while Westminster had the most homeless individuals, this was not necessarily due to its high level of gentrification. I do not see the gentrification/homelessness relationship as cause/effect, but rather the former creating more (displacement) pressure upon the service hub and affordable housing; in other words, understanding that gentrification cannot be divorced from displacement (Smith, 1996; Slater, 2006), but, by the same token, gentrification can occur and be amply threatening without the paroxysms of punitiveness and revanchism, and be effectively counterbalanced by currents of care, survival and resilience. These points will be revisited in detail in Chapter Eight with regard to Los Angeles.

By the time my research began in late 2008 (Table 6.1), Westminster's homeless policy was dominated by coercive care and anti-begging strategies, focusing on highly touristed areas like Covent Garden, Soho, Charing Cross and Victoria, as implemented through the report, *An integrated approach to reduce begging in Westminster* (Westminster Council, 2004: 1): 'Begging ... blights London's landscapes. Visitors to London cited aggressive begging as the number one reason they would not return to the capital ... By tackling begging, Westminster residents, businesses, tourists and those working in the City will all benefit.' In conjunction was the use of ASBOs (Anti-Social Behaviour Orders) that could be deployed against transient populations, potentially resulting

Table 6.1: Interviewed voluntary-sector organisations in Westminster

	Displaced	Displacement pressure	Entrapment	Owned/rented	Service
W1	No	No	Yes	Owned (1924)	Shelter
W2	Yes	Yes	No	Rented (2003)	Shelter
W3	No	No	Yes	Loaned (2005)	Housing
W4	Yes	Yes	No	Rented (2005)	Advocacy
W5	No	No	Yes	Rented (2006)	Food
W6	No	No	Yes	Rented (1988)	Drop-in/shelter
W7	Yes	Yes	No	Rented (2007)	Health
W8	No	Yes	Yes	Rented (1995)	Elderly care

in prohibitions on behaviour and/or a return to certain public spaces (Cameron, 2007). The Local Connection criteria were not only used to rid Westminster of unwanted rough-sleeping people from elsewhere – it also anchored the wanted to local services to obscure and reduce their visibility in prime urban spaces, a meshing of coercion and care. But Westminster continues to act as a magnet for those who sleep rough, who do not qualify for housing or other benefits at all, usually from the Eastern European nations of Poland and Lithuania, which have only just recently accessed the EU. This left-out population had become increasingly dominant in the emergency services landscape of Westminster by the late 2000s, and the focus of deportations in the run-up to the 2012 Olympics.

In particular, the transient and service-rich Victoria area appeared increasingly anomalous amid the uber-wealth and ambitious regeneration plans. Since gentrification has been ongoing in these areas since the 1970s, the voluntary-sector organisations serving homeless people had adjusted to the pressures of displacement, which may explain the low proportions of facilities experiencing displacement pressure and the high rates of resilience. Indeed, seven of eight facilities proved spatially resilient over the study period, despite three suffering from an episode of displacement. Of those seven resilient organisations, only three had felt displacement pressure, on the low side for the entire three-city sample. A good example of these tendencies was the story of a day centre for people sleeping rough (W6): it had been in Westminster since 1988, and its highly central location is but a stone's throw from Trafalgar Square and the Strand (DeVerteuil, 2012). The day centre has been instrumental in helping, each year, more than 5,000 people sleeping rough stay off the nearby and heavily touristed streets. Since its beginnings, the local church (St Martin-in-the-Fields), which owns the facility, has charged £1 rent per annum. Even when the building was redeveloped in 2007–08, the organisation remained in a temporary building nearby so as to stay close to its clientele – who would not move far to access services. The organisation continues to enjoys wide community support, as there is little in the way of a residential community nearby and thus relatively little NIMBY. However, displacement pressures cannot be ignored: beginning in May 2008, pavement space on the Strand and Fleet Street was subject to forced cleaning, usually between 2 am and 3 am on a weekly basis (Lane & Power, 2009). The issue of a relatively stable (yet spatially constricted) clientele found parallels in a domiciliary respite care service organisation in Soho (W8), which mentioned that its clientele of elderly homeowners were very stable, but effectively trapped in place – large-scale displacement had already occurred more than 20 years previously, along with the first waves of gentrification, with new layers superimposing but not necessarily adding to the pressure upon what is by now a well-entrenched service.

Yet clientele stability came at the cost of being invisible in public spaces. An outreach service (W3) for vulnerable people, and a gateway to housing, recovery and mental health services, as well as 'reconnection' to the proper borough services, could not help but notice that its street-based clientele were under pressure to remain discrete, while resisting the need to beg and drink in public spaces. Renting from St Mary's Hospital, the organisation clung to its centrally located and easily accessible locale, as well as sending its clientele on to nearby services in the Westminster service hub. Already gentrified when the organisation moved in 2003, the area has seen increasing NIMBY sentiments, with the growing sense of entitlement and territoriality of the incoming gentrifiers. While part of a larger service provider that ensured a sense of protection, the outreach service could not easily relocate within Westminster or replicate the service hub connections. As the Director said: "We could not relocate to Marylebone, and there is too much NIMBY in Victoria. Our umbrella organisation bought a lot of cheap locales in Inner London in the 1950s, but they could not do that today."

Since Westminster is seen as the London borough with the most obvious concentration of both rough-sleeping people and the services upon which they depend, certain unique issues have arisen. The first is the particular vulnerability to displacement of services that are not Council-supported and vetted. An example was an advice service for homeless and precariously housed Scottish people living in London (W2). Serving more than 400 clients a year, the organisation had already been displaced in the study period in 2003 when rents became untenable in the Grosvenor Gardens area. Lacking Council support and relying almost exclusively on private donations, the organisation remained vulnerable to further displacement in its rented accommodations within walking distance of Victoria Station and Victoria Coach Station, where Scottish people at risk of rough sleeping may pass through. Without an identifiable Scottish enclave in London, the organisation reasoned that this was the most accessible location. Another example was the domiciliary respite care service (W7), which received only perfunctory Council support and had been displaced in 1997 and 2007, both due to rapid escalations in rent due to gentrification in the Westbourne Gardens and Paddington areas, respectively. In 2007, the organisation moved to the Tottenham Court

Road area, but foresaw moving again in 2016 when the building will be torn down for the new Crossrail Station.

A second issue particular to Westminster was the density of soup runs. Soup runs constitute mobile food distribution in public spaces at designated times. Their very public and visible nature makes them quite vulnerable to NIMBY and community pressure: 'For some, soup runs are a valuable, life-saving resource that help to feed and support rough sleepers and other vulnerable people. For others, soup runs represent an outdated, poorly targeted and uncoordinated service that supports and sustains damaging street lifestyles' (Lane & Power, 2009: 3). The geography of soup runs is necessarily complex, a fraught negotiation between being too visible for the community and not visible enough to attract clients: 'they must operate in spaces that are marginal enough to minimise the stigma associated with the public provision of alms and conflict with those that oppose their activities, but not so marginal as to render them invisible to potential clients and compromise the safety of volunteers and service users' (Cloke et al, 2010: 111). These tensions came to a head in 2007, when Westminster Council attempted to ban soup runs altogether from the borough (DeVerteuil et al, 2009a). Although this attempt was a failure, soup runs face pressure from both the Council as well as other 'housed' voluntary organisations that they attach too few strings upon client behaviour (especially if anti-social), are too prominent in public space, are too numerous, and seen to be amateurish. In the run-up to the 2012 Olympics, there was a second (failed) attempt to ban food distribution and rough sleeping altogether (Butler, 2011):

> Conservative-controlled Westminster sought to introduce a byelaw this year allowing officials to fine people in and around the Westminster Cathedral piazza if they 'lie down or sleep in any public place', 'deposit bedding' or distribute free food and drink. It was the council's second attempt to introduce a byelaw banning soup runs in recent years. The council argued that the soup runs provided a magnet for homeless people and encouraged begging, crime and antisocial behaviour in the area.

Once again, this attempt failed due to strong opposition on the part of the voluntary sector and advocates for the needy, lending credence to the sense that while they compete over scarce resources and squabble over models of service delivery, they will band together when faced with draconian threats to their clientele.

An organisation that combined both Westminster-specific issues was a soup run (W5) with its food warehouse near Paddington and undertaking public feedings at Westminster Cathedral (near Victoria Station) twice a month, with up to 80 persons, as well as providing street outreach as a gateway to more permanent services. The organisation had no Council support and was completely reliant on individual donors, very much following a grassroots model. The founder himself had spent time on the street on Los Angeles' Skid Row – which we will visit in Chapter Eight – and had brought his street knowledge to Westminster. Having survived the 2007 attempt to close down soup runs completely, he still complained about unrelenting pressure to get off the street – from the police, established services and building-based services (for example, hostels, harm reduction), all of whom 'had it in for an insurgent movement like ourselves ... we are cutting out the middle-man and delivering straight to the poor'.

For him, holding on to the area's accessibility was of utmost importance, as Victoria was the first point of contact for many of London's precariously housed people, but simultaneously undergoing significant regeneration that, along with the long-overdue infrastructural improvements, sought to 'design out' anti-social behaviour in its environs and possibly even relocate the Victoria Coach Station outside of the borough entirely (City of Westminster, 2013). While planning to move to a less prominent area near Victoria (rail) Station, the organisation had already spent three years (2006–09) establishing itself and was in no rush to move just yet. Although never located in Westminster, I also interviewed a second soup run associated with the Hare Krishna sect. They had already been displaced out of Camden (by King's Cross station, another area of redevelopment; Campkin, 2013) and into Islington in 2006, unable to secure planning permissions to get a permanent site and under pressure to leave. They subsequently found Islington Council to be beneficially hands-off. Renting a modest storefront on Caledonian Road, the soup run could also provide on-site referrals, internet access, yoga and drug counselling; most of its clientele were still coming from Camden. In the words of the Director, "There was lots of pressure from Camden Borough to clean up the King's Cross area, and that included soup runs like us."

Both examples are powerful reminders of care 'without strings' in urban space, but also bring up the fine line of making poverty visible (Heynen, 2010) while seeking to protect the dignity of those being fed (Cloke et al, 2010). This is both a social justice issue but also a social planning and voluntary sector one.

Less specific to Westminster were the quotidian examples of spatial resilience – although given the established nature of upgrading in the borough, some of the facilities I interviewed were puzzled by my research project: naturally we are resilient, everyone has to be in Westminster! There were examples of how resilience enabled the support of surplus populations while offsetting some of the coercive tendencies in place since 2003. An interview with an advocacy centre for elderly residents in Soho in Westminster (W8) revealed a series of adaptive strategies that had served it well since 1995, including obtaining of borough and local business support, as well as renting from a nearby church (DeVerteuil, 2011a). Still, the centre had outgrown its space and suffers from entrapment, too expensive to relocate elsewhere in Inner London. A hostel (W1) within spitting distance of the Houses of Parliament had provided 68 beds for long-term homeless clients since 1924. Owning the building was a major basis for spatial resilience, as moving was not an option within Westminster, given that it has been prohibitively expensive since the 1980s. With a stable base, the hostel enabled former rough-sleeping people to stabilise and remain off the streets. All the clientele were on benefits and identified as being Westminster residents.

Finally, all of the organisations so cherished the high-profile centrality of Westminster that they adhered to it no matter the consequences – a sort of spatial resilience out of pure obstinacy. For instance, an organisation that provided space and support for the LGBT community (W4) insisted on staying put in its Soho location. Such is the prominence of Soho to the LGBT community that the organisation would not be taken seriously without this location. This realisation had driven the organisation to stay in Soho – it had already been displaced in 2005 when the building in question was converted into residential flats. The search then for a new premises was long and painful, but as the Chief Executive Officer intimated, "We were looking for centrality to all of London, but above all to serve the Soho LGBT community; Soho is the premier location for that community and we knew it, there is a rich symbolism attached to the neighbourhood and the struggles that created it." Spatial resilience was not guaranteed in the post-2005 location, given the high and escalating rents, but also the relatively weak donation culture among the LGBT community in London more generally. In the words of the Chief Executive Officer again: "We want to stay in this area, even if financially the location doesn't make sense. We need the centrality and the identity of Soho."

Other organisations shared this same desperation to maintain centrality, even if their role was advocacy and not direct service provision. An umbrella body for housing justice in the UK, which had originally rented in Marylebone between the 1970s and 2009 but had been displaced to Islington in search of cheaper rent, insisted on the symbolic importance of being in Inner London in order to be taken seriously nationwide, but also to maintain connectedness to other London-based agencies and national charities. To the coordinator in 2009, "When we left Westminster, we needed to stay in the game as a housing player, this meant not moving too far away. Central London, and especially Westminster, is the most contested space in the UK for affordable housing, as well as issues around deprivation and gentrification."

The overall themes in Westminster primarily constituted entrapment – always provisional, given that most rented – and of centrality to both London and beyond, which in turn led to issues of saturation and magnet effects. While neither of these themes necessarily ensured spatial resilience, they certainly enabled resilience to their clientele. The pressure on the street population was more coercive care than outright punitive, and the failed soup run bans demonstrated resilience. In the next case study, of Surry Hills, these themes will reappear in somewhat muted fashion while new ones will emerge, especially the growing gap between clientele and facility location.

Surry Hills case study

Surry Hills is to the south-east of Sydney CBD, a suburb in the Sydney City LGA (Figure 6.4). Its population in 2011 was 15,342, an increase of 10% from 2001 and 47% from 1991, with somewhat higher income on average in 2011 than Sydney City, which is already among the highest in the Metropolitan area (Australian Bureau of Statistics, 2011). This dramatic population increase was due to the densification resulting from new-build gentrification and the loft conversion of old manufacturing warehouses (Figure 6.3), within a context of Sydney's building boom in the run-up to the 2000 Olympics, as well as an accelerating return to the inner city after decades of disinvestment (Daly & Pritchard, 2000). However, new-build gentrification in Surry Hills is relatively modest, given the strong preservation laws, and this condition (like Glebe to the west) sets it apart from the medium- and high-rise new-builds in Kings Cross and especially the spectacular densification of Pyrmont-Ultimo directly to the west of the CBD (Bounds & Morris, 2006).

As one of the first Inner Sydney suburbs to gentrify, Surry Hills scored highly in terms of the gentrification index (10.1%) and very

Figure 6.3 Loft conversion on Cleveland Street, July 2014

RUGBY UNION and LEAGUE JERSEYS
MADE HERE

CLEVELAND & CO

1, 2 & 3 BED WAREHOUSE
APARTMENTS FROM $595,000

bkh   CBRE   cor
                           ner
                           stone.

1800 602 900 · CLEVELANDANDCO.COM.AU

Photograph taken by G DeVerteuil

Figure 6.4 Surry Hills boundaries and key infrastructure

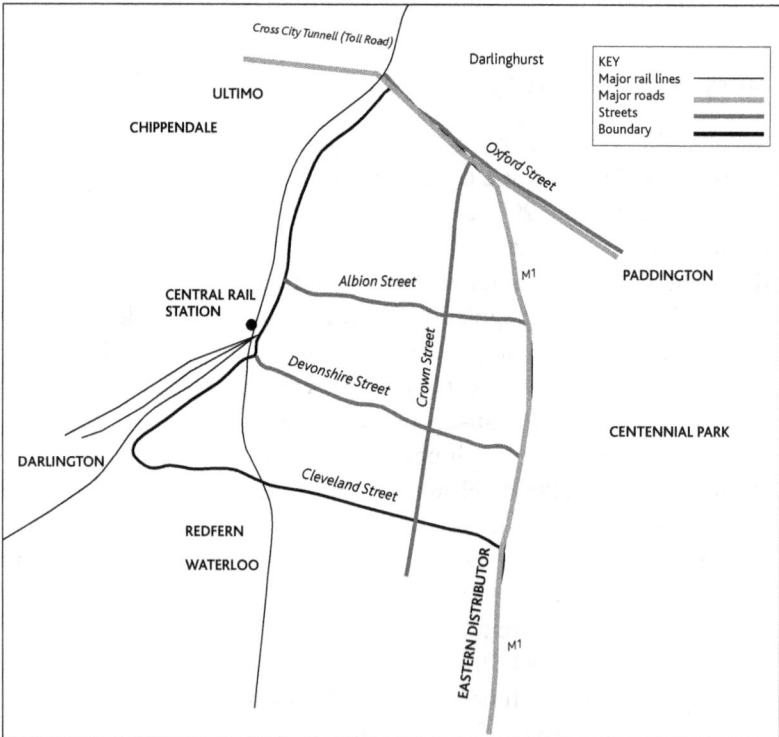

Cross City Tunnell (Toll Road)

Darlinghurst

ULTIMO

CHIPPENDALE

Oxford Street

KEY
Major rail lines
Major roads
Streets
Boundary

Albion Street

M1   PADDINGTON

CENTRAL RAIL
STATION

Devonshire Street

Crown Street

CENTENNIAL PARK

DARLINGTON

Cleveland Street

REDFERN

WATERLOO

EASTERN DISTRIBUTOR

M1

high housing prices (median price in 2014 of over AU$1 million), approaching those of the more established wealth of the eastern and northern coastal inner-suburbs that never experienced the rent gap. But unlike Westminster, well-established wealth was not to be found in Surry Hills. Rather, the area conformed to what Flood (2003: 4) identified as a pervasive trend of inner-city revalorisation, in which 'virtually every former inner slum area in Sydney, even Redfern, has now been redeveloped by stealth, and house prices have reached levels that would have been unimaginable 20 years ago'. It further epitomised this rapid turnaround from 50 years of neglect and depopulation, proving by the 1970s to already be 'too valuable to be left to the indigent and marginalised, or to industry' (Flood, 2003: 7). By the 2000s, Surry Hills was known more for its vibrant coffee culture and night-time economy than its legacy of industry and poverty (Figure 6.5) (Rose & Lynch, 2012).

Figure 6.5 Gentrification along Crown Street, July 2014

Photograph taken by G DeVerteuil

According to Shaw (2007: 7), Surry Hills was an early example of Inner Sydney rent-gap gentrification, and instructive in terms of the homogenising consequences of pervasive upgrading, and perhaps less tolerance – not so much related to racial or sexual diversity (see Forrest & Dunn, 2007) but towards perceived threats to property prices. To her, consequences manifested themselves in a range of resident activisms. Incoming residents ('gentrifiers') began to collective to drive out certain facilities and uses of urban space. These groups began to agitate against the existence of welfare services, the burning of joss sticks in an old Chinese temple, 'offensive migrant house' colours (such as 'Portuguese Pink' or 'Mediterranean Blue')'.

It is exactly this remaking/sterilisation through the displacement of pre-gentrification neighbourhood characteristics that epitomises current NIMBY campaigns. Yet, as we shall see, Surry Hills featured an extensive and largely defended cluster of voluntary organisations that predate the gentrification phase (Figure 6.6), entrenched enough to be virtually displacement-proof yet thoroughly entrapped and sometimes passionately resented (DeVerteuil, 2014).

Figure 6.6 Community service hub along Crown Street, July 2014

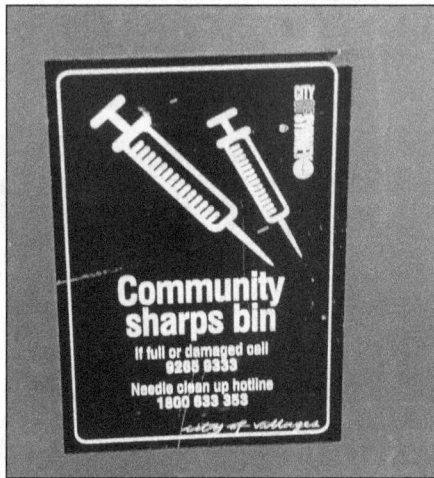

Photograph taken by G DeVerteuil

The recent transformation in Surry Hills was also of some significance nationally. Rather than homelessness and soup runs in Westminster, Surry Hills was a showcase for voluntary-sector geographies and their marooning in Inner Sydney, while the clientele sees itself displaced outwards (on the suburbanisation of disadvantage in Sydney, see Randolph and Tice, 2014).

The 10 organisations interviewed (Table 6.2) were all too aware of these larger community changes, including the realisation that the most disrupting wave of gentrification had already come and gone – the name of the game now was to actively deploy resilience despite the inability to relocate within Surry Hills. As the project manager of a youth outreach programme (S5, in Surry Hills since 1989) described:

> '... the inner Surry Hills–Darlinghurst–Paddington–Redfern areas have been increasingly gentrified. This resulted in fewer accommodation options for our clients. The accommodation that is available is very expensive and of very poor quality. As well, there has been an explosion of boutique commercial shops. This has had the effect that young persons have fewer affordable options for sourcing food and other essentials. The character of these suburbs has changed significantly, such that the young persons feel increasingly as though they cannot "belong" in these areas (ie, they feel as though they belong 'elsewhere' and are just passing through).'

Three themes emerged from the overall interview material. Like in Westminster, the first theme was entrapment, which affected all but two of the voluntary-sector organisations interviewed, among the highest

Table 6.2: Interviewed voluntary-sector organisations in Surry Hills

	Displaced?	Displacement pressure	Entrapment	Owned/rented	Service
S1	No	No	Yes	Own (1991)	advocacy
S2	No	No	Yes	Own (1982)	advocacy
S3	No	No	Unsure	Rent (2001)	Education
S4	No	No	No	Rent (1999)	Development (overseas)
S5	Yes	Yes	Yes	Rent (2006)	Youth
S6	No	No	Unsure	Rent (1987)	Shelter/drop-in
S7	No	No	Yes	Own (1976)	Shelter/drop-in
S8	No	No	Yes	Own (1989)	Drop-in
S9	No	Yes	No	Rent (1999)	Community service
S10	No	No	Yes	Rent (1998)	Advocacy, environmental

rates of the 10 study areas. This is not to say that displacement pressure was absent, however. An organisation providing accommodation, meals and support services for homeless people on the eastern edge of Surry Hills (S6), hard by the Eastern Distributor, had this to say about indirect displacement:

> '... To some extent, as boarding house facilities and private housing are withdrawn from availability (sold, redeveloped etc). Our people come from a range of locations, not just the inner city, they tend to gravitate here by reason of circumstance (mental health problems, addictions, prison background etc.). There are extensive "public housing" facilities in this area, as well as private housing stock which are increasingly being sold, redeveloped and upgraded; these are out of reach to our people.'

A Quaker development aid agency (S4) had used a Quaker facility originally built in 1903 as a mission church to serve what was considered a high-need community. This specific organisation had moved to Sydney from Hobart in 2001, and the move itself represented the greater professionalisation in development work as well as the need to be taken more seriously. The rent was extremely cheap (AU$3 a year), thus ensuring spatial resilience as well as greater links to other development agencies in Inner Sydney. However, entrapment had also occurred, as an equivalently central site would not be forthcoming in Surry Hills or other parts of Inner Sydney. Similarly, an organisation that used visual and musical arts (S5) to engage with local, disadvantaged youth paid but a notional amount (25% of the market rate) to a larger, private umbrella organisation to stay in Surry Hills. It also preferred the location given the sense that Sydney's inner city was more creative and 'funky', and thus more attractive and real to the clients. This attraction had come at a price – twice the organisation had been displaced within Surry Hills and Darlinghurst, and had moved a total of four times since 1993, but was reasonably happy with its current digs:

> 'It would be difficult for us to move now, given our special sound requirements, and the creative vibe of the area. We would never move to Western Sydney, even if more of our clients are from there, because it's not creative. But we are planning on moving nearby for an even better premises – a one-stop shop with _____.'

Its experience resonated with the LGBT community organisation, which clung on to Soho so as to be taken seriously (W4). And so pervasive entrapment had also led to increased neighbourhood management, of making the 'visible' invisible, to placate or anticipate community opposition as the area further gentrified. Again, according to the same organisation:

> 'There have been some neighborhood complaints about clients and noise, not surprising really considering what we do. We feel a need to "re-brand" our image to fit into the area, even architecturally. This meant that our building could not be covered in graffiti anymore ... Our target client group include severely disadvantaged young persons ... So we have worked very hard to develop good relationships in our community and with all levels of Government (local, state and federal). Our premises underwent a major renovation two years ago. In our submission to headquarters and council we cited gentrification of the area as one of the main reasons for our application for the refurbishment.' (S5)

For an organisation serving Aboriginal youth (S3), this image management meant a constant rekindling of community ties (and of donations, as it depended on them for 90% of its budget). For a nearby crisis service for homeless people (S7), with up to 200 staying in the shelter and another 3,000 dropping in yearly, it was essential to keep up with community concerns and NIMBY, and not give the building an institutional look (DeVerteuil, 2006). The crisis service had operated in its present location since 1976, but had become in 2005 a one-stop shop, moving beyond crisis housing to include food, legal services and health care. This process had to be managed carefully in order to win community support. Subsequent to the transformation, image management would become crucial in order to placate community concerns and retain this inner-city location, essential for a clientele who will not go far for services and who take advantage of the agglomeration benefits of nearby services. Again, ownership had ensured resilience as the area gentrified, while many of the former co-existing resources, such as boarding homes, had begun to close down in the immediate area despite the fact they became protected in 1999 (City of Sydney, 2005). Finally, the process of image management could be eased if considered a 'trendy' service that fits in well within the gentrifying yet outwardly progressive inner-city landscape. S9, a street-level community organisation serving vulnerable populations, noted that, while there was no concerted campaign to push out services in Surry Hills, those services with 'trendy' clients such as homeless youth, were more tolerated than those who served 'lost causes', such as homeless adults and those who used drugs – their next-door neighbour, a needle exchange, was viewed as particularly problematic and ill-suited to the environs. As S10, an environmental advocacy organisation, stated: "Surry Hills is ideal for trendy causes such as the environment, especially with young people … it is also attracting 'startup' not-for-profits attracted to the progressive vibe."

Following on from this last point, the third theme concentrated on the growing distance between entrapped inner-city facilities and a dispersing clientele as gentrification takes it toll. S9 noted that there are some services in the suburbs, but not enough for the demand, especially with regard to homeless people and socially housed individuals, who cannot effectively navigate the poor public transportation. Inner Sydney lacks Inner London's social differentiation and diversity, even compared to Westminster. Advocacy organisations similarly required the high visibility of inner-city service hubs, even if their clientele is more scattered and less place dependent. I interviewed three organisations (S1, S2 and S10) that acted as national-level advocates on behalf of (1) those working against nuclear weapons, (2) the Communist Party of Australia and (3) the Wilderness Society. These three organisations were very obviously advocating to remake and resist neoliberalisation, rather than only producing spatial and social resilience. The first two organisations shared a common space that had been bought in 1991 and then expanded in 2000, thereby allaying any risk of gentrification-induced displacement. The third was in a building in the garment district that specialised in not-for-profits. Critically, all greatly valued the symbolic proximity to Sydney's centre, in terms of organising and being visible through street protests (the CBD as prime protest space), rallies and pressure campaigns; the neighbourhood itself was once very working class and industrial, which had fostered a groundswell of localised sympathy. But this working-class clientele (for the Communist Party), the more radical activists (nuclear weapons) and student volunteers (environmental causes) were being displaced towards the more 'working class' areas in Western Sydney, by the deindustrialisation of local textile factories, ongoing gentrification and the destruction of local social housing in nearby Redfern (the Block) and Waterloo (high-rise towers). As the director of SI told me,

'This area is less "working class" than it used to be. There has been a debate, particularly in the Communist Party, about following our clients, the working class are now in Western Sydney, Paramatta and the like. We may want to 'cash out' and move there, but there are no plans afoot now [as of March 2011].'

This relates to the increasingly 'Parisian' model of surplus population geography in Sydney, with the western suburbs as the inevitable destination of poverty displaced from the inner city. Evidence of this displacement is everywhere in Inner Sydney, and not just in Surry Hills – directly to the south, in the suburbs of Waterloo and Redfern, once-neglected clusters of high-rise social housing are now being renewed and sold off by the urban development corporation (the Redfern-Waterloo Authority, now the Urban Growth Development Corporation) created and overseen by the New South Wales government (Searle, 2013) but presently subsumed into the Sydney Metropolitan Development Authority. The aim was to introduce more of a social mix, with predictable consequences for some of the original tenants – at least 700 units will be lost – and a diluting of Inner Sydney's largest major concentration of high-rise social housing, perhaps the last affordable refuge for surplus populations as well (Figure 6.7).

Figure 6.7 Redfern new-build gentrification in foreground, social housing in background, July 2014

Photograph taken by G DeVerteuil

The prelude to redevelopment has been marked by mismanaged (or intentional?) dilapidation of maintenance that all the more emphasises the gap with the newly gentrified landscape (Wood, 2012). This pressure on clientele makes the spatial resilience of the Surry Hills service hub all the more crucial, a testing ground for the impacts of the steadfast resilience, entrapment and marooning of the service hub in the face of clientele dispersion. The case of S5 was particularly striking – its clientele were far more vulnerable to displacement than the facility, but the organisation itself was unwilling to follow them – unless of course they all went in the same direction to the same place, which was unlikely. What is more likely is a scattering of clientele that, all other things being equal, would still require the inner city's centrality and accessibility. Moreover, organisations like S5 currently benefit from the proximity and concentration of likeminded facilities in the Surry Hills area – an agglomeration effect that would be lost in the event of a scattering. It creatively worked together with nearby organisations to ensure linked services for its youthful clientele, including shelter, food, health care and social work, thereby enabling social resilience but also ensuring a measure of spatial resilience for the Surry Hills service hub. Similarly, S9 saw the service hub as an advantage, "with high visibility and accessibility for clients, close to like-minded facilities and a community that accepts that Surry Hills is highly unequal, rich and poor but nothing in between".

In summary, the two case studies suggested how the pervasive nature of gentrification and its longstanding, seemingly irreversible effects had engendered widespread entrapment but not widespread displacement. The prominence of both locations meant that their experiences were far reaching, adding to the threat of entrapment but also coercive care mixed with real support. Both areas featured significant issues around resilience, centrality and (social) policy, as well as in/tolerance and fit within the inner city. In the next chapter, I propose several more themes that relate to spatial resilience – of how less pervasive upgrading presents opportunities to service hubs, and how large-scale, new-build gentrification (relatively rare in Westminster and Surry Hills) presents challenges to it as well.

Note

[1] Voluntary Action Councils, of which there are one per borough, grew out of the 1990s professionalisation of the relationship between the state and the voluntary sector, with the latter earning more responsibility, standards and resources.

SEVEN

Mixed place-types

Here I consider matters of service hub resilience within the four areas with mixed levels of gentrification and upgrading: the London boroughs of Islington, Lambeth and Southwark, and the Darlinghurst/ Kings Cross area in Sydney. All featured medium gentrification index scores, medium levels of voluntary-sector organisations per capita, medium levels of minority populations, and medium criminalisation index scores. In particular, I found that gentrification was more mixed than in the 'established gentrified' neighbourhoods, creating hodgepodge geographies of resilience and displacement, with gentrification counterposed with, and sometimes threatening, conspicuous areas of poverty and, in the case of London, large-scale council estates. This was epitomised by the 'super-gentrification' found in Barnsbury in Islington (Butler & Lees, 2006), set within one of the five poorest boroughs in London (MacInnes et al, 2011). Islington was not alone – both Lambeth and Southwark scored in the top third of London boroughs in terms of unemployment, households on benefits and in poor health, alongside significant (and growing) pockets of gentrification and wealth. In Darlinghurst/Kings Cross in Sydney, significant gentrification co-habited with extremes of substance abuse, prostitution and homelessness, attracted to and anchored by Sydney's traditional red-light and drugs district.

The mixed nature of these areas is partly an outcome of recent and very targeted redevelopment policies, with new-build gentrification punctuating the 19th-century and early 20th-century built environment in both London and Sydney. For instance, in Lambeth and Southwark there is now considerable new-build gentrification along the River Thames. Fainstein (2010: 126) chronicled the redevelopment of the South Bank, particularly the Coin Street and Oxo Tower project, of how 'by the mid-1990s, the South Bank was the site of a host of new projects and improvement schemes involving the public and private sectors, separately and together, and Coin Street had been redefined as both a model development and a catalyst for wider change'. Indeed, by 2014, most of the South Bank was experiencing significant new-build gentrification, spilling over from neighbouring Southwark (see case study). But along the main line from Waterloo Station to Weymouth lay several unbroken miles of council estates (Hamnett, 2003) that buffer the gentrifying zones of the riverside new builds (Davidson & Lees, 2005; Watt, 2013), including Vauxhall, pictured in Figure 7.1.

Figure 7.1 Vauxhall redevelopment and voluntary-sector organisation ('Big Issue'), August 2014

Photograph taken by G DeVerteuil

The gentrifier proxy population living along the Thames riverside of Lambeth grew by 94% between 1991 and 2001, while for Southwark it was 208% (Davidson & Lees, 2005). Riverside new-build gentrification is, however, but a more recent manifestation of the traditional, incumbent gentrification that one finds in Islington and Darlinghurst. In Islington, the super-gentrification of its southern edges is very much the product of elites working in global industries a short commute away in the City (Butler & Lees, 2006). But this has been compounded by the massive and ongoing redevelopment of King's Cross and St Pancras (as of 2014 the largest redevelopment in Western Europe) a mile to the west in Camden Borough, with impacts spilling in to Islington. As previously mentioned, an Islington soup-run organisation feeding indigent people by King's Cross Station was under pressure to rein in its public operations as the area redeveloped from the early 2000s onwards; it was eventually evicted from its rented storefront in 2006 and now occupies a marginal location at some distance from the station. While providing crucial everyday sustenance and outreach, the organisation regretted that it could no longer occupy a more central location to entice more clients into long-term care (for example, drug recovery, mental health). In Sydney's bohemian Kings Cross, considerable redevelopment had occurred since the 1990s, with high-rise redevelopment and densification punctuating the skyline to the east of the CBD, in what is already Sydney's densest area (Figure 7.2). This has brought with it a newer and less tolerant form of gentrification, with greater community opposition to existing services but also more stringent rules on its vibrant night-time economy (Nowra, 2013).

The two themes for this chapter encapsulate how more spotty forms of gentrification present opportunities for service hubs to stay put, but equally how new-build gentrification presents particular challenges to them. The case study for London will be Southwark, the site of extensive redevelopment around the London Bridge Station and Elephant and Castle areas, increasingly an extension of the financial core north of the Thames in the City (Harris, 2008). Here, I focus on the strategies whereby voluntary-sector organisations proved resilient, but also on parallel trends in Darlinghurst/Kings Cross, where recent densification and longstanding gay gentrification have put mounting pressure on voluntary-sector organisations. The resilience of these service hubs countered assumptions of outright and systematic displacement through neoliberalism/post-welfarism, and supported the residual resilience of the public city from the 1970s and 1980s. This compels us to consider a more complex vision of the inner city, which remains the ideal locus for voluntary-sector clusters.

Southwark case study

Southwark's population in 2011 was 288,300, representing a 12.3% increase since 2001, mirroring the overall trend of Inner London repopulation (UK census, 2011). Its housing prices were the tenth most expensive in London (Land Registry, 2013). Its income distribution was extremely unequal: according to the *London poverty profile* (MacInnes et al, 2011), Southwark was similar to Islington, characterised by high levels of poverty, unemployment and low-paying jobs, offset by medium levels of wealth (and some very wealthy enclaves), and making it among the top four most unequal boroughs in London. Southwark's

Figure 7.2 Juxtaposition of new-build condo tower and emergency shelter, Kings Cross Sydney

Photograph taken by G DeVerteuil

per capita measure of voluntary-sector organisations was also among the highest in Greater London, at 2.91 per 1,000 persons.

Seen until recently as a relative backwater compared with the City and Westminster, as well as being highly impoverished and marked by extensive social housing (DeVerteuil, 2014), Southwark Council has been vigorously pushing for public–private regeneration along its northern edge (South Bank, London Bridge Station, Elephant and Castle) as well as seeking to reduce, through social mixing (that is, selling off social housing to the private market so as to introduce a higher class to poor areas), its very substantial (53.5% in 2001, and 47% in 2010) (Mayor of London, 2011) social housing stock.[1] So truly a tale of two boroughs, a hodgepodge case of upgrading made even more uneven by recent redevelopment plans: the northern 20% is undergoing a spectacular restructuring of urban form and function, while the southern 80% is largely escaping these pressures of social mixing, displacement and gentrification, thereby enabling voluntary-sector organisations and poor people to stay put more or less voluntarily (Figure 7.3). This relates to the sense that gentrification in London is almost always more patchy than the US version, given the far greater supply of state-protected social housing (Butler 2007; Watt, 2013) –

Figure 7.3 Southwark boundaries and key infrastructure

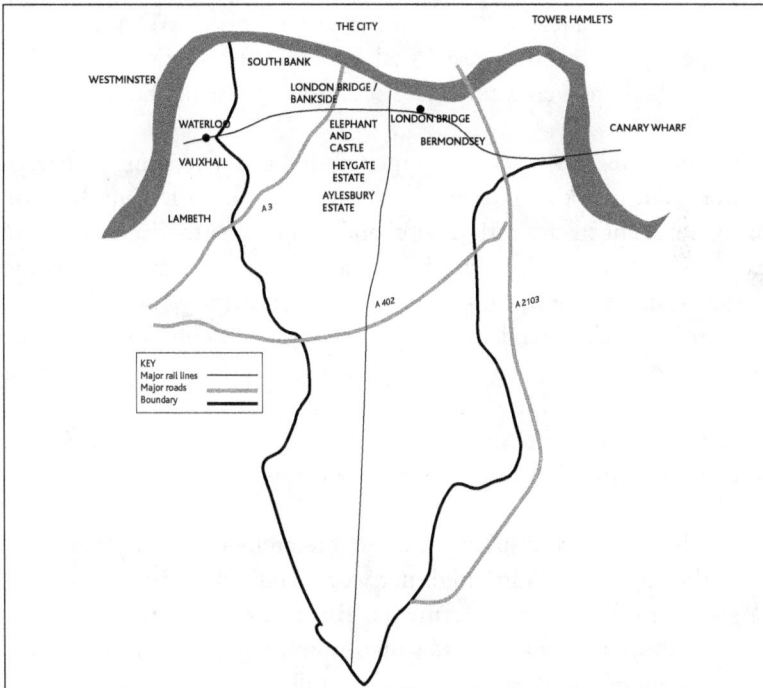

Lees (2014) duly noted that Southwark is the largest council landlord in London, the fourth largest in the entire UK and has the highest percentage of housing stock in social hands. And yet, as we shall see, some prominent council estates are currently being targeted for redevelopment, with their original inhabitants displaced.

I first focus on displacement and resilience in the northern fifth of the borough, where redevelopment and gentrification pressures were many and multiplying. The first area to consider, by London Bridge Station and dubbed Bankside, 'has benefited from the consolidation of the City of London as a major global financial centre, with its attendant generation of new wealth, consumption practices and property speculation' (Harris, 2008: 2415). This extension of the City into Bankside has been willed by an aggressive Southwark Borough Council and its redevelopment plans for the South Bank of the Thames, from the western border with Lambeth to the London Bridge Station area. Hutton (2010: 116) described the important economic re-orientation (and boosterism) inherent in this redevelopment:

> A key reference point for the new policy orientation concerns Southwark Council's aspirations to a new trajectory based increasingly on the cultural economy and creative industries ... evidenced in the popular success of the Tate Gallery of Modern Art in Bankside ... The new policy approach also seeks a larger role for Southwark in the high-powered corporate economy of Central London.

Since the late 1990s, this has included the conversion of a large power plant into the Tate Modern art gallery and the One London redevelopment in the early 2000s, and more recently the erection of Europe's tallest building (the Shard) around a regenerating London Bridge Quarter (Figure 7.4), as well as numerous new-build riverside residential developments in between, acting as beachheads for further gentrification (Figure 7.5), while displacing older, more mundane uses (Southwark Council, 2014a).

The erection of the Shard is scathingly described by Judah (2014) as a sinister symbol of London's reinvention:

> The Shard encapsulates the new hierarchy of the city. On the top floors, 'ultra high net worth individuals' entertain escorts in luxury apartments. By day, on floors below, investment bankers trade incomprehensible derivatives. Come nightfall, the elevators are full of African cleaners,

Figure 7.4 Council housing in Southwark in the shadow of the Shard, August 2010

Photograph taken by G DeVerteuil

Figure 7.5 Tate/Bankside redevelopment, August 2012

Photograph taken by G DeVerteuil

paid next to nothing and treated as nonexistent. The acres of glass windows are scrubbed by Polish laborers, who sleep four to a room in bedsit slums. And near the Shard are the immigrants from Lithuania and Romania, who broke their backs on construction sites, but are now destitute and whiling away their hours along the banks of the Thames. The Shard is London, a symbol of a city where oligarchs are celebrated and migrants are exploited but that pretends to be a multicultural utopia.

In the shadow of all this redevelopment are a variety of voluntary-sector organisations which, for the most part, preceded the reorientation but have also been buffeted by this displacement pressure while offsetting it with stout resilience (Table 7.1).

Table 7.1: Interviewed voluntary-sector organisations in Southwark

	Displaced	Displacement pressure	Entrapment	Owned/rented	Service
SW1	No	Yes	Yes	Rent (1982)	Hostel/drop-in
SW2	Yes	Yes	Yes	Rent (1998)	hostel
SW3	No	Yes	Yes	Rent (1995)	Hostel
SW4	No	No	Yes	Rent (1986)	Substance abuse treatment
SW5	No	No	No	Rent (1998)	Employment
SW6	No	No	No	Rent (2008)	Outreach
SW7	No	Yes	No	Rent (2004)	Refugees
SW8	No	No	Yes	Rent (2008)	Youth
SW9	No	No	Yes	Rent (1989)	Employment
SW10	No	No	Yes	Own (2002)	Employment
SW11	No	Yes	Yes	Own (1938)	Community support

A hostel (SW2) was displaced in 1998 through pressure from Southwark Council – the original location on Tooley Street, just across from London Bridge Station (north side) was no longer amenable due to preceding redevelopment. Further, the original location featured a larger and more visible facility. The new location was much smaller, and rented from the local authority, just a stone's throw from South Bank University and redevelopment at Elephant and Castle. The organisation had no plans to relocate, given both the centrality and convenience, married with the inability to find alternative sites nearby. Amid all this redevelopment pressure, however, were several organisations that displayed remarkable spatial resilience. First, there was the day centre (SW1) serving upwards of 200 homeless and precariously housed people with food, showers, medical care, clothing and welfare advice (DeVerteuil, 2012). A survey from 2008 revealed that 96% of the clients were male, 61% were sleeping rough, and 36% of the clientele hailed from the Eastern European countries that had recently acceded to the EU, suggesting an important gap in services as they are not immediately eligible for welfare payments or housing/hostel places in the UK. Since 1982, this day centre has remained in place because the building was owned by the Catholic Diocese of Southwark and rent free. Since the landlord was not profit-seeking, and the fact that in 2009 there was no equally central (to its clientele) location available in highly gentrified Inner London, the day centre saw no reason to move, but was also effectively trapped. In the words of the Director:

> 'while there are no immediate threats of displacement, we are conscious of the radical change offered by the London Bridge Quarter redevelopment. The Catholic Diocese is not interested in selling the plot, so it makes sense to stay in Central London. But we could not move to similar location elsewhere.'

Second, resilience was evident for a refugee centre run by a Jesuit mission (SW7). The mission remained in place as it shared some neighbouring space with SW1 and paid nominal rent to them. It had moved twice since 1998, having rented very cheaply from the Jesuits in both Hounslow (by Heathrow Airport) and Hackney. It was happier to be in a more central location now, although admitted that refugees were, as of 2009, few and far between in Inner London. However, the Director explained that, "refugees will travel long distances for services, as long as transport links are good. This is unlike rough sleepers, who will not travel very far and rarely leave the confines of Zone 1."[2]

SW7 planned on moving in the near future (the interview was in November 2009) because it needed more space, and the Diocese was planning to redevelop the site as a mixed development – the day centre was to stay, however. Locationally, the refugee centre would seek a future site with central location and good transportation links and, most importantly, attached to a Jesuit institution. There was no avoiding the latter, since for them it was the only way to obtain strategically central space in Inner London.

An outreach team for people sleeping rough (SW6) in the same area commented that there had been an increased focus on the behaviour and visibility of the homeless around London Bridge Station, but that enforcement and welfare responses remained balanced. As the team noted, "Displacement for the sake of gentrification is not good ... but displacement to change behavior in certain places may be good, as in to change the subcultures of homelessness around London Bridge Station." This obtuse reference to coercive care (Johnsen & Fitzpatrick, 2010) was the very raison d'être of the outreach team – to identify, engage, assess and connect those sleeping rough with services that effectively took them off the street. Finally, and to the south-east of London Bridge Station, there was a multi-purpose community centre (SW11) in Bermondsey for young people, those with special needs or those fleeing domestic abuse (DeVerteuil, 2012). While not run by the Borough, most of the funding was statutory, and the site was bought in 1938 as part of the settlement movement when the area was still mostly heavy industry. Despite this, and the strong council support that virtually guaranteed in perpetuity its current location, the facility could not move in to a much-needed newer and larger building, given surrounding upgrading from new-build gentrification along the Thames. The location, according to the Director, was "in between Canary Wharf, Westminster and the City, with lots of new-build and riverside gentrification. Southwark Council is eager to shed its 'basket case' aura, wants to lighten its responsibility of running council estates".

The second area to consider within the redeveloping northern fifth of the borough is directly to the south of London Bridge Station, at a crucial crossroads known as Elephant and Castle, at the very edge of Zone 1 and the Congestion Zone.[3] Given that large swathes of Inner London have already incumbently gentrified, the next frontier would be new-build gentrification threatening the many holdout council estates that conspicuously dot boroughs like Southwark (Davidson & Lees, 2010). The most prominent examples of this new frontier space for gentrification have been the Heygate and Aylesbury Estates, both near Elephant and Castle. The Elephant and Castle area has been the object of redevelopment efforts since the 1960s, when it was radically altered through large-scale, modernist renewal to produce the Elephant and Castle Shopping Centre and Alexander Fleming House. Even before the 1960s redevelopments, there was always the sense that the area had great potential given its centrality, yet perennially undervalued (Campkin, 2013). The Heygate Estate, immediately to the east of the shopping centre, is currently the focus of a massive redevelopment campaign (Campkin, 2013: 51–2):

> The £1.5 billion scheme covers 170 acres of land, much of it owned by Southwark Council. Led by Southwark and developers Lend Lease, it envisages 'a new quarter for central London' to replace what it describes as the current 'missing quarter' … The scheme is focused on creating

a new civic centre and landmark buildings, through the demolition of much of the 1960s building stock, including municipal housing owned and managed by Southwark. New housing in the area will be a mix of private, social rented and shared ownership ... The scheme is driven primarily by an economic prerogative, intended to stimulate growth through private-sector investment.

According to Campkin (2013: 85):

the decision to demolish it was taken in 2004. Since then, it has sat nearly empty, in spite of the housing shortage in the UK. ...Compulsory Purchase Orders are being currently served on the last few occupants, who have campaigned vociferously against the estate's demolition and replacement with 'affordable' and shared ownership housing association housing.

The utopian visions of the 1960s and 1970s, concretised in the form of the Heygate Estate, now seemed decidedly residual and disposable, its conspicuous size and location dooming it to redevelopment.

The two images in Figures 7.6 and 7.7 show the view from the platform of the Elephant and Castle Rail Station, looking on to the abandoned Heygate Estate.

Figure 7.6 Heygate Estate, May 2013

Photograph taken by G DeVerteuil

Figure 7.7 Heygate Estate, August 2013

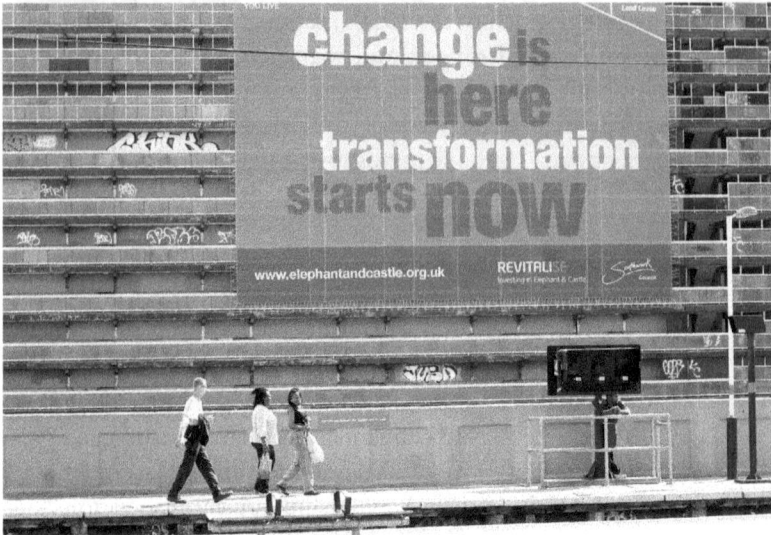

Photograph taken by G DeVerteuil

The Heygate redevelopment very much aligns with broader efforts by Southwark Council to socially cleanse the northern fifth of the borough (DeFillipis & North, 2004: 79):

> In an infamous remark, Southwark's then Director of Regeneration, Fred Manson, argued that "We need to have a wider range of people living in the borough ... social housing generates people on low incomes coming in and that generates poor school performances, middle class people stay away" (quoted in Wehner, 2002). Southwark, it was argued, suffered from having too many of the 'wrong sort' of residents: socially excluded people disadvantaged not by exclusionary labour market processes in a global city, but by 'low' aspirations and low social capital that they passed on to their children. The council's answer was managed but inclusive gentrification to bring in more wealthy residents with higher levels of social capital and labour market involvement and paying higher levels of local tax, which could be used to benefit local residents (provided they were not displaced in the process).

Several new developments have already sprouted along this eastern edge, including the 41-storey Strata Tower, built in 2008 and whose scale is entirely out of place with the medium-rise and austere concrete slabs. Directly to the south of the Heygate redevelopment along Walworth Road is the Aylesbury Estate, also a residual from the modernist, Keynesian era, but now equally threatened by destruction and displacement, an example of how 'new-build developments are pushing gentrification into the remaining working class neighbourhoods and ultra-marginal areas' (Davidson & Lees, 2010: 403). Once again, the desire to de-concentrate the problems from the inner city does little to solve poverty, but goes a long way in reducing its visibility (Reese et al, 2010). Its symbolism remains unmistakable (Campkin, 2013: 78):

> ... the Aylesbury estate is a microcosm through which we can trace the diminishing value UK governments have attached to the state provision of housing ... since their peak in the 1970s. Its history reflects successive waves of privatisation, from Thatcher's 'right to buy' policy initiated in the 1980, to New Labour's Public–Private Partnership approach of the late 1990s and 2000s, and the current Conservative-led Coalition's renewed gusto for shedding government responsibility for housing.

The Aylesbury Estate represented the high water mark of social housing in Inner London, where 40% of the total population was housed in 1981 (Hamnett, 2003). By the early 2000s, the managed disinvestment and neglect of such estates had led to an enormous (state-induced) rent gap, as they sat on highly accessible and valuable land (Watt, 2009; Lees, 2014). Unlike the Heygate redevelopment, the Aylesbury remains in limbo, yet to be demolished or tenants displaced. Rather, in 2014, a development partner has been chosen (Southwark Council, 2014b), while the Council anticipates 50% of the social stock to be saved, compared to only 25% for the Heygate (Hill, 2014). As of August 2014, the Heygate Estate was semi-demolished, with promises of only 79 social housing units and as few as 45 tenants returning to new homes in the area (London Tenants Federation et al, 2014).

Yet, despite these ambitious attempts at 'social mixing', if not extending the City's financial core southwards in a concerted, undemocratic way, the southern 80% of Southwark remains socially and economically heterogeneous, with a significant core of voluntary organisations (DeVerteuil, 2014). Even in the Elephant and Castle redevelopment zone, several voluntary-sector organisations have clung steadfastly to their locations. A frontline hostel (SW3) serving rough-sleeping people with complex needs – and with no expectation of sobriety – put up with the displacement pressures all around, but felt secure given that it had a 999-year lease from the central government:

> 'We are centrally located between London Bridge Station and Waterloo Station [located in Lambeth], and centrally for rough sleeping and networks for survival. On this last point, it is an attractive area for begging along the South Bank. But there is now more resentment towards rough sleepers, greater complaints about anti-social behavior as the neighborhood gentrifies. We feel trapped here and must carefully manage our image, keeping our clients off the front of the building as much as possible.'

Along similar lines, a drug and alcohol outreach and needle exchange programme (SW4) stayed put through a combination of image management and being embedded with the NHS, although technically still renting from Southwark Council. A combined service for long-term unemployed young people, young offenders and vocational training (SW8, SW9, SWE10) was located in the office building attached to the still-standing Elephant and Castle Shopping Centre (Hannibal House), replete with other voluntary-sector organisations. The owning of part of a floor ensured spatial stability, but of course the possible demolition of the mall loomed large. Despite the promised demolitions of nearby council estates, the clientele remained anchored to the numerous other estates further south and east.

These consistent narratives of resilience contrasted sharply with a children's charity (with a special focus on homeless young people) that found itself displaced out of Southwark entirely and into Lambeth. Funded through donations and the central government – but without council funding – the children's charity had located under the railway arches in Peckham. Within a week of moving there in 2001, a concerted NIMBY campaign began, with frequent inspectors and anonymous calls from Southwark Planning, itself under pressure from the local community. A retrospective planning review was forced upon it. In the words of the Director, "There was no help from local officials. The planning review technically forced us to move without support from Southwark Council, and without a clear alternative." While the eviction was taking place, an alternative opened up, but to no avail:

> Spacia (former property arm of Railtrack) has identified premises above Peckham Rye station as a suitable alternative to those it has provided free to the charity since 1996. But

Southwark council has yet to grant planning permission to turn the now-derelict building into a social and education centre. (Benjamin, 2003)

Again, in the words of the Director:

'It was very difficult to find a new place with all the surrounding gentrification. We were evicted, but only left once we had a new place, just across the border in Lambeth. Although there is less pressure now, we feel that the risk of further displacement is inevitable. We have no support from any local councils because our clients self-refer, they don't vote, many are BME (Black and Minority Ethnic communities), and they don't get represented by adult politics.'

These redevelopment pressures have meshed with shifts in voluntary-sector policy at the borough level. A spokesperson from the Southwark Voluntary Action Committee said the following in early 2010 about changes in the siting and management of the voluntary sector:

'Many council-owned buildings that house social services are for sale if they fail to yield enough rent, and we are thus losing potential sites that could house social services to the private market. Since 1998, 16 council-owned sites have been sold off, and this does not include all the pressure around London Bridge and Elephant and Castle and their redevelopment. There is also the emerging pressure for the voluntary sector to be more managerial – this is everywhere now, not just Southwark – with the example of council commissioning. The Council wants more affluence, beyond the Thames; but in that area it lacks pure community space, delivery space which needs to be centrally located.'

Despite these pressures, the Southwark service hub remained spatially resilient in part because of its very lack of conspicuousness so damaging to large-scale councils estates like Heygate and Aylesbury. The service hub's spread, mix and diversity ensured its continued survival. However, the pressures facing Southwark voluntary-sector organisations – and the resilience they provoked – resonated, but sometimes contrasted with, the two other mixed boroughs in London. Islington made for a somewhat muted contrast – a borough where all registered voluntary-sector organisations were, at least until 2003, provided with subsidised space owned by the council. When interviewed in 2009, the Chief Executive of the Islington Voluntary Action Council noted that the borough boasted a very large voluntary sector, comprising 14% of the workforce, with a remarkable collection of national headquarters, including the Red Cross and Age Concern (now Age UK). Since 2003, however, there have been some changes – more established organisations now pay higher rent than they did up to then, and many newer organisations have to rely on private accommodation or faith-based ventures. Such was the case for two organisations in the northern half of Islington: a Chinese cultural centre and a centre for refugees and asylum seekers. The former had been renting a property owned by Islington Council for 28 years, but in 2008 the Council decided to sell off the property in the Archway tube station area. This precipitated a desperate search for new premises, which lasted four months, without Council support. There was still a desire on the part of the cultural centre to buy a property with Council support, but this has yet to materialise. Second, the centre for refugees and asylum seekers had been using a church space rent free since 1997. The centre coordinator had noticed that fewer than 30% of the clients in 2008 were coming from Islington itself, signalling the gentrification-induced dispersion of surplus populations.

In Lambeth, redevelopment had been less aggressive than in Southwark, although still focused on the Thames riverside. The London headquarters for the *Big Issue* social enterprise, which facilitates homeless individuals become street vendors of magazines in order to earn money, advocated on behalf of the 450 street vendors and did not feel that their vendors were under increasing pressure to get off the street. Rather, it found all the new development in Vauxhall, the site of very significant high-rise development since the mid-2000s, put them at risk of displacement (Figure 7.1). The continuous and highly visible resilience enabled by this organisation, however, more than compensated for the threats to spatial stability. Further south along the Victoria Line of the underground, Brixton now stands as the epitome of 'class war' as incoming gentrifiers covet formerly radical and immigrant spaces.

Darlinghurst/Kings Cross case study

Darlinghurst and Kings Cross are neighbouring communities directly to the east of the Sydney CBD, part of what Shaw (2007) deemed the original hubs of inner-city poverty and post-war decline in Sydney, but with only limited industrialisation when compared to Surry Hills. This area includes the suburbs/census communities of Darlinghurst, Potts Point and a sliver of Woolloomooloo (the latter two comprising the Kings Cross area, with Potts Point more desirable) (see Figure 7.9). With a score of 6% on the gentrification index, the combined areas were not as far along in the process as Surry Hills, and they continued to feature strong currents of diversity and specialised service hubs that catered to specific populations Sydney-wide. For Darlinghurst, this means catering to the well-established gay community; in Kings Cross, this means catering to homeless people, and the sex worker and substance misuser populations drawn to Sydney's traditional red-light zone. The area's population growth of 15% between 2001 and 2011 (from 19,241 to 22,112) mirrored the general trend for the Sydney City LGA overall (Australian Bureau of Statistics, 2011). The area's income and housing prices were above the Sydney LGA averages. Like Southwark, Darlinghurst and Kings Cross were marked by important social and geographical polarisations, the legacy of the more generous Keynesian era increasingly surrounded by newer, denser and potentially less tolerant versions of state-supported gentrification.

Gentrification remains more patchy and varied than in Surry Hills, punctuated especially in Kings Cross by new-build high rises (Figure 7.8) that anchor a broader upgrading; as such, the displacement threat remains rather uneven. The new builds have also attracted a different

Figure 7.8 Kings Cross density, taken from Sydney Tower, July 2014

Photograph taken by G DeVerteuil

Figure 7.9 Darlinghurst/Kings Cross boundaries and key infrastructure

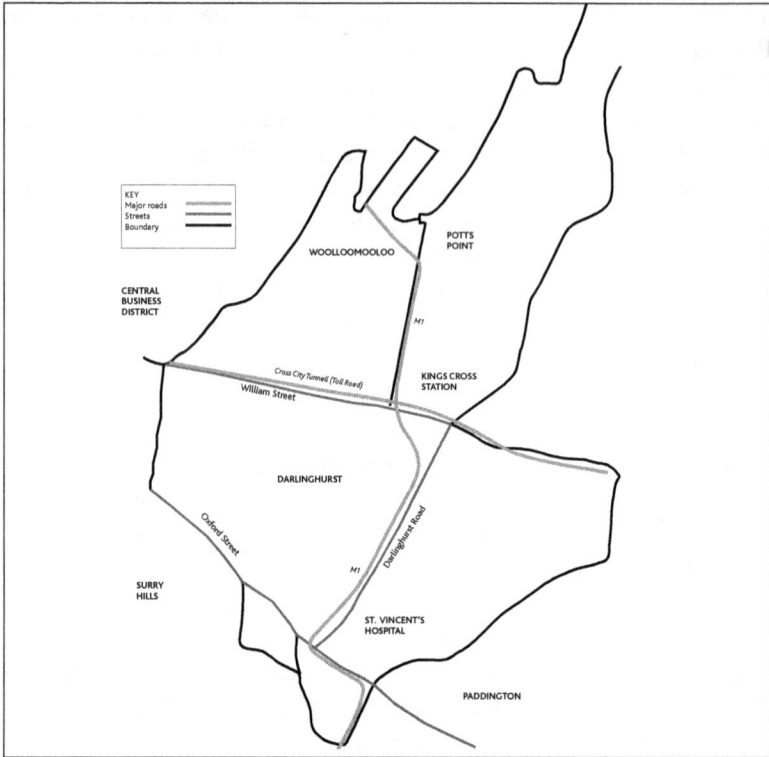

KEY
Major roads
Streets
Boundary

WOOLLOOMOOLOO

POTTS POINT

CENTRAL BUSINESS DISTRICT

M1

Cross City Tunnel (Toll Road)
William Street

KINGS CROSS STATION

DARLINGHURST

Oxford Street

Darlinghurst Road

M1

SURRY HILLS

ST. VINCENT'S HOSPITAL

PADDINGTON

kind of gentrifier, less tolerant of the deep service legacy and attendant surplus populations that flock there, and could serve as a warning for what may happen in Southwark when the new-build gentrifiers arrive in larger numbers.

Both areas were targeted for urban renewal and new-build projects in the 1970s, and both areas betrayed early signs of disinvestment in the 1950s and 1960s, including the dismantlement of the tramway in 1961 (not unlike Los Angeles in the 1950s). The Commonwealth Department of Urban and Regional Development (DURD) had some hand in redeveloping the Kings Cross area in the 1970s, as a means of stabilising what was seen to be a deteriorating inner city (Ruming et al, 2010). But, rather than slum clearance and a new expressway, the DURD sought to craft a more neighbourhood-based regeneration, saving the area from wholesale destruction, like many other inner-city areas protected by the 'Green Bans' in the 1970s (Horvath, 2004; Iveson, 2014).

This salvaging enabled Darlinghurst to emerge as a visible gay district in the 1970s along Oxford Street, and by the 1990s had become internationally renowned (Ruting, 2008). Castells (1983) was among the first to take seriously the emergence of gay districts, specifically the Castro in San Francisco. To him, spatial concentration was 'inseparable from the development of the gay community as a social movement. It brought together sexual identity, cultural self-definition, and a political project in a form organized around the control of a given territory' (1983: 157). Castells was also well aware of the links among sexuality, place-identity and class, which subsequently emerged into a fully fledged focus on 'gay gentrification' (Knopp, 1990; Lees et al, 2008), where class and sexuality fused with inner-city revitalisation and re-commodification, displacement of the lower classes and the rise of the creative city thesis by Richard Florida (2002). Building on this analysis of urban space and gay culture, Ruting (2008: 259) turned his attention to Oxford Street in Darlinghurst (Figure 7.10), which during this early era had 'emerged in Sydney's inner city, with degraded but cheap housing stocks, proximity to the city centre and the need for spatially compact communities to provide protection from wider homophobic repression'. Darlinghurst would experience successive waves of gay investment and gentrification throughout the 1990s. As Connell (2000: 11) noted,

> Despite early moral panic, tolerance enabled a gay urban renaissance ... by the time of the twenty-first Gay and Lesbian Mardi Gras in 1998, not only had the parade become more celebratory carnival than political struggle, but it had placed Sydney on a particular international tourist circuit ... Its acceptance, through far from universal, is a measure of a more liberal city ...

and arguably a more gentrified city, which could threaten the liberal one with implications for the service landscape and its tendencies to either resilience or displacement.

Yet Darlinghurst's gay scene has diluted since the 1990s, the victim of its own success, with reduced discrimination leading to a deconcentration of the LGBT community, and a further commodification of gay space with the inflow of, and some would say a new colonisation by, gentrifiers both gay and straight: (Figure 7.11)

> The Oxford Street district is unquestionably one of Sydney's 'trendy' suburbs, with many young affluent professional residents having moved in. Despite over four decades of gentrification, the district still contains a large

gay population, yet gentrification has nevertheless initiated a process of displacement and relocation of gay men and women. (Ruting, 2008: 263)

Figure 7.10 Taylor Square, Oxford Street, July 2014

Photograph taken by G DeVerteuil

Figure 7.11 New-build gentrification in Darlinghurst, July 2014

Photograph taken by G DeVerteuil

Gorman-Murray and Nash (2014) updated this finding by noting that LGBT space in Sydney has subsequently expanded directly west of the CBD, including Newtown, with a concurrent shift in voluntary-sector geography. In 1993, Darlinghurst held 73% of all voluntary-sector organisations serving the LGBT community when compared to the Inner West, but only 43% in 2012 (Gorman-Murray & Nash, 2014: 632). Despite the pressures from gentrification and deconcentration, Darlinghurst remains highly symbolic (if no longer dominant) for the LGBT voluntary sector in Inner Sydney.

If the gay enclave of Darlinghurst has faded perhaps, do its voluntary-sector organisations and their clients act as the proverbial canary in the coalmine, the first to be pushed out? Or has resilience been the dominant response? Several examples will be brought forth to survey the range of experiences in Darlinghurst, among service providers both new and old (Table 7.2).

Table 7.2: Interviewed voluntary-sector organisations in Darlinghurst/Kings Cross

	Displaced	Displacement pressure	Entrapment	Owned/rented	Service
DKC1	Yes	Yes	Yes	Rent (2005)	Shelter
DKC2	No	Yes	No	Rent (1996)	Health advocacy
DKC3	No	Yes	Yes	Rent (1997)	Legal
DKC4	No	No	No	Own (1970)	Mental health
DKC5	No	Yes	Yes	Own (1964)	Shelter
DKC6	Yes	Yes	No	Rent (2008)	Legal
DKC7	No	Yes	Yes	Own (1970)	Street outreach
DKC8	No	No	Yes	Own (2010)	Counselling
DKC9	No	Yes	Yes	Rent (1994)	Shelter
DKC10	No	Yes	Yes	Rent (disbanded in 2010)	Outreach
DCK11	No	Yes	Yes	Own (2001)	Harm reduction

The first example linking to gay gentrification was an HIV advocacy organisation (DKC2), fully funded by New South Wales Health, and catering to the following clientele:

> 'Our drop-in services are around 500 a year, with over 1000 phone calls and 2500 emails. Most of our clients are on fixed incomes (Disability Support Pension) or casual work, mostly in Darlinghurst, through its large gay community

(postcodes 2010 and 2011); 83% of our clientele last year identified as gay men.'

Unlike the street population in places like Southwark, the advocacy organisation's clientele were being displaced through changes in the real estate market of Inner Sydney. For the past 20 years, many clients on fixed incomes were seeing themselves scattered throughout Sydney as gentrification took hold, part of the slow deconcentration of the gay population overall. However, the clientele were also living longer with HIV, which worked against accessing services as frequently.

The organisation's spatial resilience was assured through a variety of factors. The first was the subsidised rent (30% of market rate), as the building was owned by the City of Sydney. Just the same, those voluntary-sector organisations that were not subsidised had slowly left the building since 1996, replaced by businesses – this included DKC6, an outreach organisation providing free legal advice to the inner-city poor people that had moved to Kings Cross. The second factor was the symbolism of being located on Oxford Street and in the former heart of the LGBT community in Sydney, as well as being 'on the radar of the Council'. The stigma attached to the gay community in Inner Sydney had long ago withered away, enabling the organisation to 'stay put' quite easily. However, the organisation did not feel entrapped, as it could co-locate with larger and more prominent LGBT community organisations nearby, and there was certainly no pressure from the community or the City council to leave.

The second voluntary-sector organisation was a mental health facility attached to the St Vincent's Hospital, and which similarly felt little pressure to move (DKC4). In fact, it had 'cashed out' in 2010 from a previous, more rundown premises and had used the proceeds to buy the next facility space. This had given it better access and proximity to clients, and better integration with mental health services. Despite its stable and protected location, the organisation had not failed to notice the upgrading all around, as well as its mixed nature – incumbent upgrading combined with the punctuations of new-build projects that radically altered the visual and social landscape, as we shall see in more detail in the next few examples in Kings Cross.

Although directly to the east, Kings Cross presented an entirely different service hub, one that builds upon the area's initial reputation as the high-tolerance 'combat zone' of Sydney, a legacy of the Vietnam War era and liberal laws on prostitution first enacted in New South Wales (Hubbard et al, 2008; Prior et al, 2012), but one also facing greater displacement pressure via the emergence of new-build gentrification. The area has always had a reputation for a transient, anonymous and service-dependent population combined with a mix of backpackers, club-goers and wild-eyed suburbanites. For those seeking services, Kings Cross can be the first resort for clients from both Sydney suburbs but also other cities and even rural Australia – a situation not unlike Westminster for London and the UK, and Skid Row, Los Angeles, for the western United States. As one homeless shelter (DKC5), in place since 1964, noted: "We've built up a lot of local goodwill and positive communication. Kings Cross' reputation has been this way since the Vietnam War – it makes sense to be here, near the longstanding community we serve."

This shelter served multiply deprived clients subject to increased surveillance and 'move on' orders from the police. These orders are citations that compel the 'offender' to not return to the same place in Kings Cross for 24 hours; if found again, fines are levied and can lead to serious debt problems. This approach was akin to the UK's ASBO project, but certainly less drastic than the street sweeps enacted in Downtown Los Angeles (see Chapter Eight). Walsh (2011) noted that there was a rough balance between legal punishment and 'make live' provisions within Australian cities for homeless people. As such, Sydney's approach to public space remained more tolerant than that of Los Angeles, but affordable housing was being stripped away by gentrification – even the old boarding houses (protected since 1999) (City of Sydney, 2005) were being redone as expensive student housing. Given its widespread nature in Inner Sydney, gentrification had made it impossible to relocate nearby, even though many of the newer, incoming gentrifiers occupying new-build high-rises were less tolerant than the more established residents and would want the shelter to move. Another shelter (DKC1), this one much smaller and entirely reliant on private donations, noted the following evidence of gentrification-induced pressure since the late 1990s:

> 'Less tolerance for "camping out" in the area; more pressure on services (especially mental health/deinstitutionalisation since late 1990s); more laws (alcohol exclusion zones and "move on" edicts; more city pressure/NIMBY; fewer squats since 1990s as buildings are now renovated; big dormitory shelters, such as St Vincent de Paul, Salvation Army have been downsized by enforcing building laws.'

A woman's-only shelter (DKC9) felt that gentrification-fuelled intolerance had forced it to keep its clients inside the facility more often, and that its original dormitory-style look had to be replaced by something more holistic and designed. This 'blending in' sought to minimise community opposition. And yet as this shelter rented directly from the State Housing Department, it was at the mercy of the government selling off its real-estate assets, as well as moving towards a 'Housing First' model[4] that would largely dispense with emergency services unless absolutely crucial in making invisible the presence of surplus populations. This Australian version of 'Housing First' corresponded with 'significant federal investment in social housing and large increases in funding for homeless services' (Parsell et al, 2013; Baker, forthcoming), presenting a potent counterfoil to uneven punitive tendencies in Sydney.

Kings Cross also boasted a highly visible and longstanding presence of sex workers, brothels and sex shops, all of which were decriminalised in New South Wales in the 1980s and 1990s (Figure 7.12), although not without some spatial prohibitions (Prior et al, 2012). In effect, selling sex was prohibited within a certain distance of schools, churches or hospitals; in Sydney's dense inner city, this meant that legal areas were informally negotiated down to very thin strips of commercial arteries such as William Street. In the immediate vicinity of the Kings Cross station – the heart of the 'high-tolerance zone' – planning rules were put in place to protect the sex industry while discouraging over-concentration and active solicitation (Prior et al, 2012). Yet several

Figure 7.12 Legal brothel on Kellett Street, Kings Cross, July 2014

Photograph taken by G DeVerteuil

longstanding services, including a street outreach unit for homeless youth and sex workers (DKC10), have noticed a shift since 1998 – there was more pressure to be off the street and into services, and the whole area was more cleaned up compared to when there were more sex workers, drugs and homelessness; short-term coercive care in the name of long-term resilience. This pressure had also extended to more stringent rules around the Kings Cross night-time economy in the wake of several lethal assaults in 2012 and 2013, but perhaps also the need to pacify the area for the incoming, less tolerant gentrification.

There has also been some direct displacement in Kings Cross. A legal aid centre for indigent clients (DKC6) had originally been renting from the City in Darlinghurst for close to nothing, between 1980 and 2008. In 2008, the City decided to renovate the building to sell, as part of a generalised gentrification of the area, and so negotiated the displacement of the centre to another city-owned building in the heart of Kings Cross – we will see a similar managed approach to displacement in Downtown Los Angeles as well, albeit on a larger scale. A shelter had also been displaced in 2005 from Surry Hills (DKC1) when the lease expired and the owner wanted to renovate. The shelter was relatively secure in its current location on the southern edge of Darlinghurst and its concentration of city-protected boarding homes that apparently can no longer be torn down or converted.

An emergency service for people who are rough sleepers and an HIV advocacy/drop-in organisation can illustrate some of the key aspects of resilience and voluntarily 'staying put' in Inner Sydney (DeVerteuil, 2014). The service (DKC7) provided food, mental health services, street-based outreach, showers and youth services for homeless people across Sydney. The increase in gentrification since the early 2000s had generated more 'move on' injunctions from the police to clients who congregated in the area, as well as less affordable housing and an influx of less tolerant gentrifiers. However, the emergency service insisted on staying in the area due to the proximity of the street-based community (who will never go far to access services), as well as city-wide goodwill built up over past decades. Resilience can also be demonstrated by Kings Cross's hallmark as a node for illegal drug use and service hub for addiction treatment. The interview with the only medically supervised injection centre in Australia (DKC11) – which opened in 2001 amid much controversy – consolidated some of the above-mentioned points about (recent) gentrification resulting in greater community intolerance, but also suggested some nuances to this process. Its very existence and location was symbolically weighty:

> The opening of this single facility represents a break in the 'War on Drugs' regulatory regime that is the hegemonic practice operating to fight the worldwide networked flow of drugs, a minor experiment with a harm minimization regime of drug regulation. I would never have even thought to mention the drug injection room because it seemed such a minor and highly localized experiment; however, when the agencies representing global hegemonic practices made such a big fuss over the injection room, I felt justified in calling it a minor difference. (Horvath, 2004: 115)

Funding was part state, part from the confiscated proceeds of drug dealers; state support was heavily dependent on showing fewer negative health outcomes stemming from drug misuse (for example, overdoses, deaths, disease). Clients were registered into a database (n=12,000 in 2011) but used the facility anonymously, and mostly lived in the immediate vicinity (postcodes 2010 and 2011). The overall goal was to entice clients to use the facility for their personal health – and to avoid using drugs in public spaces increasingly gentrifying – but simultaneously to provide gateway services if they wished to pursue long-term treatment. The location was central to the 'action', and the initial furore had dwindled among more established residents as neighbours saw fewer discarded syringes and overdoses on the street. There was absolutely no substitute for the current location – it would be unlikely that any other Sydney neighbourhood would welcome such a burdensome facility. Be that as it may, substance misuse continued to haunt Kings Cross by the very presence of treatment centres and harm reduction, and so the two cannot easily be separated except by concentrated police activity.

Stepping back, I can understand DKC11 as more than just enabling client sustenance and care; it also constituted an important abeyance structure, keeping the most marginalised injection users off the streets, while sustaining some until such time as they were willing to access mainstream substance abuse treatment (DeVerteuil, 2014). Without the abeyance functions funding would dry up, while without the care and sustenance functions, client numbers would inevitably drop to only the most hardcore users. The facility again made a sharp distinction between the more established gentrifiers from the 1990s and the most recent gentrifiers in new-builds, who despised the very idea of safe injection rooms – the new-builds effectively created a bubble environment that involved less interaction, and thus less tolerance, for certain street behaviours, with little to no memory of what Kings Cross used to be like. Butler (2003) described this same pattern of separation among gentrifiers in London's Islington, as did Clerval (2013) in Paris's east end *arrondissements*. For both cases, newly incoming gentrifiers differed markedly from the pioneer gentrifiers in the 1960s and 1970s, who attempted to personally engage with the neighbourhood at street level. Returning to Kings Cross, the more established gentrifiers had become increasingly tolerant of the site, as they remembered the 'bad old days' of overdoses in back alleys. But, as in Surry Hills, there was a sense among some of the voluntary-sector organisations that their clientele was slowly but surely scattering beyond Inner Sydney. A legal outreach centre for youth in Kings Cross (DKC8) could not help but notice the general decline in tolerance:

> 'There has been an expansion of gentrification from the eastern inner suburbs and Darlinghurst more specifically, in the form of gay gentrification. The squats have gone, there is less community tolerance for things like the sex workers on Williams Street – the newer residents are more organized and vocal, and live in new-builds. The old issues that once polarized original residents, such as the medically supervised injection site, has been superceded by newer demands ...'

This outreach had plans to move out of Kings Cross towards the Central Train Station, but only if it can replicate its current rental arrangement through the Salvation Army, which was highly beneficial but unlikely.

In summary, the examples from Southwark, Darlinghurst and Kings Cross show how resilience worked in practice across a set of neighbourhoods undergoing mixed gentrification. Revanchism, gentrification and displacement were clearly present, and yet were offset by solid levels of spatial resilience, itself enabled by the patchy and varied nature of gentrification. This mixed upgrading effectively afforded voluntary-sector organisations the ability to stay put, but the presence of new builds – whether looming in Southwark or on the ground in Inner Sydney – introduced a newer, less tolerant and perhaps more volatile displacement pressure to the respective service landscapes.

Notes

[1]   Blomley (2003) claimed persuasively that social mixing is only ever introduced into poor neighbourhoods.

[2]   Zone 1 is the most central of the travel zones in London, of which there are six. Inner London is usually contained within Zones 1 and 2.

[3] The Congestion Zone is roughly equivalent to Zone 1, where private automobiles are charged to enter during weekday peak hours.

[4] Housing First is a new model that reverses the usual crisis model of homeless services: rather than making the client 'housing ready' through a series of stabilizing means (shelter, rehab, etc.) that can drag on for months, the Housing First model provides housing in the first instance, then services designed to stabilize the client.

EIGHT

Pioneer gentrified place-types

Here I consider voluntary-sector resilience for two areas with relatively low and recent levels of gentrification, combined with traditionally very dense and robust residuals of voluntary organisations: Downtown and Hollywood, both in inner-city Los Angeles. Both areas featured high proportions of minority populations and measures that criminalised the poor (or at least contained and put them under surveillance), but also by far the highest levels of voluntary organisations per capita, with Downtown having an astounding 14 organisations per 1,000 persons, and Hollywood with 3.77 organisations per 1,000 persons. As interviews with the dozen emergency facilities emphasised, the Downtown service hub − focused on Skid Row − had become so large, dense, vested and publicly funded over such a long period that it would be a gross waste of taxpayers' money to dismantle it. Rather, the public strategy has been to compress it and gradually erode its sharp boundaries, particularly on its western and northern (gentrifying) edges (DeVerteuil, 2012). So the very conspicuousness of Skid Row's clustering of homeless facilities mitigated against its wholesale displacement; another reason may also be that Downtown's 'weak centre' gentrification and weak centrality was simply not strong enough to overcome 30-odd years of actively entrenched voluntary-sector community resilience (Reese et al, 2010). A contrasting example is given by Hollywood, where resilience was more politically supported in the form of amenable policies that made the retention (rather than erosion/displacement) of voluntary-sector organisations a priority. But, for both cases, there was a sense of ultra-marginal, frontier space (as in Southwark) being targeted by pioneer gentrification, with striking though never overwhelming parallels to Smith's (1996) account of early gentrification in the Lower East Side. In particular, Skid Row, with its large street population, dense service geography and flophouses (there is even a 'Frontier Hotel'), and purported criminality, remains the epitome of frontier space − but, even here, the forces of punitive gentrification, and the resilient and supportive responses to them were nowhere near as clearcut, predominant or even applicable as Smith portrayed them in 1990s New York.

A few words of background on Los Angeles gentrification are necessary before the two case studies are presented. The first is that, unlike London or Sydney, where centrality is not usually in question, the strongly polycentric nature of Los Angeles has produced a more fluid and perforated centrality, such that gentrification is less overspill or incumbent, and that only a few neighbourhoods can be considered truly attractive to gentrifiers, the voluntary sector *and* surplus populations. Further, most land-use policies since the 1920s have favoured a deconcentration of power and wealth. Los Angeles was the first American city to transition to a Sunbelt model, meaning that mass suburbanisation remains the dominant urban landscape, with relatively poor public transportation outside the inner city. For most of the post-war period, these accessible areas (and coincidentally the site of prominent service hubs; Wolch & Dear, 1993) – Downtown and Hollywood, but also Mid-Wilshire, Long Beach, Pasadena, Santa Monica and Venice – saw only muted gentrification and upgrading. However, by the 1990s there was a sense that high accessibility, combined with the characteristics of density and walkability (both relatively precious commodities in Los Angeles), were luring pioneer gentrifiers (DeVerteuil, 2011a; Deener, 2012). Like in Venice, gentrification of Downtown and Hollywood has 'led wealthier people, no longer simply opting to reside in the most exclusive residential enclaves [that is, gated communities], to inhabit areas with cultural diversity and dramatic income divisions' (Deener, 2012: 9). The lateness of this gentrification and its spotty nature, however, means that the process remains immature and has in many cases only sharpened pre-existing inequalities that have pervaded Los Angeles since the 1960s (Davis, 1990; Horvarth, 2004), rather than displacing them altogether. Furthermore, rather than overspill or incumbent upgrading, gentrification in Los Angeles tends to be punctuated, anchored by new-build citadels and proximity to natural amenities such as hills and beach – Banham's 'Foothill' and 'Surfurbia' ecologies respectively (1971), yet still surrounded by large areas of (working and immigrant) poverty. The primarily new-build nature of Downtown and Hollywood gentrification remains very much a work in progress, and still very mixed – the class antipodes to gated communities in Orange County or the established wealth of Los Angeles's Westside, whose congested nature means that most new and dense redevelopment will continue to be shunted to places like Downtown and Hollywood. And so Los Angeles presents an outlier to the classic Anglo-American gentrification found in London and Sydney, as well as New York, Washington, Toronto, Vancouver, Chicago, San Francisco, and so forth. The fact that gentrification is emerging at all in Los Angeles is a mild rebuke to the dystopian, LA School narrative of gang-filled inner cities, graffiti-scarred and mired in poverty and police brutality (Davis, 1990; Horvath, 2004) – but not forgetting that this gentrification introduces its own problems and polarisations.

I identified two overall themes to the case studies: (1) the contradictory role of the state and social welfare policies vis-à-vis service hubs undergoing pioneer gentrification, between state-sponsored neoliberal punitiveness and managed displacement on the one hand, and state-enabled support abetting the resilience of the voluntary sector on the other, muddling any pure instances of punitiveness and revanchism; and (2) the pressure points that come with service saturation under conditions whereby formerly neglected spaces came under the microscope and were abruptly revalorised. The first theme in particular harks back to the discussion in Chapter Three about neoliberalism and punitiveness; I do not believe that punitive measures dominate as much as they co-exist with and co-depend on more supportive measures via the voluntary sector. But, in this chapter, I go further in underlining the disconnect that counters Smith's (1996) tight coupling of state-supported gentrification and state-imposed revanchism – that the two are not always co-present, or that they can co-exist in mutated and contradictory forms.[1]

Downtown Los Angeles case study

From a traditionally low base, Downtown's population grew by 65% between 1990 and 2010, symptomatic of a recolonisation through converted office buildings and new-build gentrification. I consider Downtown Los Angeles to be inner city because the areas of interest are on the immediate outskirts of the CBD, not the CBD itself (zip code 90071), as Figure 8.1 shows.

The fate of the inner-city area is tightly linked to the fortunes of the CBD itself, which has experienced dramatic bouts of investment and disinvestment since the 1920s, with important implications for its centrality to the overall metropolitan area (Davis, 1990; Keil, 1998). In the 1920s, Los Angeles was far more monocentric, and Downtown dominated the business and commercial landscape for the entire Southern California region (Longstreth, 1997). As the power of automobile-induced deconcentration accelerated in the early post-war period, Downtown lost much of its gravitational pull, with several areas, such as Bunker Hill and Skid Row, falling into slums (Wiseman, 1970). The Community Redevelopment Agency (CRA), which had emerged in 1948, was the main vehicle with which to redevelop so-called 'blighted' areas in California. The CRA was a public body (yet

Figure 8.1 Downtown Los Angeles boundaries and key infrastructure

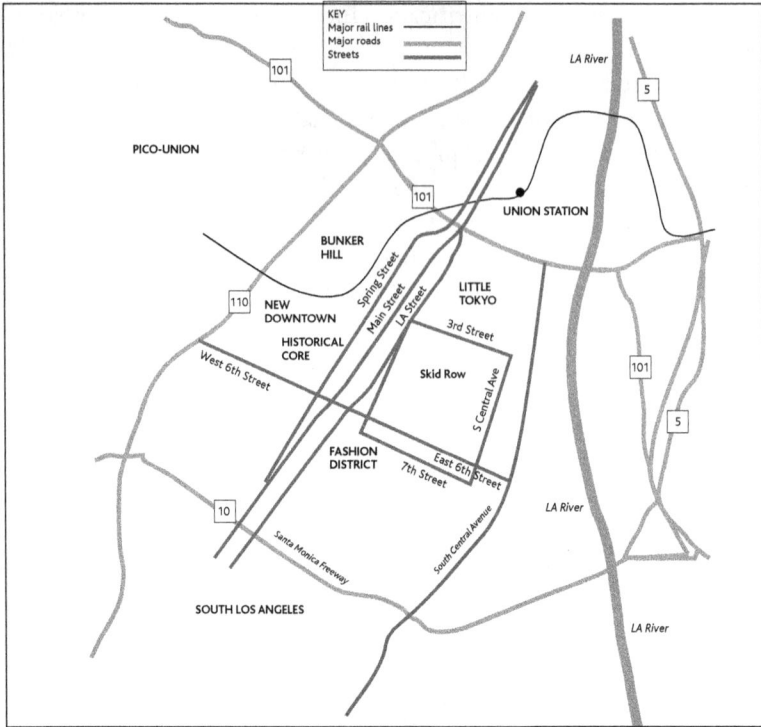

largely unaccountable) that financed itself by creaming some of the increased land taxes from redevelopment zones, a tax increment system that served it well during the heyday of Downtown demolition and high-rise reconstruction, epitomised by the Bunker Hill redevelopment from the 1960s onwards (Keil, 1998). With the CRA at the helm, the emergence of the 'New Downtown' (zip code 90071) was intensified by overseas capital (especially from Japan) and accelerated by LA's dramatic rise to global city status: 'Los Angeles absorbed part of the overaccumulation of the Japanese economic miracle. At the same time, this process created a new place: downtown Los Angeles as we know it today. This place became a chip in globalized casino capitalism' (Keil, 1998: 148). By the early 1990s, the New Downtown had more than 50 new skyscrapers, part of what Davis (1990: 228) called one of the 'largest postwar urban designs in North America'. Conversely, the adjacent Historic Core of Downtown, once the financial core, was heavily disinvested, save for the immigrant-sustained Jewelry District, Fashion District, Broadway commercial core, and Toy District.

Contradictorily, the CRA also had an important role to play in supporting the social service landscape of Downtown, and in particular spatially managing the County's most important service hub, Skid Row. This 40-block 'homeless containment zone' has the highest concentration of shelter beds, subsidised housing and rehabs in the Western United States (Reese et al, 2010), yet no official signs or maps announce Skid Row's presence as such, save for the newly painted mural in Figure 8.2.

Figure 8.2 Skid Row City Limit, San Julian Street, September 2014

Photograph taken by D Warshawsky

In 2000, Skid Row held an astonishing 25% of all the County's shelter beds, while the inner city as a whole held 57% of shelter beds but only 19.4% of the population (Goetz, 1992; Keil, 1998; CCA, 2002; Marr et al, 2009: 311). Although new shelters continue to disperse slowly to the suburbs (DeVerteuil, 2006), Skid Row remains by far the largest clustering of homeless services and people in Los Angeles County. Further, the Skid Row homeless population is particularly prominent and vulnerable. It is predominantly composed of African-Americans, who confront both contemporary racism and the accumulated disadvantages associated with past racism (Reese et al, 2010). All of these factors are exacerbated by an unwillingness to tackle homelessness with a coordinated, well-funded approach, especially when compared to certain other American metropoles – for example, Portland or even

New York (Blasi and the UCLA School of Law Fact Investigation Clinic, 2007; Wolch, 2008).

More than any of the service hubs under study, Skid Row treads a fine line between service saturation and warehousing on the one hand, and genuine support and recovery on the other; but there is no doubt as to its politically constructed (and increasingly contested) nature. The containment policy began in 1976 as an official city policy, amid a boom in commercial development of the nearby CBD (Keil, 1998; Rymer, 2001; Reese et al, 2010). The policy represented a compromise between Downtown investors and some public officials who sought to increase land values by displacing the homeless population away from redevelopment projects, and advocates of the homeless who sought to protect the homeless and increase their access to shelter space and services (Wolch & Dear, 1993). The policy of containment was largely orchestrated by the CRA, which sought to create a '24-hour downtown rivaling any world class city' (Goetz, 1992: 544), but that agreed to maintain affordable housing for the poor and services for the homeless in response to public pressure. To rehabilitate and maintain the buildings and provide affordable housing, the CRA established the Single-room occupancy Housing Corporation in the 1980s. At the street level, the homeless containment policy was selectively applied by the LAPD, using anti-loitering, panhandling and jaywalking laws (Stuart, 2014).

Many advocates of the poor did not see the policy of containment as ideal but still preferable to wholesale displacement of residents and their co-located services (Goetz, 1992; Rymer, 2001). Subsequently, the policy of containment would actually sow the seeds for future gentrification in the areas directly to the north and west of Skid Row, as well as the resilience against it. For the latter, the policy of containment created a concentrated and growing constituency of residents on low-incomes, homeless people and service providers that helped to protect it from further threat of displacement, in essence a critical mass (Reese et al, 2010). For the former, the devaluation inherent in the containment policy, especially in the spillover zone of the Historic Core, created subsequent financial incentives for developers to take advantage of an artificial rent gap, especially in proximity to already-redeveloped areas of Downtown such as Bunker Hill – the complete antipode to Skid Row and the site of the earliest displacements of surplus populations from the Downtown.

By the late 1990s, the foundations for both resilience and displacement were firmly embedded within the Skid Row containment policy. The forces of upgrading were officially unleashed in 1999 with the passage of the Adaptive Reuse bylaw, which permitted the conversion of vacant commercial structures into residential buildings, mostly found in the Historic Core (Barney, 2007; Reese et al, 2010). By the early 2000s, the Los Angeles Police Department (LAPD), under the auspices of former New York chief William Bratton, the CRA and an overlapping set of Buisness Improvement Districts – Arts District, Fashion District, Downtown Center, Historic Downtown, Central City East – began targeting Skid Row, shifting from malign neglect (Wolch & Dear, 1993) to outright interventions. As in other American cities, 'zero tolerance' policing strategies were rolled out (as part of the Safer City Initiative in 2006) aiming to 'prevent violent crime, alleviate fear, improve the quality of life in the city's residential neighborhoods, parks, and business districts, and create and support a climate in which local economic development continues to flourish' (Office of Mayor James K. Hahn, 2004; Von Mahs, 2013). No longer hidden in the shadow of the 30-year Downtown renaissance, Skid Row had become by the 2000s 'a grid of hotly competing jurisdictions, of government agencies, nonprofit organizations, and big money wrangling over a neighborhood's fate' (Rymer, 2001: 41). Since then, hardly a day goes by without some new policy and counter-policy involving community policing, homeless sweeps, BID security brutality, spatial containment, recovery models, public toilets, panhandling, patient dumping, alcohol licensing, and providing trollies for homeless people. Just to give one example of the increasingly heated level of disputes, in October 2007 the law criminalising the sitting down or laying on pavements was overturned, given the pervasive lack of affordable housing in Downtown (National Coalition for the Homeless, 2009).

How did these forces of displacement impact the 17 voluntary-sector organisations interviewed in 2009? Table 8.1 gives an idea of some of the key tendencies among the sample. The first tendency among the sample was the pervasive sense of displacement pressure, accompanied by a relative lack of actual, physical displacement. Indeed, 16 out of 17 Downtown facilities reported client displacement as an issue, particularly on Skid Row. Under the auspices of the 2006 Safer Cities Initiative, a series of street sweeps and zero-tolerance policies for jaywalking and public urination were implemented, designed to keep homeless people constantly on the move within Skid Row, and not just towards it (Reese et al, 2010; Stuart, 2014). A major transitional service for homeless men and women on Skid Row (D1) could not help but notice increasing gentrification and client displacement across Downtown, coming in waves since the early 2000s:

'Gentrification is much closer than before, only a few blocks away in Little Tokyo on San Pedro [and 4th]. Even rent for very cheap hotels is now more than GR [General Relief, which is welfare for unattached individuals; see DeVerteuil et al, 2002]. There is the police-induced displacement that has accelerated since the Safer City Initiative; more protracted sweeps through the BIDs; the physical loss of housing more consistent since 1998, including the Frontier Hotel and the Cecil Hotel.'

Table 8.1: Interviewed voluntary-sector organisations in Downtown Los Angeles

	Displaced	Displacement pressure	Entrapment	Owned/rented	Service
D1	No	Yes	Yes	Own (1984)	Shelter
D2	No	Yes	Yes	Own (1955)	Shelter
D3	Yes	No	Yes	Own (2005)	Shelter
D4	No	Yes	Yes	Own (1955)	Outreach
D5	No	Yes	Yes	Own (1990)	Shelter
D6	No	Yes	Yes	Rent (1999)	Drop-in
D7	Yes	Yes	No	Own (1978)	Shelter
D8	Yes	Yes	Yes	Rent (2009)	Advocacy
D9	No	Yes	Yes	Own (1994)	Shelter
D10	No	Yes	Yes	Own (1964)	Substance abuse treatment
D11	No	Yes	Yes	Rent (1985)	Mental health
D12	No	Yes	Yes	Rent (1992)	Employment
D13	No	Yes	Yes	Own (2001)	Advocacy
D14	No	Yes	Yes	Own (1996)	Housing
D15	No	Yes	No	Rent (2004)	Employment
D16	No	Yes	Yes	Rent (1996)	Advocacy
D17	No	Yes	Yes	Own (1999)	Employment

The punitive Safer City Initiative had taken its toll on the street-based clientele, as a shelter and transitional housing for single women on the very western edge of Skid Row testified (D7):

'In the past 9 years [for example, since 2000], we have gone from malign neglect to street sweeps that begin at 5am, so needed to open earlier to accommodate stressed-out clients.

The BIDs became more interventionist, and our location became part of a BID! More displacement now with the Safer City Initiative, the cardboard boxes have disappeared during the day.'

On this very street, I took images in 1998 and 2009 to chronicle these changes (see Figure 8.3).

Figure 8.3 4th and Los Angeles Streets, 1998 and 2009

Photographs taken by G DeVerteuil

The 2009 image clearly shows a new condo being erected. Almost all facilities mentioned the near-impossibility of expanding westwards back into the Historic Core, now that Main Street had become a gentrified barrier rather than a constituent part of Skid Row. But, even within a shrinking Skid Row, many in the business community (for example, Toy District) were against any expansion in the amount of services for homeless people.

While services bemoaned client displacement and exclusionary displacement, Stuart (2014) suggested that some of them were partly to blame by enforcing a 'recovery zone' model on Skid Row that ensured more aggressive policing of the 'shelter resistant' and 'street temptations'. One large, high-tolerance shelter, itself displaced by the CRA to the heart of Skid Row (D3), was more than happy to see client displacement *off* the streets and *in to* the shelter, which ensured more compliance with the various recovery programmes. Other large shelters concurred – the Union Rescue Mission (D9) welcomed police pressure to get recalcitrant people off the street, thereby ensuring that their services would become even more essential and obviate, albeit temporarily, the need to build permanent housing for those who were destitute. Some services had in fact emerged with but one purpose: to manage those forced off the street, in an abeyance function albeit sprinkled with some (coercive) care. One service's (D4) sole focus was to secure housing for those arrested on misdemeanour charges (such as trespassing, jaywalking or loitering, under the Safer City Initiative), in conjunction with the Los Angeles City Attorney and LAPD. If clients spent at least 21 days in emergency housing, their charges were dropped. But for those unable or unwilling to settle down in emergency services, the Safer City Initiative has done little more than scatter homeless people across Downtown and beyond, earning Los Angeles the 'meanest city' title in 2009 (National Coalition for the Homeless, 2009). Client displacement also had a clear racial component: the vast majority of the homeless in Downtown were African-American men, while the majority of gentrifiers coming in to the Historic Core were white (and sometimes Asian) (Barney, 2007).

Just the same, a spokesperson for the Downtown council member reminded me in June 2009 that gentrification, even if state-supported by the CRA, was more a rebalancing of the social mix,

> with 6000 units of affordable housing (and over 2500 emergency shelter beds) firmly arrayed against 7000 high-end units, and that Downtown could no longer be the dumping-ground of last resort for the service-dependent County-wide. (DeVerteuil, 2011a: 1576)

Some of the entrenched issues around homelessness required County-wide, rather than Downtown-centric, solutions; foremost would be the de-saturation and scattering of homeless services to other parts of the County, which is exactly the rationale for the service hub model (Dear et al, 1994). Yet it was highly unlikely that any other area would taken in the mega-shelters, which I defined (2006) as (1) located within, and reinforcing, strong service hubs such as Skid Row, (2) associated with well-funded service providers, some of whom are national or international in nature, (3) large capacity and a multi-service approach and (4) rejecting the institutional, dormitory look in favour of more welcoming and visually appealing architecture. A recent example (April 2014) of opposition was the denied renovation of an SRO-hotel on Main Street (Hotel Cecil) into 348 units of supported affordable housing; the rebuke was strongly linked to the idea that Skid Row had far too many units already, even if the renovation would have taken hundreds of homeless people off the streets (Evans, 2014), and proven a more durable solution than the emergency services that still largely dominate the service hub landscapes of Skid Row. This was a good example of the saturation effect on Skid Row that makes it difficult to add any more services or housing – a case of 'too much in my backyard already'.

Facility displacement was also an issue on Skid Row, part of an unofficial spatial compression policy, especially on its northern and western (gentrifying) edges, to thereby displace (but not dismantle) those voluntary-sector organisations that found themselves 'in the way' of pioneer gentrification deeper into Skid Row. The managed displacement (and ensuing consolidation around Skid Row) of facilities away from the northern edges of Skid Row and the expanding Civic Center began in earnest before the study period (1998–2011). Takahashi (1998) traced the trajectory of the managed displacement of the Union Rescue Mission (D9), from the 1989 CRA proposal to its ultimate relocation away from 2nd and Main to the heart of Skid Row on San Pedro Street in 1994. In 1989, this 'move by City officials reinforced informal suspicions long held by service providers involved with homelessness, that City officials were working to relocate homeless persons and facilities providing services to the homeless population from the Civic Center area further east towards the central core of Skid Row' (Takahashi, 1998: 109). But through intense negotiations as well as generous CRA relocation grants totalling US$6.5 million, the Union Rescue Mission moved into its new US$29 million building in 1994. At 225,000 square feet, the new Union Rescue Mission was three times the size of the old one (Takahashi, 1998). In my interview with them in May 2009, the sheer scale of the operation became quite apparent, with 965 beds a night, 3,500 meals a day, the largest rescue mission in the US.

The pattern of managed displacement repeated itself in the mid-2000s, this time at the behest of creeping gentrification from the west, along Spring, Main and Los Angeles Streets. The results were mixed, with several facilities displaced within the Historic Core and two facilities asked to leave (without and with a relocation grant, respectively) to the heart of Skid Row to make space for the leading edge of gentrification, a process ongoing since the early 1990s. The non-managed displacement occurred to renting organisations, including a community advocacy/legal clinic (D8). The organisation had been displaced from Spring Street by a loft conversion in 2003 – other voluntary organisations had also lost their leases in the process. For six more years, the organisations clung to a small building on Main Street, before finding newer premises further south along the same street, with this particular relocation funded by the CRA. Despite this assistance, rent was 2.5 times higher. Conversely, the managed displacement affected large and owner, not renter, organisations. The first facility, a large high-tolerance mission-style shelter with more than 200 beds (D3) was displaced in 2005 from Los Angeles Street to what the director of public affairs called Skid Row's 'central core' along San Pedro Street, and again like D9 into a larger and newer facility. This move was encouraged by the CRA and the City of Los Angeles; as previously mentioned, no other area in the County would conceivably welcome such a mega-shelter. As he stated,

> 'We sold our building at 4th and Los Angeles Street to help fund the new building, no question that area had gotten more expensive. The CRA had always encouraged us to relocate away from the Toy District to the heart of Skid Row, and we needed a new facility to expand – could not go to places like Burbank, Glendale or the San Gabriel Valley; there was even resistance to staying in Skid Row. But the CRA did help smooth the move. The advantages now are that we are closer to the central core of Skid Row, with its other services and density of clients – the old location was a bit far for some clients. We have a much larger facility now. But perhaps we are too central – we are a recovery community but immersed in street drugs.'

In 2010, the second facility (D7, the same shelter and transitional housing for single women on the edge of Skid Row) was forced to move, as the surrounding parking lot had been developed as condos (Figure 8.3). With CRA assistance, the facility moved to a city-subsidised facility in the heart of Skid Row, again to San Pedro Street. The process was described in the following terms:

> 'The parking lot has been sold to a developer for condos, and offered to buy the land around it as well and our building too. We said no, and asked the local councilor for a better deal, a larger building – the only one available it would seem was on San Pedro between 4th Street and 5th Street, and that will be our new location. We were encouraged to leave and it was incentivized, so this not really a displacement but further consolidation.'

Spatial resilience was still evident – yet more challenging – for those services remaining in place along the western edge of Skid Row, the frontline of pioneer gentrification. A gateway service on Main Street (D6), with about 275 drop-ins a week, had noticed more pressure upon the visible yet 'harmless homeless'. Once centrally located, the gateway service now felt on the fringe to its client base. Gentrification was quite evident in this area: neighbouring SRO Hotels had been lost (the Rosslyn and the Alexandria), parking fees had more than doubled, and gentrifiers outnumbered the street population. In response, D6 had plans to move to the heart of Skid Row along San Pedro Street, but without any 'official' encouragement or subsidy.

Yet, despite these displacing and punitive impulses on behalf of gentrification (both of facilities and clientele), many of the Skid Row services had remained adamantly in place (frequently and contradictorily with the support of the CRA itself), ensuring accessibility for clients while admitting to the impossibility of relocating in an equally central place in Los Angeles County. As the transitional service (D1) bluntly stated:

> 'One cannot dismantle Skid Row very easily – the impediments are many, including federal mandates on 5,000 to 6,000 affordable housing units that last 55 years; the large missions are private and own their land; there is nowhere else to go, a "safety valve" argument; and there is strength in numbers. Besides, the city created Skid Row, so why dismantle it?'

Rather than dismantlement, or wholesale displacement, there had been active and coordinated resilience. Indeed, more than half of 17 of the services owned their properties, and others benefited from supportive landlords. An employment agency on Main Street (D12) had stayed put due to its embedding in to newly built affordable housing, paying below market rent. Interestingly, the largest employer for the clientele seemed to be the Downtown BIDs, given their proximity and the clients' familiarity with Skid Row etiquette. Community solidarity also emerged as a key source of resilience – Skid Row was simply too vested and interdependent to be dismantled, although some argued that a judicious measure of dispersal might not be such a bad idea. Moreover, many of the services conceived Skid Row as a gateway to more permanent options in less fraught environments – they did not like to think that clients adapted permanently to living there, rather than as a stepping stone.

The very concentration of housing and services for low-income and homeless people on Skid Row had encouraged various forms of collective resilience to arise. This included many examples of voluntary-sector organisations working together to help clients, but also banding together when faced with outward threats, despite the pervasive squabbling and fragmentation among competing care and recovery models. This active and adaptive resilience had thus far successfully protected Skid Row; the vast majority of homeless services remaining had no plans to relocate any time soon (Reese et al, 2010). An example of adaptive resilience involved some (owner) facilities feeling the need to become more active in their advocacy in response to the gentrification-induced anti-homeless push since 2006. A transitional and permanent supportive housing service (D11) found advocacy against the criminalisation absolutely essential to ensure that its clients – many of whom had a mental illness – could be free from police harassment, and that Skid Row could become more humane, as the last major concentration of 'last resort' housing in Los Angeles. They were also inclined to criticise the 'coercive' and 'emergency' nature of many of the services, and state that there were not enough permanent solutions to homelessness. Other forms of adaptive resilience involved a grudging acceptance of poor premises and bad housing, rather than giving up the centrality that Downtown afforded. The Salvation Army (D10) was a well-funded and long-time owner, yet in an ideal world it would move to a larger, newer building in a heartbeat. It remained on the eastern edge of Skid Row and put up with an older and cramped premises in an 'unsavoury' area that was very challenging to its clients in detox and treatment. It was even approached in 2007 to sell the building for condos, but again there were no alternative sites in Skid Row given the rise of gentrification-induced NIMBY and the gentrification-induced rise in land prices. Another example was a Filipino community and workers advocacy centre (D13) just west of Downtown, far from the intense battles over space found in Skid Row. As owner, the centre refused to contemplate a move elsewhere, despite the creeping overspill of Downtown gentrification that made any relocation impossible. It wanted to stay in the area, "because of the clientele, which remain largely in the area and have knowledge of services. There are roots in the area, and even if the population disperses, it's best to remain in the old hub."

A community service in Little Tokyo (D14) felt the same way, sticking to its hub even though the majority of the Japanese/Nikkei community had long moved out of Downtown, leaving behind mostly elderly people and clients on low incomes, but also a rich legacy of fundraising and Japanese-American cultural capital. In existence since 1979, the current facility had been custom built in 1996. Any new expansion, including new-build affordable housing, had occurred outside of Downtown.

So the very conspicuousness and solidarity of Skid Row's concentrated homeless facilities mitigated against its displacement alongside some support from the CRA, even if it sometimes meant suffering from managed displacement. Skid Row may appear to most outsiders as a dead-end, last-resort dumping ground, or Hell's half-acre (see Vergara, 1995), but it remains a key node of survival and support for the most denigrated of surplus populations. A saying on Skid Row is that everyone is there for a reason – but I would like to think that the reason is structural, rather than individual. Skid Row sustains, but also enables, individual resilience by providing (and protecting) some of the most string-free services and affordable housing in the entire County. The very clustering does, however, make it difficult for the impoverished individual to escape, for there is no equivalent elsewhere (Von Mahs, 2013).

Another reason for spatial resilience may also have been that Downtown's 'weak centre' gentrification was simply not strong enough to overcome 30-odd years of stubbornly entrenched resilience on the part of the Skid Row voluntary community (Reese et al, 2010). The relatively late start and staccato nature of gentrification in Downtown Los Angeles was far from a 'relentless march' (Slater et al, 2004), at least in 2009 when the interviews took place. In effect, the post-2008 slowdown had put many new developments and conversions on hold. By 2014, this lull seemed more like a temporary blip in the steady gentrification of Downtown – construction cranes had returned with a vengeance, with numerous new-build constructions to the south and east of the CBD, creating the conditions of what Marcuse (1985) would deem exclusionary displacement. Atkinson et al (2011) captured this stage as in between the partial and full gentrification of a neighbourhood, and before wholesale displacement of the former residential population.

While it is difficult to argue that displacement pressures and actual displacement were not linked to the revanchism that, according to Smith (1996), invariably and necessarily creates the space for gentrification, counter-evidence was plentiful: the concentrated presence of voluntary-sector organisations, itself propped up by the CRA, becomes an effective barrier to deeper incursions by gentrification while ensuring community survival and continuity (Clerval, 2013). In sum, wholesale gentrification had not occurred as of 2009 (nor by 2014), and Skid Row remained spatially resilient (albeit shrunken along its northern and western borders), not out of inertia or lassitude but due to a continual adaptation to shifting redevelopment priorities, as well as a dense thicket of likeminded voluntary-sector organisations that provided a critical mass and a critical bulwark against a pointed yet sometimes ambivalent punitiveness.

Hollywood case study

Hollywood is several kilometres to the north-west of Downtown, and like many other older nodes in Los Angeles (for example, Venice, San Pedro) was once its own municipality before being annexed in 1910. Hollywood emerged in the first three decades of the twentieth century as the world's most prominent production and office cluster for the motion picture industry. From the 1950s onwards, as Los Angeles suburbanised and the movie studios escaped to Burbank and the San Fernando Valley (Longstreth, 1997), Hollywood endured a long descent. By the early 1990s, all pretence of Hollywood glamour had evaporated, replaced with more mundane concerns around homeless young people, drugs, crime and abandonment. Davis (1998: 395) qualified the endgame of this desuetude in typically hyperbolic terms: 'the real Hollywood has gone from picturesque dilapidation to hyperviolent slum' (Figures 8.4, 8.5).

In response to this decline, numerous efforts have been deployed to regenerate Hollywood, from the 1977 Hollywood Revitalization Plan to the 1986 CRA Redevelopment Plan and subsequent amendments and expansions in the 1990s, the 1991 Social Services Plan, as well

Figure 8.4 Abandoned apartment building off Yucca Street, April 1997

Photograph taken by G DeVerteuil

Figure 8.5 Recovery services on Sunset Boulevard, July 1996

Photograph taken by G DeVerteuil

Figure 8.6 Hollywood boundaries and key infrastructure

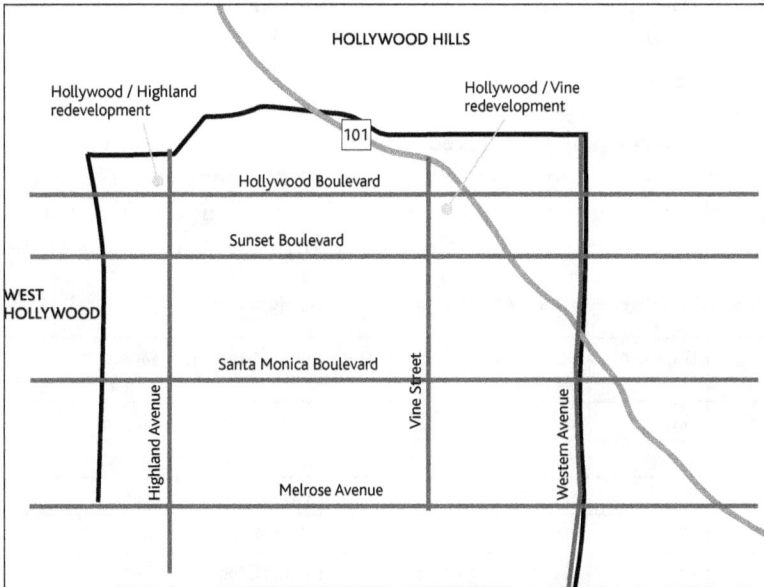

as the founding of the Hollywood Entertainment District BID in 2004 and its expansion in 2009 as far east as the Hollywood Freeway (#101). Revitalisation was only truly consolidated from the early 2000s onwards, anchored by the catalytic mega-projects at Hollywood/ Highland and Hollywood/Vine, along with new Metro stations, commercial developments and substantial residential densification (Figure 8.6) (DeVerteuil, 2011a).

These redevelopment plans would have crucial implications for the location (and relocation) of voluntary-sector organisations. Just the same, redevelopment and state-sponsored gentrification have not led to the wholesale displacement and dispersal of the service hub. Rather, the Hollywood CRA, along with the police and local BID, have ensured that significant redevelopment and social service preservation were not mutually exclusive; therefore there has been less managed displacement when compared with Downtown and less displacement pressure overall. The consensus was spelled out in the 1991 Social Services Plan: the CRA would set aside 10% of the tax increment to be expended on programmes and projects that fulfil a social needs purpose, which included direct grants to voluntary-sector organisations in Hollywood (CRA Los Angeles, 1991). The Social Services Plan also recognised that voluntary-sector organisations were essential to Hollywood's redevelopment and prosperity, and as such should not be pushed out by said redevelopment. But more informally, interview material from the voluntary-sector organisations (Table 8.2) made clear that partial displacement from the redevelopment area directly along Hollywood Boulevard (essentially between Highland and Vine) was encouraged and subsidised by the CRA. I will return to some of these cases of managed displacement in a few paragraphs' time.

The CRA's policies evolved in response to Hollywood emerging in the 1980s as a regional service hub for two distinct constituencies: homeless young people and the LGBT community. In the case of runaway teens, Ruddick (1996) argued that the clientele forced the

Table 8.2: Interviewed voluntary-sector organisations in Hollywood

	Displaced	Displacement pressure	Entrapment	Owned/rented	Service
H1	Yes	Yes	Yes	Own (2008)	Drop-in
H2	Yes	Yes	Yes	Own (2001)	Shelter
H3	Yes	Yes	No	Own (2007)	Food
H4	No	Yes	Yes	Own (1992)	Health
H5	No	Yes	Yes	Own (1998)	Health
H6	No	Yes	Yes	Rent (1995)	Shelter
H7	No	Yes	Yes	Rent (1997)	Shelter
H8	No	Yes	Yes	Own (2004)	Shelter
H9	No	Yes	Yes	Own (2002)	Housing, development
H10	No	Yes	Yes	Mobile (2005)	Food
H11	No	No	Yes	Own (1963)	Advocacy

services to relocate, a switch from the usual 'drift to services' implicit in the service-dependent ghetto model (Dear & Wolch, 1987). However, once those services clustered in Hollywood, they faced the delicate task of maximising access to their clientele, who usually haunted heavily-touristed streets such as Hollywood Boulevard, while lowering their visibility. As Ruddick explained (142):

> Social services evolved a complex spatial strategy in relation to the community itself. First, they chose locations to enhance possibilities of attracting youths off the boulevards and into their programs ... Second, these services extended the reach of their programs with street outreach, on foot or with mobile vans ... Third, the programs began to choreograph the social space of runaway and homeless youths within the larger community, setting up curfews and even designating certain parts of the community 'off-limits' to their clientele. These strategies were intended to modify the behaviors of the youths within the community, and to manage their image within it.

Kenney (2001) underlined a second institutional constituency in Hollywood – the LGBT community, and its ability to self-organise and create grassroots voluntary-sector organisations separate from the traditional hub in West Hollywood, directly to the west but its own municipality (Keil, 1998). More specifically, organisations such as the Gay and Lesbian Center and AIDS Project Los Angeles filled crucial gaps in the service landscape, enabled safe spaces for the community, but also extended beyond to include important political work and, ultimately, a say in the redevelopment of Hollywood itself, including the inclusion and retention of voluntary-sector organisations more generally. The spectre, however, of replicating the extreme saturation of Downtown Skid Row compelled both organisations (through the CRA) to locate near, but not on, Hollywood Boulevard, at the edges of the redevelopment zones. This locational strategy paralleled the homeless teen organisations in the 1990s.

The displacement that did occur in Hollywood was mostly managed but on a much smaller scale than Downtown. While similar in terms of prodding voluntary-sector organisations to vacate zones of redevelopment, the Hollywood case focused on reducing the visibility of services for homeless young people, which traditionally congregated on Hollywood Boulevard (Ruddick, 1996). Two facilities for homeless youth were displaced from more central locations in Hollywood to more marginal locations eastwards (DeVerteuil, 2011a). The first voluntary-sector organisation (H2), a day centre for street kids, was evicted in 2001 near Hollywood and Vine; this occurred at a similar time to a needle exchange nearby on Selma and Cahuenga being disbanded entirely. This was a site of significant state-subsidised gentrification, including a new W Hotel, condominiums and loft conversions, rising rents and more proactive BID security, all of which led their clients to feel no longer welcome 'on the Boulevard'. The centre bought a smaller building on the eastern fringes of Hollywood and paid it off in 2008. The Associate Executive Director let me know that this fringe location was a compromise – still accessible for the provision of care and sustenance, but also part of a local abeyance strategy to keep homeless teens (and their services) off central Hollywood Boulevard (DeVerteuil 2011a). In her words,

> 'our clients have been pushed eastwards and away from the redevelopment, along with the location of the facility. However, our clients are not being punished – rather, there are more connections for them in terms of the local service community. We are off the prime area, but still close to clients, and in an anonymous part of Hollywood but still on the Boulevard, which is essential to attract new clients. Still, the odds of getting a larger premises equally located is almost impossible.'

The second facility, a drop-in for street kids and travellers' aid (H1), was displaced eastwards in 2008 beyond the Hollywood study area entirely, when it could not find an appropriate and affordable replacement for its rented site. The drop-in, which had been in service since 1983, was disbanded at the same time. In the words of the Executive Director:

> 'Our original site on Hollywood Boulevard was converted into condos and office space for the entertainment industry. We went to the CRA to propose a different site, staying within Central Hollywood. It was a hopeless search, given the NIMBY and escalating land costs. Local homeowners prevailed in excluding the drop-in entirely, so we had to disband it. We spent 10 months looking, and the CRA finally suggested, and agreed to subsidise, our move to East Hollywood, but we had to pay top dollar for the new house ($800,000). Perhaps it's better anyway, as poor people are being shunted eastward?'

An example of a non-managed displacement occurred with a food delivery programme for homebound people with HIV/AIDS and other debilitating diseases (H3). Once located on Sunset near the border with West Hollywood, the facility moved in 2007 as the rent had gone from $38,556 in 1996 to a whopping $252,000 in 2006, an increase of more than 600%! The new location, in a cheaper and more southern part of Hollywood, still proved central enough even though clients were also being displaced:

> 'We serve about 2,300 individuals, 50% of whom have HIV/ AIDS. But they too are being displaced to cheaper parts of Los Angeles and out of Hollywood, West Hollywood and Silverlake. We remain centrally located for delivery and near our volunteer base. There is no immediate pressure here, although the area is getting more expensive.'

Conversely, Hollywood was an excellent example of how a supportive local government structure could prop up spatial resilience. Council members, businesses in the Hollywood Entertainment and Sunset/ Vine BID and planners in the CRA made the retention of voluntary-sector organisations a priority. A spokesperson for the Sunset and Vine BID mentioned that there is no umbrella policy to evict agencies; the spokesperson for the CRA confirmed that the redevelopment plans in the 1990s and 2000s all conserved an important voluntary-sector service component (DeVerteuil, 2012). For instance, a shelter for homeless women and families (H6) in the heart of Hollywood had managed to hold on to its location since 1995 due to its rental from the Hollywood YMCA, as well as predictable funding from the federal Housing and Urban Department (HUD). But a key source of resilience for the shelter had also been to ally directly with the Hollywood BID to keep homeless individuals out of key areas – this experience paralleled a larger shelter (H8) at the very eastern edge of the BID, which had moved there in 2004 despite strong NIMBY sentiments. A measure of 'coercive care' was thus in operation, forcing the homeless to become more attached to services or risk displacement entirely. Similarly, a health care clinic (H4) on the eastern edges of Hollywood Boulevard had managed to avoid being displaced – or even being asked to leave – by maintaining a low profile, ensuring that its youth clientele 'have learned to be invisible' in public space. The facility felt entrapped, as it could not expand and could not move within Hollywood; but it does own the premises, and felt that Hollywood is more supportive than Downtown, with excellent relationships with the BID and the CRA. To this facility and others, the advantages of staying with the Hollywood service hub outweighed the disadvantages. A Thai community development and social service agency (H9) – the only one in Los Angeles County – had held on to its very central location by buying an entire building in 1995, when it was very cheap, and then converting most of it into affordable housing.

Another source of resilience came from the very concentration of LGBT-orientated services in Hollywood, which have traditionally received help and support from Hollywood politicians and the CRA (Kenney 2001). This is what a service hub ought to be – a concentration of likeminded organisations sustaining a network of clients while offsetting punitiveness and NIMBYism. A drop-in centre for LGBT youth on Santa Monica Boulevard (H7) spoke to this very issue. Founded in 1997, the organisation was well aware of Hollywood's long-running attraction to homeless or runaway young people, including not just the supposed glamour but also the higher degree of tolerance and the availability of specialised services. As a result, most clients were not from Hollywood itself but the poorer and more underserved areas of Los Angeles, including the traditional African-American areas of south Los Angeles. Gentrification in this part of Hollywood was increasing:

> "All around there is gentrification. One symptom is the new la Brea/Santa Monica complex just down the road, where there used to be squatting – clients did not disappear but instead came for services" (H7).

Being part of the Los Angeles Gay and Lesbian Center network ensured a certain stability of funding and reputation. Moreover, the facility rented from a 'reasonable' landlord, and enjoyed support from the CRA, even if its location was not trouble free.

Finally, the Hollywood CRA and BID have been instrumental in ensuring the survival, if not always the locational integrity, of voluntary-sector organisations. One example was an organisation that used public feedings (H10) to entice homeless people into more long-term services. But even this arrangement took some time and effort – the original feeding site was in front of the Hollywood Library, proving too visible. Although legal to feed in public spaces, this original site was dropped in favour of a less prominent place a few blocks away at Hollywood and Argyle, in the shadow of the Hollywood/Vine redevelopment.

In summary, I return to the two main themes that have crosscut the Downtown and Hollywood case studies. The first was the contradictory role of the state and social welfare policies, of punitiveness and gentrification-induced displacement, versus state-supported policies abetting voluntary-sector resilience. A superficial reading of the managed displacement in Downtown, and to a lesser extent Hollywood, would suggest punitiveness and revanchism, but a careful investigation revealed the contradictory support behind them, the punitive and the supportive in co-dependent kinship. The cost to organisations was (managed) displacement but not disbandment, which adds yet another layer of complexity to understanding inner-city dynamics. Gentrification was not always accompanied by revanchism, and sometimes revanchism was robustly counterbalanced. So even in Downtown Los Angeles, punitiveness was not unadulterated, and demonstrates how local social policy can make or break service hubs. The second theme focused on the pressures of service saturation when ultra-marginal places like Downtown and Hollywood became revalorised. The case studies diverged in this respect – Downtown was far less supportive of any growth or spread of services, while Hollywood remained generally supportive of its service hub. Both service hubs used their very concentration to enable survival and social resilience – the next chapter focuses on this very process, with specific reference to immigrant enclaves.

Note

[1]   Nor does gentrification cause homelessness per se – although it can be a contributing factor, it need not be a determinant one. For instance, in Los Angeles, mass homelessness in the 1980s preceded any meaningful gentrification by 25 years.

NINE

Immigrant enclaves

Here I consider the spatial resilience of immigrant-orientated voluntary-sector organisations – and how they enabled resilience socially – set within a predominantly immigrant community space: Pico-Union in Los Angeles and Tower Hamlets borough in London. The two most important immigrant groups in these enclaves are made up of Central American and Bangladeshi people,[1] respectively, and both consider these areas their original settlement hubs. Accordingly, I focused on the service hubs that have emerged to cater to an immigrant clientele. While Sydney is most definitely a migrant metropolis and the primary magnet for Australia (Forrest & Dunn, 2007), its inner city has been gentrified to the point where many immigrants now head directly to the (inner-western) suburbs, particularly within 20 kilometres of Auburn CBD (Lalich, 2006). More generally, inner-city Australia has been, using Shaw's term (2007), 'white-washed' (see Walters & McCrea, 2014, for Brisbane; Van Hulten, 2010, for Melbourne; and Byrne & Houston, 2005, for Perth). In Sydney, the obvious exception to this trend has been Chinatown, but beyond it there was a generalised evacuation of immigrant community space that was more advanced than Inner London and most certainly for inner-city Los Angeles.

Threats of displacement in Pico-Union and Tower Hamlets came in two forms: the threat of absolute homelessness for what are two very vulnerable groups – the response to which involved the voluntary sector enabling and transferring social resilience to the community – as well as broader threats through gentrification and redevelopment, which involved voluntary-sector spatial resilience. Sometimes forgotten by proponents of professionalisation (Hamnett, 2003), immigrant community space is crucial in that it reflects the polarisation endemic to global cities, but also contains the very voluntary-sector organisations designed to allay its worst tendencies. Moreover, the relationship between immigrant community space and gentrification seems woefully understudied (but see Walks & Maaranen, 2008), and certainly worthy of further consideration. For instance, different models of relationships can be proposed: for Sydney, it was a suburban model whereby immigrants shun the gentrifying inner city; for London it was more of a bubble model, whereby gentrifiers have moved into inner-city immigrant community space but have yet to displace it entirely, relying instead on a spatially proximate but socially apart existence (May, 1996; Butler, 2003; Clerval, 2013); and for Los Angeles, inner-city immigrant communities tended to act as a barrier to gentrification, but also sometimes afforded the space for wealthier immigrant groups (for example, Koreans) to gentrify their own enclaves. These scenarios suggest an important relationship between race and gentrification, one that has been broached (for example, Shaw, 2007) but lacking the added complexity of immigration.

This chapter therefore considers a different kind of neighbourhood (the immigrant enclave) and a different kind of voluntary-sector organisation (immigrant serving, but still arranged in service hubs). Immigrant communities like those composed of Central American and Bangladeshi people suffer from deep poverty and spatial exclusion, and may be considered part of the 'postindustrial precariat' (Wacquant, 2008). Yet their community space is more an enclave than a ghetto model. Marcuse (1997: 242) defined enclaves as 'a spatially concentrated area in which members of a particular population group, self-defined by ethnicity … congregate as a means of enhancing their economic, social, political and/or cultural development'. Immigrant enclaves can be seen as voluntary and self-segregated spaces, defensive clusters designed to ensure daily survival. As Phillips et al (2007: 219) aptly put it, 'the more positive aspects of minority clustering, namely, the social and cultural capital inherent in supportive social networks, and the better health and well-being associated with community support in otherwise deprive inner urban areas, tend to receive less attention'. This attention to enclaves does not, however, deny that some elements of the more pejorative ghetto models of immigrant settlement were also in effect in London and Los Angeles. To Marcuse (1997: 231), ghettoes were seen as 'spatial concentrations used to separate and to limit a particular involuntarily defined population group (usually by race) held to be, and treated as, inferior by the dominant society'. By this notion, immigrant ghettoes are confining and involuntarily segregated spaces, and reflect an overall powerlessness and racist intent on the part of larger society. Keith (2005: 267) captured this double-edged sword: 'the ethnic enclave is potentially both a testament to institutionally racist exclusion and a source of social capital and networking'.

Immigrant enclaves and immigrant community space are obvious co-platforms and enablers of the immigrant-serving voluntary sector. In his pioneering study of the Mission District in San Francisco, Castells (1983: xviii) identified the emergence of a Latino-orientated service hub for the local population that was culturally focused and culturally competent, self-organised and arising in response to deficient local provision from the state, in 'defense of cultural identity associated with and organized around a specific territory' (see also DeVerteuil & Wilson, 2010, on catering to the Aboriginal population in Winnipeg). From these humble beginnings, many inner-city enclaves developed extensive networks of immigrant-serving voluntary-sector organisations attuned to the needs of their specific immigrant clientele (Martin, 2011), and in so doing 'differ from other social-service providers in that they explicitly incorporate cultural components, and a consciousness of ethnic or national-origin identity, into their mission, practices, services and programmes' (Cordero-Guzman, 2005: 894). Immigrant enclaves become service hubs for a very distinct and place-bound clientele. Moreover, as subsequent generations moved beyond the enclave they periodically returned to use this bespoke service hub, with organisations providing evidence of innovation, specialisation and a certain independence from the mainstream welfare state. As Keil (1998: 125) noted, 'immigrant communities have consistently tested and challenged the boundaries of the social welfare state'; this does not mean, however, that they can dispense with the larger welfare state entirely, as we shall see with the cases of the Bangladeshi and Central American communities. Finally, valorising these two Global South communities and their fate in Global North global city-regions constitutes a certain 'worlding' of cities (Roy, 2009; Baker & Ruming, forthcoming), of 'transnationalism from below' (Smith, 2001), of paying closer attention to Global South models – in this case, approaches to survival and producing/enabling social resilience – imported to the Global North global city-region.

While differing culturally, Bangladeshi and Central American people shared certain 'informative similarities' (Hasson & Ley 1997) that enabled comparison (Allen & Turner, 1997; Davis, 1998; Amin et al, 2002; Dench et al, 2006; Peach, 2006). First and foremost was that each immigrant community only significantly expanded during roughly the same period of intense post-Keynesian national welfare state restructuring, with the greatest inflow occurring throughout the 1980s, substantially enlarging the modest original settlements (DeVerteuil, 2011b). Second, both communities remain among the poorest and most segregated groups in London and Los Angeles, although the settlement patterns reflect both externally imposed segregation and self-segregation for cultural, economic and protective purposes (DeVerteuil, 2011c). Third, both groups remain decidedly 'inner city' when compared to less densely settled, suburbanised immigrant clusters. Indeed, 73% of London Bangladeshi people remain confined to Inner London (UK census, 2011), the only Asian population more numerous in the inner city than in Outer London. And, fourth, these hubs constitute 'extraterritorial spaces' (Roy, 2009: 827), in that they have strong links back to homelands, economically (via remittances) (see Figure 9.1), politically (via hometown associations and voting in national elections) and socially (via transnational support). They also represented the largest settlements outside their respective nations (Bangladesh, El Salvador and Guatemala).

Figure 9.1 Remittances, Brick Lane, November 2012

Photograph taken by G DeVerteuil

Yet each group displayed a uniqueness that makes for informative differences. More than 80% of Central Americans in Los Angeles consisted of Salvadorans and Guatemalans who involuntarily fled civil wars in the 1980s in large numbers to settle, usually undocumented. They constituted a textbook case of 'clandestine chain migration' (Landolt, 2008: 53). Conversely, as economic migrants, Bangladeshi people arrived in large numbers in the 1970s and 1980s to Tower Hamlets, fleeing crushing poverty in the Sylhet area. According to 1991 and 2001 census data, Bangladeshi people were among the poorest and most segregated immigrant groups in London (Peach, 1996; 2006); according to the 2011 UK census, 30% of London Bangladeshi people lived in deprived neighbourhoods, more than any other ethnic group in the UK.

Both immigrant groups were clearly resilient in terms of avoiding street homelessness (although not hidden homelessness, such as doubling up) by strategically deploying voluntary-sector organisations, social networks, state subsidies, overcrowding and relative immobility within segregated (yet also protective) community immigrant space, an apparent 'ethnic density effect' that also facilitated self-catering and self-provisioning. In 2008, in London, those sleeping rough were 63% white British-born, compared with 17% black and less than 5% Asian (National Centre for Social Research, 2009); this was despite the fact that more than half the poverty population in London was of a BME background, with Pakistani and Bangladeshi people among the most poverty stricken (MacInnes et al, 2011). Similarly, a County-wide study in Los Angeles revealed that, while immigrants, Latinos and Asians all suffered from impoverishment (more than half of all poor people in the County were Latino in 2003), they were under-represented in their use of shelters; conversely, African-Americans were four times more likely to use shelters (38% of all users) than the total proportion of poor in Los Angeles (9%) (Shelter Partnership, 2000; Institute for the Study of Homeless and Poverty, 2004). The three largest mainstream shelters in Los Angeles (D3, D9, D10) were interviewed as to whether they accommodated a Central American clientele; all said very few, recognising (1) the social networks that kept this community off the street, (2) the distrust of mainstream services given the lack of documentation, and (3) the lack of culturally competent services on Skid Row. As the Salvation Army (D10) noted, "we haven't seen a Salvadoran or Guatemalan in 2 years, except for feedings". In effect, only a few day labourers [2] or young people may end up on the street, cast off as marginal within the larger community. As the director of a Central American organisation (PU1; see Table 9.2) explained:

'I think that when we talk about key issues, homelessness is not an issue that comes up a lot within the community of service providers in our own planning. So I think kind of from that I would assume that there isn't a large issue of homelessness. We don't hear about it from our community. I think the only part of the community where we hear about homelessness is within the day labour population but those are recent arrivals and there's a high transiency rate. But again, I think that what we see more often is those men might all chip in and pay for a 1 bedroom apartment and you'll have like ten of them [Laugh] living in them but they are not living on the street.'

A worker at T4 (see Table 9.1) explained that, for the Bangladeshi community,

> 'because of the strong, close-knit between the community members, it is difficult, you know, to identify the homeless from those who have homes because I mean living with your relative, who has got, who is already overcrowded and living in a small property, is quite normal. If the culture is different from Bangladeshi, you would have been sleeping on the street ...'

Tower Hamlets

As a migrant metropolis, London has been characterised as 'hyper-diverse' (Wills et al, 2010), with a recent wave of newcomers joining a strongly Commonwealth-infused base. As befits the UK's only truly global city, London consistently attracts a higher number of migrants than the rest of the UK – one third of the population in 2011 was foreign born, with people from 179 different countries speaking up to 300 different languages (MacInnes et al, 2011; Wills, 2012). According to 2011 UK census data, Tower Hamlets' population had grown by more than any other borough since 2001, from 196,106 to 254,000. Bangladeshi people constituted the largest single ethnic group, with 32% of the population. According to *London's Poverty Profile 2011* (MacInnes et al, 2011), Tower Hamlets ranked among the four most deprived boroughs in London for almost half of the socio-economic indicators, including homelessness, unemployment, child poverty, premature mortality and low educational attainment. This may be partly explained through the persistent poverty of London's East End, consolidated by the strong presence of both social housing and impoverished immigrant groups. The surge in immigration of the 2000s, especially from Eastern Europe, put greater strain on those that had arrived in the 1980s and 1990s (Wills et al, 2010), and further eroded the employability of the older BME groups that had flocked to London in the 1960s, 1970s and early 1980s from ex-Commonwealth countries such as Jamaica, India, Pakistan and Bangladesh. As such, Bangladeshi people have found themselves increasingly shut out of the London economy,

> '... caught in the cross-fire of the city's reinvention. On the one hand the employment generated by the new growth is not for them; it is a different class project entirely. This is

London "global city" as a capital of neoliberalisation. On the other hand, as their old jobs disappear, other workers arrive from around the planet to compete for the few economic opportunities that do remain to them. This is London "global city" as cultural mixity. The old London working class (already ethnically mixed), caught between the two world citydoms, feels itself under threat from both directions.'

And within this ever-dynamic migrant metropolis, Tower Hamlets has always had a special role to play (Dench et al, 2006: ix):

> The East End of London has always been the door to Great Britain: it was a haven for the Huguenots fleeing persecution in France and Irish escaping from famine, and has welcomed Jewish refugees from Central and Eastern Europe. And in the second half of the twentieth century their descendants have been joined in Tower Hamlets by Bangladeshi immigrants – who now represent the largest concentration of a single minority group in any locality in Britain.

The Bangladeshi symbolic centre in Tower Hamlets is the Brick Lane/Spitalfields/Banglatown wards just east of the City of London (Glynn, 2005; Dench et al., 2006; Peach, 2006) (Figure 9.2). This area is now the site of complex political contestations among state secularisation, Muslim faith-based community mobilisation, and partnership governance (Back et al, 2009), but it is also a site of substantial voluntary-sector clustering, a service hub that must transcend longstanding exclusion, poverty, insularity and self-reliance among Bangladeshi people (Amin et al, 2002). Bangladeshi overspill has advanced eastwards and northwards to the adjoining boroughs of Newham and Hackney, but Tower Hamlets remains the focal point of the community, now into its third generation.

Given its close proximity to the City, as well as containing the authoritarian redevelopments of Canary Wharf and parts of the Stratford 2012 Olympics redevelopment (Hamnett, 2003; Fainstein, 2010), it should come as no surprise that Tower Hamlets is also experiencing gentrification and 'increasingly integrated into the buoyant economy of London' (Amin et al, 2002: 83). One source of protection against gentrification has been the heavy reliance on social housing: while 24% of the Greater London housing stock was socially rented in

2010 (Heywood, 2012: 14), the proportion in Tower Hamlets was 42% (Mayor of London, 2011), and Bangladeshi people were heavily dependent on this resource. Moreover, Tower Hamlets Council has been both welfare-orientated and welcoming to immigrant groups, and funded on average 75% of the budgets of the seven immigrant-serving organisations interviewed.

Figure 9.2 Tower Hamlets boundaries and key infrastructure

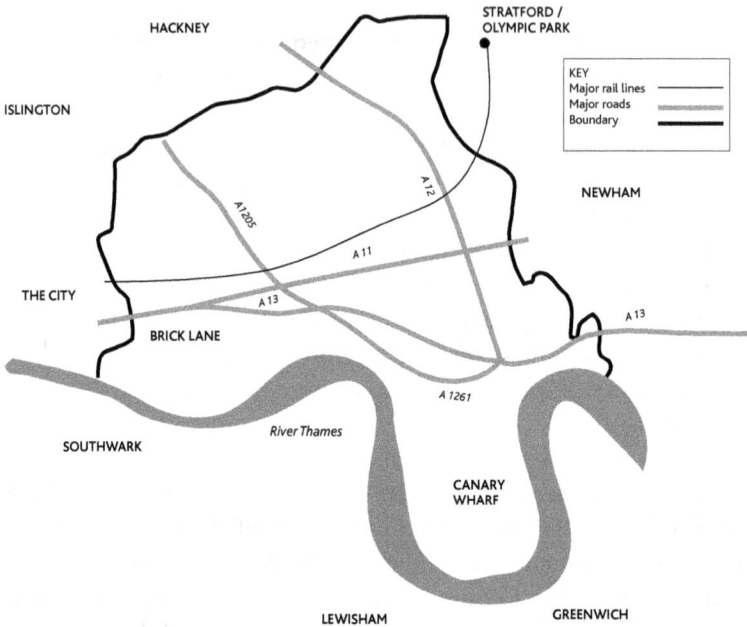

Table 9.1: Interviewed voluntary-sector organisations in Tower Hamlets

	Displaced	Displacement pressure	Entrapment	Owned/rented	Service
T1	No	Yes	Yes	Rent (1992)	Housing association
T2	No	Yes	Yes	Rent (1984)	Housing association
T3	No	No	No	Own (1983)	Community centre
T4	No	No	Yes	Own (1998)	Advocacy
T5	No	Yes	Yes	Rent (1998)	Housing association
T6	No	Yes	Yes	Rent (2000)	Women's group
T7	Yes	Yes	Yes	Rent (2000)	Youth/community group

And yet that council support was the result of years of contestation; in the beginning, there was only the grassroots, first emerging in the 1970s and continuing well in to the early 2000s, as a worker from T6 (a women's organisation, located in the vast Ocean's Estate, paralleling the Aylesbury and Heygate in Southwark) recounted:

'Where we started in the beginning was all Bangladeshi clients and then the Somali women came. When they came it was ... at the beginning it was like our women were like sisters ... hugging and you know ... outside ... but then there was this sort of resentment ... dislike of each other because they see ... they think that too much is happening for Bangladeshi women. And what the Bangladeshis say is that it didn't happen to us. I explained to them it didn't happen to the Bangladeshi community overnight. After 30 years, this community has been ... in Tower Hamlets. When we came there wasn't the mosque ... there wasn't a community centre available for us, you know! It took time. Now they have everything ready. It's for all, not just Bangladeshis like these sewing classes, you know! In the 1970s my own mother couldn't access these sewing classes! It wasn't available locally, you know! Today here in every corner there are sewing classes available.'

All the other Bangladeshi organisations recounted similarly modest beginnings, propped up by defensive residential clustering. Resilience was enabled directly and indirectly at the social scale – frequently piggybacking on existing community resources, both endogenous and exogenous, as well as fought over and earned at the scale of the enclave. This enabling of resilience was deeply implicated in my previous discussions about poverty management, care and sustenance (see Chapter Three), but also about transferring specific resources for social reproduction, especially housing – which is always a scarce resource in the global city-region – that subsequently frees up energy and funds to secure other resources. In terms of direct enabling of resilience, I could identify several mechanisms of transfer, including (1) direct services provided by the immigrant-serving voluntary sector, admittedly serving only a modest role in enabling their clientele to avoid street homelessness but crucial for overall social reproduction, and (2) the spatial concentration of said sector, which served as an important sustaining role for the community (DeVerteuil, 2011b). For the first mechanism, a housing association (T2) provided 389 units of affordable housing: its clientele was 99% Bangladeshi from Tower Hamlets. Originally set up to deal with homelessness and overcrowding in the 1980s, the organisation emerged as a key resource for those unable to put up with the very long waits for council housing – Tower Hamlets has the third-longest list of any borough, with 20,000 households in 2012. Once housed, its clients preferred to stay in Tower Hamlets because of the pronounced accessibility to services and cultural amenities. For another housing association, its mission was clearly linked to enabling the most destitute to avoid the streets (T1):

> 'the prime service we provide is a residential housing association, set up in 1979 by activists for the Bangladeshi community to relieve overcrowding and insalubrious conditions. We currently hold 650 properties (of which 645 are in Tower Hamlets), almost all new-build, this is social housing with HCA [Homes and Community Agency] funding to develop sites to subsidise rental housing. We also provide employment services. With 650 social housing properties, this gives about 3,000 clients, mostly low-income at around 70% on housing benefits. About 75% of our clientele is Bangladeshi; it used to be more, but now the Council decides who's on the waiting list, so we have some Somalis now.'

While some organisations were more secular, others were expressly linked to the faith-based sector (T4):

> 'The mosques actually serve the Bangladeshi communities like any other organization, like any other … they also … you know some of them are organised as groups and they get funding from, you know, different sources for the service they provide. They also get help and support from us, as part of the voluntary sector we're dealing with. We help them, like others, with fundraising, we help them with how to manage, in an appropriate way, the mosque they're dealing with and how to deal with their clients.'

For the 'spatial concentration' mechanism, the director at T2 stressed the importance of a central Tower Hamlets location:

> 'Advantages include clients living nearby and nearby properties; the historical legacy of Bangladeshi community

in Tower Hamlets; the social networks in place; and the fact that many people prefer to live in Tower Hamlets because of its good accessibility. However Tower Hamlets has gotten expensive and gentrified, making it hard to do new-build and giving a sense of a need to leave. The 2012 Olympics are particularly problematic, worried about a Canary Wharf repeat.'

And T7 lauded its location right on Brick Lane, the heart of the immigrant service hub (Mavrommatis, 2006; Alexander, 2011):

'... we could be anywhere, but here because this is considered to be the heartland of the Bengali community. Everybody tends to come here and, and you have access to everything anything Bengali, um it it's very well connected in terms of public transport so it's easier for, for people to come here, it's on the map, everybody knows where Brick Lane is, it just makes life easier.'

A second way in which immigrant community space enabled and reinforced resilience was by spatially concentrating everyday household reproduction and, more specifically, by enabling dense social networks and overcrowding. All seven organisations pointed to, and indirectly buttressed and enabled, the strong social networks that meant few were at risk of street homelessness, since there was always some friend or family member to take them in (DeVerteuil, 2011b). For the Bangladeshi community in London, 53% lived in overcrowded conditions according to the 2001 UK census, compared with 17% of all London households (Dench et al, 2006: 160). Overcrowding to survive and avoid homelessness – and, early on, to protect against racist attacks – had a long pedigree in Tower Hamlets. As Glynn (2005: 536) described,

Like the Jews before them, the [Bangladeshi people] crowded together, relying on their own community networks for the infrastructure of daily life and for physical protection. Like the Jews, they crowded into Spitalfields, close to the docks, the point of arrival for the ... lascars (seamen) who became the first Bengali settlers. The Brick Lane area presented them with a warren of workshops and privately owned rented old houses and tenements that had deteriorated to such a state that no one would choose to live in them.

Overcrowding was a natural response to a lack of housing and a key way to avoid absolute homelessness, but also an example of Global South strategies being imported to, and adapted for, Global North urban space. Overcrowding also worked hand in hand with strong social networks. As one Bangladeshi housing association worker (T1) reminded me,

> '... family ties are strong, and so would never put members on the street – strong stigma attached to this. Services are also important, as we use the existing social networks in the community for people to double up, so overcrowding does occur, in both public and private housing. This service taps the social networks, but does not necessarily provide the housing – we contact local housing, social housing.'

To the director of T7, social networks were essential in maintaining housing:

> 'Most people who are here, who came here initially came here through kinship, so the first ones who came here in turn brought their relatives or people from, from the same village or same area [for example, Sylhet]. So even today you'll find most people are from one specific district of Bangladesh, um from rural background and, and from certain areas of that district as well, so there's a very strong network amongst people in the community from those areas, and they all know each other because they've all come from the same area and from the same background.'

More than half of the organisations noted that the barriers to using more mainstream services were slowly weakening for the newer generation, although conversely they also tended to work in the immigrant-serving voluntary sector. Finally, the issue of spatial resilience, entrapment and displacement pressure in the face of creeping gentrification was noted by all the organisations, although only one had actually suffered from spatial displacement itself (Table 9.1). State-induced displacement is nothing new in Tower Hamlets: Watt (2013: 103) argued that, 'East London has been one of the main laboratories for post-war UK urban policy ... from slum clearance, to property-led regeneration in London Docklands, community participation and, more recently, the redevelopment of council estates involving either their partial or full demolition.' While gentrification clearly came from large-scale new-builds, such as Stratford City and Canary Wharf, as well as redevelopment of certain so-called problematic council estates (for example, Ocean's Estate on Mile End Road), there was also a sense of being a victim of one's own success. This was in terms of promotion of commodified ethnic spaces such as Banglatown along Brick Lane, which pulled in tourists and packaged diversity in a way acceptable to gentrifiers seeking edgier and more exotic locales (Phillips et al, 2007; Alexander, 2011), attracting white gentrifiers to formerly minority space. In the words of the Director of T7, there had been a rebranding of the area, but especially Brick Lane itself:

> 'The Council has, I think it was in the 90s, rebranded this area as Bangla-Town and the whole idea was to bring in tourism, visitors and they put in a number a number of initiatives, like the, we have the Brick Lane festival which brings in large number of visitors to the area.'

While the Central American population in Pico-Union was largely ignored (or worse) by the state, the Bangladeshi population in London was far more prominent. This commodification of ethnicity had even led to pressure upon organisations who were on Brick Lane (T7):

> 'You're right, I mean this whole place has been regenerated, and the whole place has been you know done up, refurbished. This is now become a place for visitors, for tourists to come to. The top half of Brick Lane has become very trendy in terms of it really becoming an artist's quarter. You have very trendy bars and, and pubs so you have a lot of young artists who tend to congregate at the top of end of Brick Lane. And then this part of Brick Lane is easily … you get the city professionals who tend to come in here for lunch or the restaurants. And then Tower Hamlets has also put the prices up of, of properties here, you know the rent rate has gone up. As you say the last 10, 20 years it's really rocketed.'

The director of T5 echoed these sentiments: 70% of its properties were within two miles of the head office in Tower Hamlets, but it had become virtually impossible to find new properties, caught between looming gentrification and the poorest and most overcrowded borough in London. For another organisation (T1), Tower Hamlets had become too expensive, and so it focused its efforts on securing the more affordable (and social) housing for its clients in Hackney, many of whom are overspill from the original hub neighbourhoods.

Although the Bangladeshi service hub was located primarily in Tower Hamlets, it was not entirely located therein, which afforded some spatial resilience in reserve – theoretically every London borough could support a Bangladeshi association or community centre provided by the voluntary sector, and many do, including Camden, Croydon and Hackney (DeVerteuil, 2011b). For instance, T3, an important community centre, was located near Notting Hill in Kensington and Chelsea, the legacy of an early purchase in 1983 with assistance from the Bangladeshi government. Of course, none of these far-flung associations could possibly replicate the density of services in Tower Hamlets, nor could they replace the sentimental value of this community space for Bangladeshi people London-wide.

Pico-Union

Los Angeles has, since the 1960s, become one of the world's premier migrant global city-regions, not in terms of super- and hyper-diversity (such as London and Sydney; see Forrest & Dunn, 2007; Hugo, 2008; Wills et al, 2010) or even in terms of proportion (such as Miami and Toronto; see Nijman, 2007; Lo, 2008) but rather in terms of the sheer quantity and extensive spatial coverage (Benton-Short et al, 2005; Soja, 2010; Vicino et al, 2011). Los Angeles boasts some of the largest diasporic communities outside of the respective nations, including Armenian, Korean, Persian and Thai people, alongside Mexican, Guatemalan and Salvadoran people. With regards to Latino immigration, Davis (2001) deemed their settlement pattern a 'city within a city' to the east and south of the Downtown CBD, with more than 2 million people almost entirely from Mexico, an immigrant space without equivalent in the rest of the US. With less than 3% of the national population, 11% of all Latino people in the US in 2010 lived in Los Angeles County (US Census Bureau, 2010). Further east, the San Gabriel Valley now constitutes the most important node of Asian immigrant population in the US. To the west of the CBD, however, is a more mixed zone of relatively recent immigration (Smith, 2001). This area, variously known as Westlake, MacArthur Park and Pico-Union (see Figure 9.5) is the symbolic and demographic centre for Central Americans (comprising 25% of all Central Americans in Los

Angeles County in 2000). Nationally, 22% of all Salvadoran and 21% of all Guatemalan people lived in Los Angeles County in 2010 (US Census Bureau, 2010). Zilberg (2002: 32) marked Pico-Union (Figures 9.3, 9.4) as fundamental to the Central American experience in both Los Angeles specifically and the US more generally:

> In the 1980s, Pico-Union served as a major entry point for Salvadorans and other Central Americans fleeing their war-torn countries. Today, it is Salvadoran Los Angeles' symbolic, if not demographic, center. I say symbolic, because while Pico-Union is predominantly Mexican and Mexican-American, it is also home to nearly every Central American community organisation, has served as the central stage for their political protests and cultural production, and is saturated with the signs of that diaspora. *Pupuserias*, street vendors selling green mango with lime and chili, *botanicas'* windows filled with plaster of Paris figurines of saints popular to Central Americans and courier and travel services to Central America dominate the landscape.

The very proximity of immigrants, however, enabled a certain level of self-sustaining survival through shared background and circumstances, a sort of 'reactive ethnicity' deployed to combat discrimination and

Figure 9.3 Mural in Pico-Union, September 2007

Photograph taken by G DeVerteuil

Figure 9.4 Grocery store on Seventh Street in Pico-Union, June 1998

Photograph taken by G DeVerteuil

Figure 9.5 Pico-Union boundaries and key infrastructure

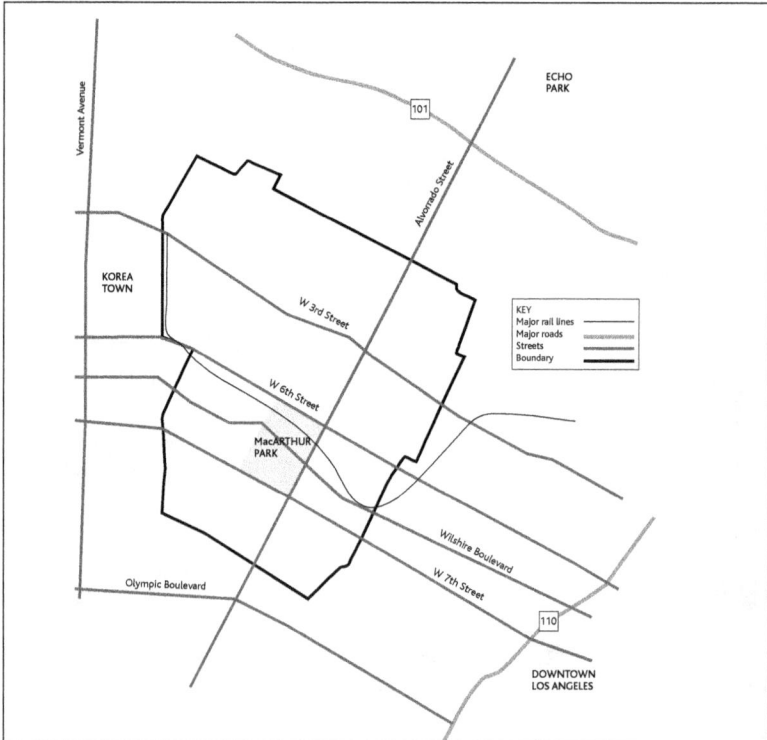

state abandonment (Popkin, 1999). And this survival, if not resilience, was enabled by a gregarious density so rare in American cities. As Zilberg (2002: 44) noted, 'the barrio is one of the few spaces in LA's contemporary built environment where pedestrianism exists outside the postmodern theme parks and shopping malls of Universal City Walk or 3rd Street Promenade in Santa Monica'. It has also become central to the Central American community and voluntary-sector organisations (PU2):

> '...this is an iconic district in the city of Los Angeles. Why? Because even though you are right, Mesoamericans and Central Americans have gone to cheaper places where they can rent cheaper ... and they can buy cheaper properties and bigger properties in, you know, run down areas of the city. And, they are changing rapidly because of the economic activity. So why do the people come here even if they cram into a very small apartment? It's because they find jobs here that do not demand from them that they speak in English. And so this is like their first step into the American experience as immigrants ... newly arriving immigrants.'

The nine voluntary organisations interviewed (Table 9.2) were primarily serving the Central American community, providing services such as legal counselling, affordable housing, transnational political projects, case management, immigrant rights, medical services and the like.

Table 9.2: Interviewed voluntary-sector organisations in Pico-Union (zip code 90057)

	Displaced	Displacement pressure	Entrapment	Owned/rented	Service
PU1	No	Yes	Yes	Own (2000)	Community centre
PU2	Yes	No	Yes	Rent (1983)	Legal
PU3	No	No	Yes	Own (1989)	Families/women
PU4	No	No	Yes	Own (1983)	Medical
PU5	No	Yes	Yes	Rent (2003)	Employment
PU6	No	No	No	Own (1993)	Food
PU7	No	No	Yes	Own (2001)	Shelter
PU8	No	No	Yes	Own (1995)	Education
PU9	No	No	Yes	Own (1999)	Community centre

All organisations had cultural competence with their respective community, although some now promoted themselves more as 'pan-Latino' rather than purely Central American. Unlike in Tower Hamlets, state funding was harder to come by: only 34% of total funding came from the state, compared to more than 75% for Bangladeshi organisations (DeVerteuil, 2011c: 1140). In turn, the Bangladeshi immigrant-serving voluntary sector was smaller and more specialised, covering less in terms of enabling resilience among its clients. The Central American immigrant-serving voluntary sector needed to enable more resilience in the absence of state support by serving more clientele, having larger budgets and becoming more pan-ethnic in nature (DeVerteuil, 2011c). The American federal government had never accepted Central American people as legitimate refugees (Landolt, 2008), with many still lacking the basic resources of citizenship and little access to the welfare state. Social housing in Los Angeles is a scarce resource, comprising less than 1% of the housing stock (DeVerteuil, 2006). Finally, the nature of the inner-city space itself was different. While Tower Hamlets boasted a richly layered, longstanding legacy of welfare provision, immigrant-oriented welfarism, and extensive local authority social housing in East End London (Amin et al, 2002), Pico-Union was forced to be more grassroots and radically DIY, according to this medical service provider (PU4):

> 'a totally different ballgame back then, you know. We, I think, this operation and other operations in the area were sponsored by the Solidarity Movement, political movement within the religious organizations and the history says that the first grant, received by this _____ was from this group of churches, that was the first one. It was until this organization was founded in 1983, and I believe it was until 1988 that, you know, the year that I arrived at _____, that the administration decided to look for government grants; it was only back then.'

This grassroots beginnings very much reflected the desperate circumstances of the incoming migrants, but also the desire to push for transformative politics through immigrant and citizenship rights:

> 'There was a war going on in Central America, El Salvador where I am from, Guatemala was affected, Honduras to some degree and Nicaragua, but the majority of the people came from El Salvador to Los Angeles and many

of us came to this country without knowing the system here and without knowing how to tap into resources in the community. So some political missionaries, some community activists with some vision decided to, you know, get together with some professionals in the community and they founded this and other projects in the area.'

Once established, other services (for example, PU9) moved to the Pico-Union service hub in 1999 from East Los Angeles, to a building that had a long history for the Central American community:

'The building used to belong to the United Methodist Church and during the 1980s it was a sanctuary for various Central Americans fleeing conflict in their own countries and they used to be like dormitories. There was like two restrooms and two showers and then there were ... about eight families were living here.'

Given that many of the migrants themselves were undocumented, there was a deep-seated reluctance to seek government funding (PU8):

'And that's what happened with us with the Central American organisations. We didn't know the government had the money for non-profits, we didn't know the city had money for non-profits! We learned in the process but we said we need this so we have to do it!'

In terms of directly enabling resilience, I identified several mechanisms of transfer that broadly followed those in Tower Hamlets. These included (1) direct services provided by the immigrant-serving voluntary sector, and (2) the spatial concentrating of the immigrant-serving voluntary sector (DeVerteuil, 2011b). There was a limited legacy of immigrant settlement and service hub provision in Pico-Union, which resembled many American inner-city areas forsaken by white people in the 1970s and 1980s, and organisationally abandoned (DeVerteuil, 2011b), lacking the longstanding tradition of innovative and generous welfare provision, immigrant welfarism and extensive local authority social housing like Tower Hamlets (Amin et al, 2002). Nonetheless, Pico-Union acts as a transformative space for right to citizenship, with MacArthur Park as the stage for protests for living wages and against police brutality, while also continuing to be an essential location for immigrant-serving voluntary-sector organisations:

'Well as a Central American organisation it made sense to go
to Pico Union because when we were founded, Pico Union
had the highest density of Central Americans outside of
Central America so ... in and near our community.' (PU1)

This was counterposed by a continued desire to take advantage of a
spatially concentrated (and loyal) clientele (PU4):

'This is an immigrant neighborhood and consistently acts
as one. People come here and get their feet on the ground
and often times end up moving as life gets better ... but
they still come back to the community for various events
and socializing and I think even just to come to the clinic
because that's where their medical help is.'

Most of the organisations that I interviewed provided important
interventions into client survival and ultimately resilience. As a
community organiser (PU1) explained:

'We're not emergency intervention, we don't do that so I
think it's hard for us to speak to it because we, for example,
partner with an organization called Inquilinos Unidos ...
tenants united is what the translation would be ... and
basically we do workshops on 'Know your Rights as a
Tenant', we would support our community in organizing
against a landlord that was maybe wrongfully evicting them.'

These interventions were, however, particularly consequential for the
social resilience of new arrivals (PU2):

'I think the role of community services or organisations
is a supporting role in helping you with that transition ...
arriving here in a new culture and new economy, a new set
of rules. These organisations help you transition in providing
critical information, advice sometimes ... support, access
to services that you otherwise would not have access to. So
it is a critical helping hand for new arrivals. That's where
I define the role of these. And in terms of civil rights and
political rights, it's also an empowering role because we
provide guidance, we provide organisational methodology
and we provide critical information so people know what
their rights are and how to defend them.'

Some organisations provided more tangible resources, such as this community organisation for women and families (PU3):

> 'We provide 600 units of affordable housing, and 8,000 families enrolled in our programmes. I oversee the Family Development Network. And what that is that we provide services to the families who live in this area, who are low income and the services are case management, information and referral, we also provide workshops in parenting skills, financial literacy, nutrition and physical education. We also refer families to immigration referrals, government benefits such as applying for welfare and applying for food stamps; we have a subcontractor who prides medical and dental services free of charge, computer literacy classes and ESL classes, after school programs and child care services.'

An organisation that provided emergency housing (PU7) was particularly focused on hard-to-serve and isolated individuals:

> 'The shelter provides emergency overnight services for any youths who come in, but like you said, we'll provide services to any youth but we particularly receive unaccompanied immigrant minors and refugee minors. We do long-term transitional care, which includes social services; we do tutoring, educational services, medical assistance with any kind of social program we can apply for them. I guess, almost anything across the board because we're specifically a social service organisation and it kind of applies to any way that we can help them transition into independent living.'

Beyond these direct services, the voluntary-sector organisations also enabled – by freeing up resources such as housing, food, shelter and medical care – the sustaining of well-honed survival skills via social networks and overcrowding. This indirect support was captured by the medical clinic (PU4):

> 'I think, you know, although we provide medical services, another organisation provides social and legal services, there is a political element too and so, I think the main objective of projects like this is to empower people and to provide services, but to make them more politically and socially aware of the resources that this country offers.'

Of course, this assistance was conditional on the clientele remaining in Pico-Union, or at least willing to travel there every so often – otherwise this produced and enabled resilience was likely to be lost in the more mainstream spaces of Los Angeles County and beyond. For Central Americans, social networks and overcrowding were, as in the case of the Bangladeshi people, deployed to ensure resilience and avoid homelessness. As I argued previously (DeVerteuil, 2011b), the astonishing concentration of immigrant-serving voluntary organisations in Pico-Union was itself important in enabling and transferring resilience to clients. A community organisation (PU9) made it clear that the density of services and clients was absolutely crucial in their locational decision making:

> 'I think the reason why we picked this area is because it's really well known. A lot of immigrants from Central America arrive in this area, mostly because downtown is close and there are more opportunities for jobs. And the transportation issue, it's more convenient for them...and before, their rent was cheaper! Now it's more expensive than other areas ... that's one of the reasons...and we know there are a lot of Central American in this area.'

All the organisations were supportive of social networks and overcrowding as ways to avoid absolute homelessness. The director of PU2 told me that,

> '... it's a balance between pride and space needed to survive ... from my own experience when I was a refugee here in Los Angeles back in 1980, we sucked up that pride stuff and even if it's in very crowded conditions we team up resources and we live under one roof and we manage to live and survive there until things get better, you know.'

He was not alone; all those I interviewed expressed willingness to or had actual previous experience in taking in needy family members or friends. Throughout, community space enabled these well-honed survival skills and ability to secure housing for all, although as we shall see in more detail in Chapter Ten, the Bangladeshi community did this from a more cushioned, state-supported position (DeVerteuil, 2011b).

The most vulnerable group in the Central American population – and the one least likely to access these immigrant-serving organisations – was the day labourers. For them, given the lack of family attachments and services, they resorted to extreme overcrowding, as the Director of PU5 explained in 2009:

> 'Yes, officially due to what's going on with the whole economic crisis right now, a lot of them had been going, staying, well starting to be homeless now. They just can't find work anywhere, so a lot of them are going to be homeless, going to shelters. So what they try to do to avoid that is that they try to group with each other in apartments.'

Gentrification-induced displacement seemed a distant threat to most of the facilities in Pico-Union, given that the very large and visible presence of working-poor immigrant people had effectively created a strong barrier to gentrification, not unlike the *banlieues* of Paris (which admittedly had the additional barrier of a degraded built environment). And, like the *banlieues*, there had been widespread damage during urban unrest, especially the long shadow of the 1992 'Justice Riots' (Jencks, 1993) and the privatised 'Rebuild Los Angeles' that had cast the area in a negative and uncertain light: 'RLA's spatial-cultural discourse constructed Pico-Union as a particular kind of object of knowledge: a neglected area, a zone of need, and the ignored poor, isolated inner city' (Zilberg, 2002: 37; see also Davis, 1998). As such, the strongly immigrant nature of Pico-Union, its long-time reputation for crime (and police corruption), alongside a lack of new-build redevelopment, has formed a barrier to all but the most pioneer forms of gentrification. And yet there were some inklings of pressure in the late 2000s and early 2010s, mostly through the overspill of a gentrifying Downtown to the east, and a revitalising Koreatown to the west, with gentrification as much Korean as white. As the Director of a longstanding community centre (PU1) put it in 2009,

> 'These days those demographics are changing. The cost of living in this area is skyrocketing ... housing specifically is the issue ... and so we are seeing a decline in the number of recent arrival Central Americans in the area. So, I would say in the next 5 to 10 years we are going to have to re-evaluate whether or not this is the best place to be.'

Gentrification was limited to modest redevelopments along the western edge of Downtown (especially outwards from the Staples Center) and the eastern edge of Koreatown at Vermont and Wilshire. But all Central American facilities noted the increasingly expensive rents in the area, long known for its cheapness, and that day labourers were under more pressure to reduce their visibility. As the Day Labor Site (PU5) mentioned:

'If day laborers are now harassed by the police, it is not about immigrant status [which led to our designated site]. It is about being too visible and competing with each other … We currently stay in this City-owned site rent-free, but could be asked to leave at any point! I think the only disadvantage is … it hasn't presented itself but we predict that soon … our community will start to not be so close.'

As of 2014, Pico-Union was a long way from its 1992 nadir, when the east–west commercial streets of 3rd, 6th, Wilshire, 8th, Olympic, Pico and Venice, and the north–south arteries of Alvarado and Vermont were systematically ransacked. Rather, it is a inner-city neighbourhood on a slow trajectory upwards (Figure 9.6):

'We're about walking distance from the Staples Center. Definitely gotten more expensive, with a lot of the while, kind of like the Figueroa Corridor; it's been revitalised, although some might say on the backs of the community that's here, but definitely it is getting more expensive …

Figure 9.6 New-build Downtown tower and Pico-Union street scene, March 2009

Photograph taken by G DeVerteuil

fortunately, we own the building so we don't have to leave this place.' (PU10)

Overall, the two immigrant enclaves were similar (for example, grassroots beginnings, enabling resilience to social networks, and overcrowding) and dissimilar (for example, levels of government support, levels of gentrification, and displacement pressure). Their geographical stability ensured a measure of social resilience. In Chapter Ten, these comparisons will be focused on the exogenous sources of enabling resilience – and to a lesser extent spatial resilience – and particularly how radically differing levels of state support have led some to argue that the spatially resilient presence of Bangladeshi people in Tower Hamlets is a state creation, underpinned by abundant social housing and long-term unemployment benefits (Glynn, 2005; Dench et al, 2006), while Pico-Union remains bare bones and DIY.

Notes

[1] People of Central American origin or identity (Guatemala, El Salvador, Honduras, Nicaragua, Costa Rica and Panama), although for the purposes of this study, the focus is on Guatemalan and Salvadoran people. People of Bangladeshi origin and/ or identity, the vast majority of which are Muslims. The terms 'Bengali' is not used since it can also refer to people of West Bengal in India.

[2] Day labourers are usually unattached men who seek daily, piecemeal work outside of hardware stores and construction sites, and found primarily in immigrant areas of American cities.

TEN

Comparative analysis and summary

In Chapter Five, I began the comparative analysis by placing inner-city London, Los Angeles and Sydney side by side. In this chapter, I analyse similarities and differences in voluntary-sector resilience (spatial and social) *across* the 100 organisations embedded within four place-types and three global city-regions, using the three hallmarks of my comparative approach in Chapter Four, while suggesting lines of research for comparative resilience. As a starting point, and emerging organically from the results from Chapters Five to Nine, I propose *three prevailing strategies of spatial resilience.* These strategies built on and somewhat reworked literatures on (1) the barriers to gentrification (Shaw, 2005; Ley & Dobson, 2008; Walks & August, 2008) and, more specifically, (2) the geographies of anti-displacement, based primarily on the work of Newman and Wyly (2006: 28), who sought to explain why gentrified neighbourhoods in New York City do not always produce displacement – 'that after two generations of intense gentrification, any low and moderate-income renters who have managed to avoid displacement are likely to be those people who have found ways to adapt and survive in an increasingly competitive housing market'. I have little interest here in overt residential resistance to gentrification (for example, Sakizlioglu & Uitermark, 2014) – rather, I privilege the active outflanking and persistent outlasting of gentrification via the production of institutionalised resilience.

For the first strategy of resilience – which I deem the 'private' – Newman and Wyly (2006) identified a variety of active residential strategies, such as overcrowding, enduring high housing costs and poor housing quality, and owner-occupation that consistently inhibited displacement. For voluntary-sector organisations, these private strategies can be translated into (1) owning your own building, or (2) leasing it from a supportive landlord that is not profit seeking. These became barriers to gentrification-induced displacement as they involved removing oneself from the vagaries of the private real estate market. Leasing from supportive landlords could include larger umbrella voluntary-sector organisations, as well as faith-based organisations, whose religious infrastructure can be remarkably central and accessible.

As the coordinator of Housing Justice in London commented, "churches are not in the business of flipping real estate, they are in it for the long haul, so they act as a barrier to gentrification".

The second strategy – which I deem the 'voluntary sector' – drew strength from the efforts of community mobilisation and entrenched community solidarity, producing 'cultures of alternative values' and 'a politics of resistance' that are facilitated through concentrated place-embeddedness within a supportive inner city (Shaw, 2005; Newman & Wyly, 2006: 181; Ley & Dobson, 2008; see also Gilbert, 1998). Such strategies beneficially joined place (for example, the service hub) and territory (for example, the inner city), bearing witness to and taking advantage of 'sustained and proximate interaction over time [that] can create strong trusting relations among actors, which can then be drawn on to enable collective action' (Nicholls et al, 2013: 4). This place-based and territorially-bound solidarity counteracted and transcended the fragmentation and dog-eat-dog competition over scarce resources, funding and clients that purportedly mars the voluntary sector. The conspicuous concentration of likeminded voluntary-sector organisations and their clientele have proven invaluable (if unacknowledged) in preserving Vancouver's Downtown Eastside (Lees et al, 2008; Ley and Dobson 2008), San Francisco's Tenderloin (Hutton 2010) and Sydney's The Block (Shaw, 2007). Facilities may also be protected if they were firmly embedded within a larger, overarching and resource-rich voluntary-sector network, such as the Salvation Army or the Catholic Church (DeVerteuil, 2012). More broadly, community solidarity and place-embeddedness defended place-based fabrics of support that included service hubs, and thus limited the uncompensated losses from gentrification (Betancur, 2002). As the results have already suggested, it was not the *size* of the service hub that ensured its resilience, but more its *concentration* and the advantages that flowed from it.

For the third strategy – which I deem the 'political' – Newman and Wyly (2006) pointed to the vital role of local state interventions such as public housing and rent stabilisation schemes in guaranteeing that some poor renters in New York City stayed in place. Shaw (2005: 181) referred, in the case of Melbourne's St Kilda, to the extraction of 'substantial state support for the fledgling community housing program – an act that was instrumental in perpetuating a culture of egalitarianism'. Resilience is always political, the result of decisions and non-decisions to prop up (or not) certain latent tools of past residuals of the state. But, more specifically, local government interventions that sustained spatial resilience can include:

Direct financial support to services, land use controls and dedicated space that guarantee a persistent and legally legitimate base for services, a recognition that central locations are essential for non-profit social services in terms of maximising visibility and client accessibility (despite also rendering them potentially vulnerable to gentrification-induced displacement), and the fact that charitable organisations may pay reduced property taxes where otherwise they would have been priced out with pervasive gentrification. (DeVerteuil, 2012: 209)

Spatially resilient facilities in London, Los Angeles and Sydney used varying combinations of these private strategies (especially property ownership), voluntary-sector embeddedness (the strength of community mobilisation and entrenched community solidarity facilitated through concentrated emplacement) and public-sector support (reliance on direct and consistent statutory funding from local government and subsidised leases to rent space in publicly owned buildings).

While the chapter's focus is on using resilience to compare voluntary-sector organisations within particular territories (inner-city place-types, and ultimately global city-regions), my research also contributes modestly to the act of comparing resilience itself (Vale & Campanella, 2005; Hall & Lamont, 2013). Lessons from comparative urbanism – such as the balancing between difference and similarity, the encompassing approach, and comparing as a strategy – will be discussed at the very end of the chapter, as a tentative contribution upon returning to the three hallmarks of my comparative approach. Before such time, I will emphasise instances of endogenous and exogenous resilience that readily mapped on to the three strategies, with endogenous resilience figuring strongly for private and community-based strategies, and exogenous resilience connected not just to local support but also to broader structures such as the welfare state and voluntary state regimes.

Armed with these conceptualisations of spatial resilience strategies, I return to my central problematic: directly comparing and interpreting the 'how' of voluntary-sector resilience in the face of gentrification-induced displacement at the scale of the voluntary organisation across the four place-types and the three global city-regions. With the process and production of resilience at the core of this subsequent comparison, the inner-city areas themselves will not be explicitly compared (but see comparisons in Chapters One, Four and Five), and so I will not add much more except to consider the role of inner-city space in the three global city-regions more generally at the end of Chapter Eleven. Also of note is the particular case of producing social resilience (Chapter Nine), itself enabled by a stable geographical base through which to provide care and sustenance for client survival. My comparison of the production of social resilience will focus largely on the immigrant enclave experience, particularly how the similar survival outcomes between the Bangladeshi and Central American communities were so differently supported by the state.

Table 10.1 identifies a universe of resilient (immobile, either voluntarily or involuntarily) organisations as they responded to exogenous threats (for example, gentrification) and supports (for example, local state) across the 10 areas and four place-types by private, voluntary sector or political strategies of resilience. As outlined in Chapter Four, my approach was an encompassing one: I sought both similarities and differences for organisational resilience across each place-type, with the overarching process being resilience as a response to the threat of gentrification-induced displacement, as part of an

Table 10.1: Resilience strategies by voluntary-sector organisation across the place-types

	Resilience: in/voluntary immobility	Resilience: private strategies	Resilience: voluntary-sector strategies	Resilience: political strategies
ESTABLISHED GENTRIFIED	16 out of 18	8 out of 16	14 out of 16	6 out of 16
Westminster	7 out of 8	3 out of 7	5 out of 7	3 out of 7
Surry Hills	9 out of 10	5 out of 9	9 out of 9	3 out of 9
MIXED	26 out of 38	11 out of 26	13 out of 26	17 out of 26
Lambeth	5 out of 8	1 out of 5	1 out of 5	3 out of 5
Southwark	8 out of 11	4 out of 8	5 out of 8	6 out of 8
Islington	5 out of 8	2 out of 5	2 out of 5	4 out of 5
Kings Cross/ Darlinghurst	8 out of 11	4 out of 8	5 out of 8	4 out of 8
PIONEER	25 out of 28	21 out of 25	22 out of 25	7 out of 25
Downtown	15 out of 17	12 out of 15	13 out of 15	5 out of 15
Hollywood	10 out of 11	9 out of 10	9 out of 10	2 out of 10
IMMIGRANT ENCLAVE	14 out of 16	9 out of 14	5 out of 14	7 out of 14
Tower Hamlets	6 out of 7	2 out of 6	3 out of 6	6 out of 6
Pico-Union	8 out of 9	7 out of 8	2 out of 8	1 out of 8
TOTALS (percentage)	81%	60%	66%	46%

incomplete neoliberal/post-welfare system, and in the global city-region inner city.

Comparing voluntary-sector resilience by place-types

Table 10.1 identifies differing profiles of voluntary-sector resilience. All organisations featured strong proportions of resilience save the 'mixed' place-type, a pattern that reflected less the agency of voluntary-sector organisations and more the variegated nature of the gentrification threat itself. The resilience strategies very much adapted to the variegated nature of the gentrification threat that differed according to place-type, and suggested that resilience was indeed relationally adaptive. Resilience was more assured in the established gentrified place-type due to the longstanding nature of gentrification, which had in turn enabled a more experienced set of voluntary-sector organisations. Conversely, gentrification was more tentative in the pioneer and immigrant enclave place-types, which also ensured a certain level of resilience. It was organisations in the mixed place-type that proved least resilient, perhaps because of the punctuated and new-build nature of the gentrification that made it difficult to respond to; and perhaps as well, the sense that incoming gentrifiers in the new-builds were less tolerant of service hubs and their clientele than more long-term gentrifiers, as seen in Kings Cross in Sydney. In effect, this patchwork style of gentrification, with its sharp contrasts, lowered tolerance and volatile nature, was found in the mixed (for example, Southwark's redevelopment of Heygate and Aylesbury estates) but also enclave (for example, Olympic-branded revitalisation in Tower Hamlets) and pioneer gentrified place-types (for example, Downtown Skid Row), frequently catching voluntary-sector organisations off guard and ill-prepared.

Now that the overall patterns of resilience have been analysed, the remainder of the comparative exercise is explicitly framed by the three strategies of resilience. Across the 81 resilient organisations, private and voluntary-sector strategies (60% and 66%, respectively) were more likely than political strategies (46%), suggesting that state support was less forthcoming and, as we shall see, heavily concentrated in London rather than Los Angeles or Sydney. This is the first of several crosscutting themes that will animate the analysis; the others will include the crucial role of local social policy and the voluntary sector in managing the common challenge of social and spatial polarisation in the global city-region, and the unavoidably politicised nature of resilience.

For the *established gentrified* areas, 50% of organisations used private strategies, 88% used voluntary-sector strategies and 38% used political strategies. There were no major differences in resilience strategies between Westminster and Surry Hills. The overriding themes of saturation, entrapment and the dispersion of clientele all helped to frame these resilience rates. The high prevalence of voluntary-sector strategies related to the well-established and entrapped nature of the service hubs that required constant vigilance and active resilience, not just against displacement but also against the ill-effects of saturation. While on average the organisations had not been in their current locations any longer than for other place-types, their average age was greater than any other place-types save Downtown Los Angeles, which lent a certain maturity paralleling the maturity of the gentrification process itself, as if in lockstep but lagging as well. The relatively modest rates of political strategies suggested at best grudging support for the service hubs; in particular, Westminster Council was eager to avoid saturation effects from both organisations and clientele, and tailored most of its social policies around this goal. Finally, the relatively modest rates of private strategies suggested the difficulties in buying properties in highly gentrified areas, making renting the only alternative. Since the days to buy are now long gone, the best option was to remain (stuck) in place.

For the *mixed* areas, 42% of organisations used private strategies, 50% used voluntary-sector strategies and 65% used political support. The London organisations enjoyed more explicit state support for their spatial resilience, while Sydney organisations were more likely to use private and voluntary-sector strategies when compared to the London average. The service hubs in these areas were not as well established as for the entrenched gentrified place-type, such that fewer voluntary-sector strategies were used. Moreover, the patchy and new-build nature of gentrification perhaps prevented large-scale service hub solidarity and awareness, but also sometimes downgraded the threat of gentrification-induced displacement (less so in Islington and Lambeth). The Sydney case study of Darlinghurst/Kings Cross did reveal some pioneer tendencies – that is, new gentrifiers with lower tolerance that compelled organisations to actively use private and voluntary-sector strategies more than those in London. This will resonate in the ensuring pioneer place-type, where gentrifiers had little experience in dealing with well-established, clustered and self-aware (and self-organising) service hubs in Los Angeles.

For the *pioneer* areas, 80% of organisations used private strategies, 88% used voluntary-sector strategies and a paltry 28% used political strategies. Since both pioneer areas were in Los Angeles, it was easy to discern the more privatised and voluntary-sector nature of the resilience strategies. In particular, the high levels of ownership reflected the need for caution and protection. Skid Row and Hollywood were protective service hubs, their sheer density and common purpose ensuring a certain level of solidarity – although the Hollywood service hub enjoyed explicit political support that Downtown lacked. This did not mean, however, that all organisations agreed on everything – we have already seen the gap emerging between services pushing for coercive care on Skid Row to swell their own client numbers against those railing against the street sweeps and other displacement pressures on clients (Stuart, 2014). This protective tendency also blunted the punitive tendencies found in the expressly displacing logics of Downtown gentrification and, to a lesser extent, Hollywood gentrification. Indeed, gentrification is not always accompanied by revanchism (see Clerval, 2013, in the case of Paris) or even displacement. Even with managed displacement and an increasingly intolerant gentrification, both Downtown and Hollywood still represented havens of acceptance. To incoming pioneer gentrifiers, a place like Skid Row would be a true test of tolerance, and it has proven resilient partly because the 'no Skid Row' scenario is too detrimental to easily envision, and partly that Downtown gentrification remains somewhat novel and thus muted. This connects to the grudging public support for Skid Row through a CRA that offered both the punitive and supportive in offsetting measures, demonstrating the crucial difference that social policy made.

Finally, for the *immigrant enclave*, 64% used private strategies, 36% used voluntary-sector strategies and 50% used political strategies. Here, the similarities and differences between the case studies were perhaps the most stark and most worthy of greater consideration, with similar enabling of resilience stemming from very different levels of exogenous support. Both the Bangladeshi and Central American immigrant-serving organisations experienced similar grassroots beginnings as a way to address unmet community needs and an unresponsive welfare state. Inner-city community space worked in similar fashion, with clustering key to social networks, overcrowding and the voluntary sector itself, producing similarly low levels of street homelessness. This legitimised the perspective that the inner city continues to act as an enclave space in terms of self-segregation, the pooling of social capital and social innovation, and resilience, counteracting perspectives that dwell only on social disorganisation, crime and ghettoisation (see Phillips et al, 2007; Wacquant, 2008; DeVerteuil, 2011b). But the organisational comparison diverged regarding the crucial nature of exogenously supported resilience, which also hinted at some cross-city and cross-national differences to be explored later in this chapter. Table 10.1

showed 100% political support (seven out of seven) for the resilient Bangladeshi organisations, but only 12.5% for Central American ones (one out of nine). Tower Hamlets Council was especially generous when compared to the stingy (and now declining, given the post-2008 budget crisis in California) outlays of the City and County of Los Angeles. So although most Central American services received some state support, the proportion of the total funding was much lower and more recent in nature (DeVerteuil, 2011c). By contrast, the Bangladeshi community had embedded itself into a much stronger local welfare state in Tower Hamlets (as well as the national UK welfare state), especially social housing, in turn helping to explain their strong segregation pattern and clustering around the original point of entry (Peach, 1996; Hamnett, 2003; Glynn, 2005). From very modest beginnings with squatting quite common, by 2001, 62% of Bangladeshi people in Tower Hamlets (and 59% of the London Bangladeshi population) lived in local authority housing, compared to 17% for the population of Greater London as a whole, the result of the Bangladeshi community making the best of a challenging housing situation (Amin et al, 2002; Glynn, 2005; Dench et al., 2006). Overall, in 2009, 73% of London's Bangladeshi community were dependent on benefits (Mayhew & Harper, 2010).

In effect, Bangladeshi people were among the last immigrant communities to take full advantage of the (Keynesian) UK welfare state before it began to tighten in the 1980s with broad cutbacks, the 'Right to Buy' legislation that allowed tenants to buy their council flats, and stricter rules on residency and citizenship:

> Between the 1950s and the 1980s, immigrants from the Caribbean, India, Bangladesh and Pakistan arrived with strong traditions of collective organization that were coincident with a growing new Left in Britain. Over time, different organizations were able to forge alliances with each other, securing space for anti-racist politics and practice in the wider body politic. For a period in the 1970s and 1980s, shared political identifications of 'black' and 'anti-racist' united a wide range of individuals, organizations and communities in a struggle for justice. In the wake of this political organization, the UK largely came to accept itself as a multicultural polity, albeit one in which socio-economic disadvantage continues to shape the lives of most minority ethnic Britons today. (Wills et al, 2010: 163–4)

Comparing voluntary-sector resilience by global city-region

Recapping Tables 5.3 and 10.1, there were some key similarities and differences across London, Los Angeles and Sydney in terms of voluntary-sector resilience. Different rates of resilience were found, with London's rate of 74% coming in somewhat lower than Los Angeles's at 89% and Sydney's at 81%. The main explanation for this difference was that rates of resilience for two boroughs in particular (Islington and Lambeth) were lower than for the other three (case study) boroughs, which brought the overall rate down. Counter-intuitively, the results suggested that London organisations were more likely to depend upon political support to prop up their resilience (see below), but that London organisations *without* public support were more vulnerable (and spatially non-resilient) than those in Los Angeles and Sydney because they were less likely to deploy alternative private or voluntary-sector strategies. Summaries from Table 10.1 broadly supported this contention. Private strategies were used at a rate of 39% for London organisations, 85% for Los Angeles organisations and 47% for Sydney ones; for voluntary-sector strategies it was 57%, 73% and 82%, respectively, and political strategies were at 78%, 24% and 41%. What is striking is the lack of consistency across the strategies and the global city-regions. London and Sydney both had similar proportions using private strategies; Los Angeles and Sydney were similar in terms of voluntary-sector strategies; and London was a clear outlier in terms of political strategies, while Los Angeles acted as one in terms of private strategies. Let us now consider these organisational differences by strategy and global city-region in more depth.

The use of *private strategies* was mixed, with Los Angeles organisations most likely to employ them. This was certainly not by design, but more likely the result of an American ownership culture and the larger size and greater fiscal capacity of Los Angeles organisations, although this too was uneven, with the smaller 'storefront' services particularly vulnerable to displacement pressures (alongside those services not attached to well-funded causes or populations, such as the LGBT community). The greater reliance on ownership in Los Angeles was also more out of desperation, given the scant governmental supports and greater displacement pressure overall, exacerbated by a more (racially) stigmatised clientele, especially in Downtown (DeVerteuil 2012). In London and Sydney, private strategies were more likely to involve cheap leases. These advantageous private arrangements enabled the voluntary sector to stay put, but at the cost of entrapment.

While gentrification had only gently reorientated centrality towards Downtown and Hollywood, it had further consolidated centrality in inner London and Sydney, and as such the ability to purchase properties had come and gone in these latter two global city-regions. Overall, the active and sometimes aggressive buying of property, particularly in Los Angeles, suggested that the voluntary sector could behave more like a corporation, moving it away from the state and the informal community and nudging it towards a more explicitly market orientation. This is akin to the 'empire building' that characterises many other non-state actors in the US – universities, foundations and faith-based entities.

Sydney organisations were most likely to use *voluntary-sector strategies*, followed closely by Los Angeles. While the overall profile of organisations that used voluntary-sector strategies was quite heterogeneous, especially with regard to funding and ownership status, spatially they tended to operate within very constrained service hubs or clusters, benefiting from the strength of numbers even when clientele were dispersing outwards, with examples offered by both Surry Hills and Darlinghurst/Kings Cross. Protectiveness in the face of gentrification was also out of a certain precaution: Los Angeles was crucially short of walkable, transit-orientated, dense and accessible neighbourhoods – neighbourhoods that surplus populations seek to access (Glaeser et al, 2000) but that are now being menaced by pioneer gentrification. Indeed, for the second half of the twentieth century, places like Downtown, Hollywood and Pico-Union were easily accessible to the poor, but this accessibility may in the near future become compromised if it is not stoutly defended. When compared to poor people in Sydney – who have increasingly been banished to far-flung western suburbs, either priced-out or pushed out as public housing estates are scattered – poor people in Los Angeles have always had more accessibility to a weak yet still active centrality, and the inner city of Los Angeles has always maintained a certain diversity of income and race. Inner London represented a middle ground, where the poor have always rubbed shoulders with the rich through the stalwart presence of social housing, but where a variety of private and policy pressures are currently conspiring to overturn this longstanding mix (see Chapter Twelve). While a North American construct (see Milligan, 1996, on the applicability of the service-dependent ghetto to Scotland), the reality of the highly clustered service hub is more applicable to places like Sydney, with its newer built environment and more segregated land uses, than in the more spatially heterogeneous and organic European cities like London. And so, community solidarity around the service hub was least evident in London, due to its unplanned and relatively unclustered (or expressly de-clustered, in the case of Westminster) nature, but also due to the greater and more consistent political support, especially in boroughs like Tower Hamlets. Even Westminster's grudging support, with echoes of the CRA in Downtown and Hollywood, outstripped what was offered in Los Angeles or even Sydney.

As a final point, voluntary-sector strategies of resilience intersected with notions of abeyance, care and sustenance in interesting and surprising ways. In Los Angeles, voluntary-sector organisations were more likely to be forced into abeyance by the local state, in the interest of redevelopment/gentrification; in Sydney and London there was less pressure to do so, although more so with the London soup runs. More generally, the advent of gentrification was accompanied by a crosscutting pressure to obscure highly visible and stigmatised clientele. Virtually all 81 resilient organisations – and the remaining 19 as well – displayed co-existence between abeyance and care/sustenance imperatives; while not everything the voluntary sector did was supportive, much of the abeyance was offset by the provision of everyday sustenance as a way to entice clients into voluntary-sector spaces of care. Sometimes this care was coerced for the sake of abeyance – that is, removing the abrasive presence of surplus populations from the sight of gentrifiers and city officials, ostensibly for their 'own good'.

For *political strategies*, there was a higher degree of local council intervention, ownership and rent subsidisation in London (and to a lesser extent Sydney) when compared to Los Angeles, not to mention greater governmental funding of day-to-day operations that further ensured locational stability and resilience to gentrification-induced displacement (Watt, 2009). The far greater local council intervention, ownership and rent subsidisation in London differed somewhat by borough: Islington was generally the most supportive, while Southwark, with its redevelopment ambitions for a 'second City', was probably the least, with Westminster not far behind (DeVerteuil, 2012). Resilience in the immigrant enclaves was more state supported in Tower Hamlets than in Pico-Union, with Bangladeshi people enjoying far more housing and welfare support from the state, a legacy of strong Keynesian residuals. Indeed, the level of state involvement could not have been more different: the more explicitly multicultural (Koopmans, 2010), accommodating and (residually) generous UK welfare state diverged sharply with the threadbare US welfare state and its inherently disadvantaging treatment of immigrant groups. Conversely, support for the voluntary sector in Los Angeles reflected a more laissez-faire,

Sunbelt model of government intervention, meaning that gentrification in Los Angeles was potentially more destabilising, especially taking into account the uneven revanchist tendencies in places like Downtown. Although difficult to measure, the role of 'race' was potentially profound, given the assumption that service-dependent populations in the US were frequently (and sometimes wrongly) assumed to be racial minorities and that their reliance on the voluntary sector may be a further source of NIMBY and displacement (Takahashi, 1998; Betancur, 2002; Slater, 2004). Sydney occupied more a middle ground, sometimes supportive like London but also sometimes more prone to lackadaisical support as found in Los Angeles. Contradictory and ambivalent social policy crosscut all three global-city regions. In Los Angeles, but also in London and Sydney, there was a tension between implicitly not wanting to eliminate the service hub given its usefulness (care, sustenance but also abeyance), and explicitly not wanting it to become too visible, too conspicuous so as to scare off gentrification entirely – leading to a politically compromised muddle. So, even in supposedly revanchist Los Angeles, there was no serious talk about dismantling Skid Row – and no real talk of dismantling any other service hub either.

Local governance structures also helped to explain differences and similarities on whether to employ political strategies of resilience. The more uneven and autonomous, yet increasingly skeletal, US local welfare settlement contrasted sharply with the more supported and centralised (yet relatively inflexible) Australian and UK systems. While the City of Los Angeles was more generous to its citizens than many of the other surrounding municipalities (Law, 2001), it could not afford to be too generous lest it become a magnet; some would argue that it already has become magnetic through its many service hubs, above all Downtown. These fears reflected the fragmented and highly competitive nature of local governance in large American global city-regions. By comparison, the London boroughs enjoyed considerable support from the Greater London Authority – at least until 2013 – and reasonably good levels of subsidies to support local welfare, housing and health benefits. The support was even more solid in the 1980s when the Bangladeshi population essentially captured the local welfare state in Tower Hamlets. However, Glynn (2010) cautioned against over-romanticising this capture of the state, since it still involved a struggle marked by racism, setbacks and persistent segregation. The wealthier and more generous Inner Sydney LGAs were crucial in ensuring the denser matrix of voluntary-sector organisations when compared to the more far-flung, and increasingly needy, suburban areas to the far west.

While my comparative approach has been to embed patterns of voluntary-sector resilience to specific places (for example, service hubs) and territories (for example, inner city), my ground-level results can further offer a window into the possibilities of convergence and divergence of welfare state policies nationally and locally, of the multiscalar connections between the voluntary sector, and the local and national settlements that underpin it, as outlined in Chapter Five. In particular, the stark differences in the political strategies of resilience mapped (but sometimes not) on to larger debates about the convergence and divergence of specific national and local welfare state settlements across Australia, the UK and the US. I now use the results to shed light on the four hypothetical points made in Chapter Five about an isomorphic 'Anglo-Saxon' liberal welfare state regime: the threadbare US welfare state; the US-orientated directionality and convergence of welfare policies; the dually influenced nature of the UK welfare state; and the in-between-ness of the Australian welfare state. While confirming the anaemic US model, my results largely challenged purported convergence, confirming rather the path-dependent outcomes and a lack of Americanised post-welfarism in the London and Sydney case studies. The clearest example was the glaring differences between levels of state support for London Bangladeshi and Los Angeles Central American voluntary-sector organisations that most clearly reflected previously entrenched differences in the national welfare state settlement (DeVerteuil, 2011c). With its smaller size and greater reliance on the state, the Bangladeshi-serving voluntary sector reflected the generous legacy and reach of the larger UK welfare system as well as a favourable local settlement in Tower Hamlets. The weaker and more dependent Bangladeshi sector contrasted with a more robust and gap-filling Central American voluntary landscape, the product of a residualised American welfare state combined with the lack of legal recognition. Though the UK is less supportive than other European nations (see Koopmans, 2010), it remains more committed to a multicultural welfare state than the US, with its intense devolutionary impulses yielding a competitive race to the bottom (DeVerteuil et al, 2002), as well as more outwardly anti-immigrant resentments that were a central plank in the 1996 PRWORA (Hero & Preuhs, 2007). So, despite the more recent *rapprochement* between American and British welfare state restructuring, there remained substantial differences within the purportedly residual Anglo-Saxon welfare model, or 'folk concept'. So we must reject the equally balanced duality of the UK welfare state – it was more European for the time being, despite the rhetoric around its Americanisation (but see Chapter Twelve).

These differences were also due to the presence of strong residuals in the welfare landscape of the UK, including but not limited to social housing and entrenched tendencies towards redistribution, community solidarity, nationalised health care, and multiculturalism (Peck, 2001; Wacquant, 2008; Koopmans, 2010). Australia similarly enjoyed some of these social policies, such as nationalised health care and efforts at redistribution, but lacked any meaningful presence of social housing – witness the 2014 talk around scattering the public housing in Millers Point (Sydney CBD) and Glebe (Inner Sydney). As such, transpacific convergence was limited, as Inner Sydney did not take on some of the more unevenly punitive and obviously threadbare tendencies of the American model grounded in inner-city Los Angeles (Horvath, 2004). Australia has yet to fully Americanise its welfare state settlement, and Sydney has not followed suit either. Weller and O'Neill (2014: 123) forcefully argued that Australia's developmental trajectory has only partially emulated US-style neoliberalism, and found that Americanisation was more (electoral) rhetoric than reality, that much of Australia's experience over the past 40 years exceeded any recognisable version of variegated neoliberalism: 'our assessment is that the changes do not accord with a retrenchment of the state by roll-out neoliberalism, a hollowing out of the nation state, [or] a roll back of intervention'. Inner Sydney was quite generous, protective even, with less of the fear of becoming a welfare magnet than in Los Angeles or London, and no explicit agenda to push out services (S9).

But what about the points of convergence and divergence from Salamon and Anheier's (1998) voluntary-sector regime framework that I outlined in Chapter Five? Here I could see even more divergence than for the welfare state regimes, with the results suggesting considerable internal variation. The US version of the 'liberal model' regime, with its greater autonomy and fundraising capacities, translated into a more independent, if not fully fledged player in locational decisions, such as in Hollywood. Conversely, the UK regime was better funded, coordinated and controlled by the central government, yielding much less independence and more vulnerability to (1) those organisations that fell outside government favour – such as the LGBT community – as well as (2) those organisations overly reliant on government funding. In Chapter Twelve I will consider this issue in some depth, as this has been occurring in the UK since 2010. The Australian version of the regime seemed more aligned to the US model of proactivity and independence; certainly in Sydney, the desire to use the service hub for protection was twice as likely as it was in London. Whether by emulation or design, Sydney voluntary-sector organisations tended to be less reliant on government funding and more ready to fundraise and own their properties, which explained why the LBGT organisations in Darlinghurst were more dynamic and similar to the Hollywood hub than to the Soho hub.

The three-way results and comparisons robustly challenged the wisdom of seeing a unitary, Anglo-Saxon liberal welfare state (and voluntary sector) regime both transatlantic and transpacific, as well as an all-encompassing neoliberalism exploiting the voluntary sector. However, residuals of the national welfare state settlement are by nature lagging, such that differences between the US and the UK are perhaps now outdated – Chapter Twelve will update the post-2010 period and the shift in the UK welfare state towards a more blatantly US model that threatens to unevenly reconstitute roll-back neoliberalism, with the potential for more convergence with the residual US (Hamnett, 2014). The Australian context is also of concern, with the new Abbott government promising fundamental cuts to disability support pensions and Newstart (income support, with calls for it to be conditional upon workfare as it was before the Rudd and Gillard federal Labour governments) to fix the so-called 'unsustainable' welfare system (Jabour, 2014; O'Connor, 2014). Interestingly, the cuts are being proposed as a way to avoid the fate of the supposedly bloated European welfare state (which subsumes the UK model), despite the fact that Australia is already more stringent in terms of eligibility and in far better fiscal shape overall. So the cuts are more ideologically driven than budgetary driven.

Thinking about comparison/resilience

I have used the comparison of voluntary-sector resilience as a way to extend and apply some of the many innovations that have marked comparative urbanism of late. Returning to the three hallmarks of my comparative approach outlined in Chapter Four, the first was on the tension between difference and similarity. Now that the comparisons have been made, I return to Nijman's (2007b) idea of 'deep analogies' to recast the comparative results. I have studied several serially replicated reference points – neoliberalism/post-welfarism, gentrification-induced displacement, and service hub resilience – as a way to understand the inner cities of Global North global city-regions like London, Los Angeles and Sydney, and the service hubs therein. There was significant diversity within each inner city, as these generic forces were differently filtered through locally unique historical legacies, voluntary-sector regimes and cultures, welfare state regimes and local governance structures. The initial aim was to capture the idiosyncrasies of each site, the local specificities as influenced by state, regional and local agents in a temporally sensitive approach (Boudreau et al, 2007). This was a more deductive approach, moving from the general to the particular, and ultimately about highlighting local difference. What I found was an interesting set of differences: between London's more state-supported yet perhaps exclusionary experience as compared to Los Angeles's more privatised and menaced, yet remarkably resilient and clustered, experience; and Sydney's middle-of-the-road experience, which combined some of London's levels of support with a more Americanised laissez-faire approach. The nature of the threat itself differed: in Los Angeles, gentrification was newer yet more punitive than in London and Sydney, although Westminster certainly approached Downtown Los Angeles in circumscribing the movements of homeless people.

Yet, crucially, Nijman (2007a, 2007b) also emphasised the generalities that crosscut understandably and inevitably unique settings. This connected to the second hallmark of my comparative approach, that of the encompassing method, which followed on both from Nijman's deep analogies and Bollens' (2009: 2) concept of the 'dual focused comparative approach', in which intensive case studies were joined to a limited number of research questions and reference points, seeking to 'generalize findings by going beyond single case studies'. Here I was interested in generalising beyond the local specificities, inductively from the particular to the general. There were several crosscutting similarities in the results: how inner-city space was similarly beneficial for service hubs in all three global city-regions; how the voluntary sector, despite legal permutations across Australia, the UK and the US, performed similar caring, sustaining and abeyance roles with regard to surplus populations in need (and beyond); how service hubs were forgotten places but now subject to renewed attention; and the pernicious effects of gentrification upon service hubs, their clientele and a tolerant inner city more generally.

The third hallmark returns to the idea of comparison as strategy. Carpenter and Lees (1995) noted that comparison *questions* complex patterns and generalisations of urban processes such as gentrification and its outcomes. I wielded my comparative approach as a strategy to query the received wisdom of certain taken-for-granted depictions and representations within the Global North, such as transatlantic and transpacific convergence of welfare models, as well as the premise of Anglo-American gentrification. For the former, there was limited evidence of convergence, and much evidence of immobility and path-dependency, at least while the study was being undertaken. However, the sense in 2014 was that convergence may be more forthcoming (see Chapter Twelve). For the latter, Los Angeles emerged as clear outlier, lacking the strong centre that structures inner-city gentrification. Sydney and London were more similar in these regards, although London gentrification faced more residual barriers.

Crucially, I used comparison as a political opportunity to valorise certain ordinary agents – the voluntary sector in particular – whose ordinary practices have traditionally been stereotyped and downplayed within hegemonic understandings of the neoliberal and punitive city (May & Cloke, 2014) *and* the global city (Sassen, 2001). So while my geographical comparative focus took place within over-studied global city-regions, the agents were themselves marginal, and have been largely ignored by critical and mainstream geographers alike. Their humble existence was in the shadows of a gentrifying and glamorising inner city, clinging to the (stagnant or shrinking) ordinary spaces of the global city-region; the ordinary in the global city-region, if you will. As Abu-Lughod (2007) rightly pointed out, too much of comparative work among global cities uses macro-data that privilege global industries and corporate agents, and hive off just a small section of urban space to represent its global city status (for example, for Sydney, only the CBD and North Sydney CBD; McNeill et al, 2005; Baker & Ruming, forthcoming). I provided instead a view from below – so rather than data on headquarters, accounting, advertising, banking, financial law and the like (for example, Beaverstock et al, 1999), I favoured putting (relatively) unremarkable and ignored service hubs under the microscope, ordinary spaces and practices certainly, but certainly not in ordinary cities. This was akin to Zukin's (1992) focus on the global city's vernacular landscapes, alongside and in relation to glitzy global-city power landscapes. I hope that this strategic orientation towards urban backwaters and ordinary agents and practices can somewhat mollify Robinson's (2011b: 1090) broader critique of urban studies – and by extension urban geography – for its narrow comparative palette, 'risking irrelevance if it continues to set agendas and build theorization on the experiences of relatively wealthy cities'.

The final and more tentative point is my contribution to comparative resilience (via the voluntary sector) as a nascent field of study in and of itself. Much of resilience research is implicitly approached in a comparative way – why do certain places or phenomena prove resilient while others prove vulnerable and not long for this world? This question inherently involves comparing the resilient from the non-resilient, the saved from the drowned. Some works on resilience were explicitly comparative (Vale & Campanella, 2005; Hall and Lamont, 2013) but surprisingly quiet about how exactly comparison is methodologically approached, of how resilience presents special issues, of how resilience may mean different things in different places. For instance, the Hall and Lamont edited volume *Social resilience in the neoliberal era* (2013) lacked a final chapter to draw together the comparisons. My key lessons for comparative resilience include the following: being more explicit about specific approaches to comparison, from the encompassing to the variation finding; appreciating that many urban phenomena are quite fragile and require exogenous support; the importance of comparing resilience across the unlike to find similarities; acknowledging the role of the local in filtering globally recurring phenomena (such as neoliberalism); focusing on marginal vehicles of resilience, rather than just the nation state, regional or city-wide level; and employing comparison as a strategy to explore, for instance, exogenous versus endogenous resilience. Just like cities, resilience can be approached in a more relational way; after all, resilience is produced and a process, but also a condition and a state of being, such that it can be transferred and emulated as a flow and as a connection, rather than being solely place-based. These lessons could be used to inform future studies of comparative resilience, which should be sensitive to the local but also wide ranging enough to be used in and across many different places. On the latter point, typologies are particularly useful in developing more generic approaches. With regard to voluntary-sector comparison, the field would similarly benefit from more explicit and rigorous approaches taken from comparative urbanism, such as recognising difference and similarity, the need to tie in the sector to welfare state and voluntary-sector regimes, as a strategy to valorise marginal yet crucial vehicles for social reproduction, and the need to learn across empirical case studies rather than strive for particularism. In Part Three, I will revisit the concept of resilience itself, underlining my primary innovation of the 'critical resilience of the residuals'.

Part Three
Conclusions, critical resilience, commons and austerity

Here I critically evaluate the utility of social and spatial resilience to the voluntary sector in residual service hubs, both in terms of resilience as a phenomenon to be studied in its own right but also its utility for social and critical geography, and for the study of the voluntary sector. I will argue in Chapter Eleven that resilience can be seen as a social and spatial struggle as important as any effort to secure the 'right to the city' (but garnering far less attention), with at least some critical potential. While much of the chapter is concerned with the real-world application of previously developed concepts about resilience, survival and gentrification, my centrepiece innovation is the presentation and consolidation of a new perspective on resilience captured by the 'critical resilience of the residuals'. But Chapter Eleven by no means gives carte blanche to resilience – it is both a deconstruction *and* reconstruction of resilience, a stress-test following the Burawoy et al (1991) extended case study. Indeed, the results suggested some shortcomings to the concept which are difficult to surmount, prompting the need to supplement resilience with alternative concepts such as 'commons'. In Chapter Twelve, I recast service hubs as commons before considering the more acute pressures from the post-2008 crisis of neoliberalism and emerging (post-welfare) arrangements within a context of 'austerity urbanism' (Peck, 2012) in the UK and US, but less so in Australia.

ELEVEN

The critical resilience
of the residuals

I first argue that resilience has been ignored by critical geographers perpetually seeking spectacular evidence of transformation, however unlikely or sporadic. From critical approaches to disasters such as heatwaves (for example, Klinenberg, 2002, on how poor Chicago neighbourhoods avoided high death rates) to the survival of surplus populations (for example, Li, 2010, on why Kerala provides for poor people while Indonesia does not), 'staying put' (for example, Shaw, 2007, on the Block in Sydney's Redfern), and persistence of older immigrant enclaves (for example, Li et al, 2013, on the survival of Chinatowns in Boston, New York and Philadelphia), resilience both social and spatial has rarely been named or understood, much less interpreted in a critical sense. These examples suggest the pressing need to construe how things survive without disappearing, moving beyond inertia and persistence to embrace active, adaptive resilience under conditions of chronic and acute threats. Rather than one more study using Lefebvre's 'right to the city', perhaps it is time to apply concepts of resilience as a way to better grasp the full nature of urban struggle. Mitchell (2003) and Harvey (2012) both argued that the right to the city was the best normative platform to ensure the geography of survival, but resilience could be equally useful and sometimes more realistic for marginal vehicles like the voluntary sector, and in cases where overturning the system is not viable or possible; resilience more as a *precursor*, a prerequisite for eventual transformation. In this way, the crucial 'resilience stage' in the evolution of potentially transformative action may act as a foundation for survival and existence itself. That survival requires both social *and* spatial resilience seems obvious to geographers – to be, and a place to be – but relatively ignored by other resilience scholars who fail to connect the two.

Returning to each of the seven proposals generated in Chapter Two, I will reinforce the critical intention of the production of resilience – as a means to preserve crucial yet residual arrangements of social support in the inner city; as a means to capture the everyday and active nature of persistence; as evidence of caring and sustaining, but also coercive care and abeyance; and as a complex yet useful term, laying the foundations (but not more) for transformation, resistance and remaking. If anything, service hubs have proven more than just resilient – in a sense they are *spatially recalcitrant*, featuring an obstinate desire and ability to 'stay put' that parallels the survival strategies of the equally besieged immigrant communities under study, and more than making up for the revanchism and punitiveness that purportedly so permeates urban space and urban social policy. My results have shown that the process (the 'how') of resilience is always complex and incomplete, and locally contingent. Throughout, I have striven to interpret and reveal resilience as an important, on-the-ground process, understanding the neglected agents that actively produce resilience and with what consequences across different (inner-city) spaces.

But I also relied on the rich comparative material to critically appraise the empirical and conceptual advantages *and* disadvantages of resilience, further expanding the range of consequences of gentrification beyond displacement, and breathing life into the idea that resilience is more than the 'in the meantime' filler before inevitable displacement – it can become an alternative to displacement itself, or constitute the status quo after the first wave of displacement. My encompassing comparison necessarily yielded crosscutting yet also contradictory variations, and thus performed a vital empirical filtering of the resilience concept. At the very least, resilience was the dominant response to gentrification-induced displacement: there was precious little talk of reworking or resisting the threat, and relatively little overt contestation. I will identify some real-world drawbacks, particularly the case of entrapment among voluntary-sector organisations and the double-edge reality of enabling resilience but limiting social mobility. By applying resilience to a stagnant (or even dwindling) number of service hubs, I unavoidably emphasise (if not celebrate) stopgap, protective and rearguard action and 'militant particularisms'; but, in response, I supplement resilience with something less preservative and more generative – that is, the 'commons' found in Chapter Twelve that recast service hubs as potential springboards for transformation.

Resilience requires a threat (acute or chronic)

The results reinforced the general consensus that gentrification-induced displacement represents a systematic, chronic threat to service hubs that is now spatially and temporally generalised across the ten inner-city areas, a colonisation run amok, strengthening after each plunge in the real estate market, and widening the gap between gentrifiers and the left-behind. As a consequence, social policy reorientates towards the incoming groups, and the service hub becomes harder to defend spatially and politically within a gentrified and purportedly punitive context. Atkinson (2000: 322) noted that the more middle class an area becomes, the less pressure there is to provide public services for the poor, or make room for service hubs more generally; the less resistance (and resilience?) there is to gentrification. In the case of Inner London, 'perceived levels of need were lowered, while the distance of needy residents to services set up by local authority and voluntary groups was increased'. Davidson (2008: 2392) found similar patterns of neighbourhood resource displacement in new-build gentrification along the River Thames: 'not only does the neighbourhood social balance change, but also local shops and services change and meeting-places disappear. The places by which people once defined their neighbourhood become spaces with which they no longer associate'.

Both neoliberalism and gentrification were themselves resilient, albeit increasingly crisis prone; in Chapter Two, I implied that resilience on its own is not inherently positive or negative, and while I have strenuously promoted the positive, resilience admittedly maintains a dark side in which undesirable systems become entrenched (Slater, 2014b; Weichselgartner & Kelman, forthcoming). Just because a system is resilient does not mean it is a good system – some of the most evil systems ever devised proved remarkably resilient. Take Stalinism, for example: during its 25-year existence, it proved resilient (at enormous human cost) to both internally generated crises (forced collectivisation, purges) and externally generated (the Nazi invasion of 1941, the Cold War). Presenting gentrification as darkly resilient signals that class conflict is alive and well across urban space (Davidson & Wyly, 2012). In this respect, the urban working class continue to cling to urban space despite all of the froth around professionalisation, 'creative cities', super-gentrification and the like, while partially mutating into a precarious surplus population dependent on the voluntary sector, itself under extreme spatial and social pressures yet surviving in the unlikeliest of ways and, crucially, in the most overlooked of places.

My results confirmed that gentrification was more than just about physical displacement, but also a spatial discourse and imaginary (Miller, 2013) that promises emancipation, density, diversity and urbanity, yet ultimately stifles them through cultural, social and spatial entitlements that progressively devitalise vibrant neighbourhoods (Deener, 2012; Harvey, 2012). Once seen as potentially liberating when compared to suburban life (Caulfield 1994), my results suggested that gentrification was now trending in the opposite direction. While earlier gentrifiers proved tolerant of inner-city residuals such as service hubs, the impression from the voluntary sector was that newer gentrifiers viewed them with disdain, their vision of inner-city space conceived solely in terms of exchange use, and thus introducing suburban-like NIMBYism and privatisation to the inner city. The evidence was apparent across all the case studies, even in Los Angeles where the inner-city and suburban landscapes are thoroughly blurred. This evidence must also be set within a broader renaissance of privatised urbanity that has become increasingly dominant in the early 21st century. Steffen (2013) noted that, given 'a revival in middle-class cultural preferences for urban living and the booming wealth of global economic hubs, cities are straining at the seams'. This is occurring not just in global city-regions like London, Los Angeles and Sydney, but even extending to traditionally anti-urban heartlands like the US Sunbelt, where data are showing declines in car sales, increases in public transit use and gradual repopulating of cores, lending credence to the (temporary?) slowing down of the suburbanisation and de-concentration of US cities (Luce, 2013). While gratifying at one level, these trends are also increasingly exclusionary, with only a small, fortunate group of gentrifiers enjoying the exemplary walkability, accessibility and centrality that comes with inner-city residence. The rest must put up with long commutes, inaccessibility and perhaps fewer voluntary sector services as well, since they continue to be arranged in resilient inner-city hubs. That the benefits of this newest renaissance fall almost exclusively to the gentrifiers and to already gentrified areas applied especially well to London and Sydney, where there was the risk of the 'hollow city' in which traditional inner-city diversity falls prey to the *embarras de richesse* that Glass (1964) warned about 50 years ago.

My own results confirmed this well-documented hollowing-out and 'bubble effect' (for example, May, 1996; Butler, 2003; Clerval, 2013). But we know appreciably less about gentrification's threat to (1) established centrality and accessibility, and how the threat involves (2) reinvigorated scrutiny of passed-over places in the inner city, and with what consequences. For the first gap, pervasive gentrification raises the spectre of a Parisian model of urbanism, with the poor banished to suburbs and the (depopulating) inner city the preserve of the wealthy (Dikec, 2007; Clerval, 2013). Sydney already resembled this model – as do most Australian capital cities – and London is surely on its way, accelerating in the post-2008 period (see Chapter Twelve). Los Angeles remained an outlier in this regard, with exceptional class and racial diversity still marking its inner city, and with gentrification perhaps *adding* to this diversity rather than subtracting from it. While maintaining accessibility for the inner-city poor, this state of affairs may not last much longer either – the rising cost of living in Los Angeles's inner city is pushing the poor outwards to the Inland Empire, currently America's largest bedroom community and hard hit by the real estate crisis of the post-2008 period – and woefully under-serviced by the voluntary sector, which continues to favour more established areas (Luce, 2013; for an earlier perspective, see Davis, 1990). As such, gentrification reinforced the longstanding centrality in Sydney and London, but in small measure reintroduced a lost centrality to Los Angeles and its dubious attachment to the Anglo-American model of gentrification.

Despite being residual, monocentric and agglomerative, centrality continues to structure service hub location. This circumstance should not be ignored in the headlong rush to understand new urban forms and to decipher the 21st-century city as increasingly fragmented and multiple-centred (Soja, 2000; Roy, 2009; Merrifield, 2013). While multiple centralities have been and are surely now at work on urban space, blithely ignoring residual continuities and the spaces they help structure in no way help us understand issues of accessibility for surplus populations. Service hubs anchor surplus populations to the inner city, and depend upon residual centrality to boost their accessibility; mass gentrification threatens to rearrange this condition. What I am arguing here is that the very de-centred nature of 21st-century cities makes the resilience of residual centralities and accessibilities like service hubs all the more precarious and thus precious. By narrowly celebrating new and renewed urban forms, we give up on a century of centrality and agglomeration effects that were struggled over and that have still important residual effects (Soja, 2010). As Harvey persuasively argued (2012: xvii), 'the traditional centrality of the city has been destroyed. But there is an impulse towards and longing for its restoration, which arises again and again to produce far-reaching political effects, as we have recently seen in the central squares of Cairo, Madrid, Athens, Barcelona …'. Focusing on left-behind and residual centralities structuring, and structured by, service hubs is arguably less dramatic to urban theorists but crucial to the lives of surplus populations.

For the second gap, gentrification was consequential because it introduced a new scrutiny to once forsaken inner-city spaces and populations; its own version of centrality inevitably clashed with the residual centrality of the inner city and the service hub. Once ignored in the shadows of the centre, these backwaters are now being revalorised, with every square centimetre under the microscope. Voluntary-sector organisations were being increasingly pressured to take on the roles of abeyance and coercive care to hide the poverty of their clientele by keeping them off the streets. This was very apparent in cases like Westminster and Surry Hills, but also on Skid Row. In the face of all these threats, the issue was not whether service hubs could prove resilient – we know this to be true. Rather, of importance was the interpretation of said resilience, both in its positive and negative consequences. From the case studies – and especially the established gentrification ones – the interpretation was that gentrification has tended to freeze service hub geographies rather than disrupt or displace them, leading to barriers to further displacement (DeVerteuil, 2011a). This entrapment laid the foundation for a rough co-existence, the modalities of which were characterised by countervailing practices: of increasing community NIMBY and entrepreneurial politics on the one hand, voluntary-sector solidarity and uneven (yet crucial) political support on the other. As such, the legacy of the public city and its voluntary sector geographies cannot easily be remade (or undone) by gentrification in the uneven post-welfare city, despite the inherent vulnerabilities and displacements around the edges (DeVerteuil, 2012). Holding one's ground was a way to block punitiveness, enable social resilience and lay the foundation for survival not just of service hubs but also the surplus populations that depended on them.

But while it was better to be resilient than not to exist at all, there were still downsides to service hubs and their clientele in the form of entrapment and reduced mobility, both spatial and social, which alerts us to other consequences to gentrification beyond immediate or eventual displacement punitively framed. Whether active or passive, spatial resilience and 'staying put' implied a variety of disadvantages (DeVerteuil, 2012) usually ignored in the fervent celebrations of spectacular occupations and rebellious cities. First and foremost was the inability to find feasible locational alternatives in a gentrified city, thereby locking in facilities to their locations (and locking out newcomers), and making it impossible to seek alternative yet equally central locations. Second was the inability to expand in situ due to gentrification-infused NIMBYism; here the vast majority of the resilient facilities complained that gentrification had increased the level of community opposition and locational conflict, making it necessary to improve their external image and micro-manage their clientele even more, to the point of implementing coercive care. Third, there was the inability to seriously challenge residual, but by now deeply entrenched and inequitable, voluntary-sector geographies across urban space, particularly services for certain stigmatised surplus populations. In other words, the saturation of service hubs such as Downtown Los Angeles and Westminster cannot easily be disentangled in a gentrified city, and so these service hubs can become traps. This confirmed Dear's (1980: 219) incisive remarks on the public city: the concentration of clients and facilities seems to provide a supportive environment for the user, but this environment is dominated by society's wounded. From the exclusionary community's viewpoint, however, the containment of 'deviants' in the transient, variegated city core probably seems the least threatening and most convenient solution (see also Fairbanks, 2009). So, in the case of Downtown Los Angeles, it was literally all or nothing – either Skid Row institutions became entrapped, or they disappeared entirely, since no other neighbourhood would accept such a burdensome clustering (Reese et al, 2010). While lauding the resilient clustering intrinsic to some service hubs, there was no doubt that some service hubs would benefit from a bit of equitable *de-concentration* to other parts of the global city-region, which is fundamental to a equitably functioning service hub model. This is not an easy conundrum to escape in an increasingly off-limits inner city and gentrified-induced NIMBYism (DeVerteuil, 2013). Fourth, staying put meant that facilities stood their ground and actively contested displacement while the clientele themselves were displaced further away to cheaper and more 'socially amenable' locales. This was particularly a problem in both inner-city Los Angeles and Sydney, which lacked the density of social housing when compared with London (Watt 2009), but it could also apply to homeless people who have been 'moved on' by street clearances, a problem common to all three global city-regions. In Sydney, the suburbanisation of poverty was most advanced, and thus the dilemma of centrally located services and dispersed clientele will only worsen over time. For these four reasons, entrapment constituted a concealed and uncompensated cost and consequence of gentrification.

In terms of enabling resilience, there was a double-edged reality: the ability to survive by depending on proximate service hubs overlapped with the inability to truly thrive and attain upward mobility (DeVerteuil, 2011b). Immigrant enclaves ensured resilience and survival but simultaneously reproduced segregation, a frequently unacknowledged disadvantage to social buffers and social capital. Moreover, the precarity associated with overcrowding is understood to cause significant social and physical stresses within the household, as well as create a lack of residential stability, destitution and limited long-term life chances (Kissoon, 2010). Language and citizenship barriers frequently served to constrain survival patterns to areas like Tower Hamlets and Pico-Union, especially for new arrivals. All of this problematised the staying put inherent in forms of resilience, but also highlighted the adaptive behaviour needed to get to such a point, the subject of the next proposal to revisit.

Resilience can be adaptive, and is more than just 'bouncing back' or persisting

Resilience is ultimately about how things continue to survive, to carry on, and to learn from experience. I detected some evidence of managed persistence (Smart, 2001) in the case studies on the part of the local state – Skid Row and Hollywood come to mind. I can interpret this as managed persistence because service hubs performed important roles as abeyance containers, minimising the spillover of surplus populations in prime urban space. According to this functionalist perspective, it was neither feasible nor popular to dismantle service hubs, yielding a 'policy of convenience and precedent' (Smart, 2001: 41). This perspective also acknowledged co-dependency: service hub resilience may rely on state funding and protection, but at the same time the service hub is compelled to perform irreplaceable abeyance functions. The variegated nature of the gentrification threat itself proved important for resilience, in that it was adaptive and thus relational, working against the threat presented via the lens of the four place-types.

But my results suggested that passive measures were *no longer* sufficient in response to the exigency of the threat of neoliberalism and gentrification-induced displacement. Rather, I argue for the absolute necessity of an active and adaptive process on the part of voluntary-sector organisations, to outflank rather than merely outlast. As the case studies have shown, service hubs were unplanned (for example, Tower Hamlets, Pico-Union) and even unruly (for example, Skid Row), actively resisting attempts to micro-manage and regulate them. As the agent of resilience, the voluntary sector – both on its own and in solidarity with others in service hubs – occasionally proved independent of neoliberalism, the market and the shadow state. This brings up the idea of the 'margins', whereby Wolch (1999: 26) implored the voluntary sector to shed its partnership model with the state, to decentre itself 'away from dominant institutions, powerful groups and privileged places', and move to the margins as a way to maintain its innovativeness and traditional focus on social justice, inclusion and alterity (see also Amin et al, 2002; Fyfe, 2005). My results suggested that the voluntary sector was somewhat self-organising and partially independent, operating as a stable and resilient source of survival.

With managed persistence no longer enough to guarantee spatial resilience, voluntary-sector organisations must now be proactive to maintain their coherency and centrality through learning, image management, solidarity and lobbying. The overall results suggested significant measures of adaptability. Examples were numerous: the youth centre in Surry Hills that adapted to, if not pre-empted, community opposition by changing its façade; the tight (but not patronising) relationship between Hollywood voluntary-sector organisations and the political elite; the solidarity shown by Westminster facilities when faced with severe threats to the survival of their (hungry) clientele; and the savvy image management performed by the safe injection site in Kings Cross. There was a mix of private and voluntary-sector strategies, some high profile, others low. Privately, organisations had the foresight of buying property when it was cheap, or seeking amenable landlords in accessible areas. Active solidarity with other organisations in the service hub also promoted resilience, in terms of lobbying as a common front, as well as capitalising on governmental support and confronting governmental policy if need be. In an age of splintering and privatising urbanism, service hubs are potent reminders of the legacy of the Keynesian (inner) city, particularly its public nature and class compromises that favour, and never to solely punish, the downtrodden.

Resilience is a process, not an endpoint

This particular proposal returns us to the central plank of the book – how to interpret the means of resilience through the agent (and agency) of the voluntary sector, of how resilience is produced via service hubs for their own survival and the survival of their clients. Given current trends, we know already that the Keynesian/public city is unlikely to return to its full glory, so it is well worth fighting for its residuals – this is a struggle without end, what Castells (1983: 335) considered to be essential to urbanisation itself, 'cities as the result of an endless historical struggle over the definition of urban meaning by antagonistic social actors'. The empirical material covered close to 15 years of struggle during a period of consolidating yet incomplete neoliberalism and uneven post-welfarism, and showed a wide range of strategies and outcomes.

Resilience must therefore be seen as a social and spatial struggle at the heart of critical geography, no longer on the periphery or ridiculed as comically out of touch with critical scholarship (for example, Slater, 2014b). The case study material amply demonstrated the downsides but also the benefits of staying put – in terms of maintaining centrality and holding on to previous gains – and the challenges in staying put, with various private, voluntary-sector and political strategies employed in the face of pervasive threats. The focus on resilience itself was a positive one, endlessly searching for the 'cracks in the city' (Moyersoen & Swyngedouw, 2013) rather than dwelling on the largely negative, seemingly overwhelming power of neoliberalism, gentrification, punitiveness and revanchism. This paralleled Gibson-Graham's (2006) trenchant critique of 'strong theory', that is 'critical urban scholarship that provides explanations of the processes of urban restructuring that seem all powerful, all pervasive and impossible to challenge' (Lees, 2014: 923).

If resilience has no endpoint, does it work against urban dynamism, the creative destruction so common to urban spaces under (restructuring) capitalism? Yes, if ensuring the spatial stability of service hubs and other resilient residuals locks in certain land uses and shuts out others, guaranteeing city-wide diversity and the survival of key services and populations (Fainstein, 2010). While gentrification is the sharp edge of this dynamism, its displacing effects are not inevitable if barriers are sufficiently strong. But, by the same token, rich neighbourhoods – some of which were once in the pioneer gentrification stage – artificially protect themselves from change as well, even in the pressured inner-cities of global city-regions, through well-organised NIMBY campaigns, wars of attrition over zoning and 'appropriate' land uses, and exclusionary built environments with eye-watering real estate prices. Examples were rife in the case studies, from the difficulties in maintaining service hub coherency in Westminster and Surry Hills, where there was a growing gap between affordable housing and the service hubs themselves, to the entitlements that gentrifiers felt when they opposed new services in places like Downtown and Kings Cross. If powerful urban actors persistently use enclavism to defend their existence and privileges, why not the less powerful?

Resilience can be enabled, shared and transferred

Spatial resilience provided the platform for the producing and enabling of social resilience, last-ditch spaces of care, refuge, sanctuary, difference, collective consumption and social reproduction (DeVerteuil, 2011a). These residuals of the public city proved resilient and sometimes slyly, sometimes openly, challenged the class remaking of the inner city. In this sense, entrapment worked against concepts of annihilation, revanchism and collapse; service-dependent populations can never disappear entirely as long as there is a stable service geography to underpin them (see also DeVerteuil et al, 2009b). In my examples, the voluntary sector enabled everyday survival through care (sometimes coercively) and sustenance. The results suggested that social resilience can be *institutionalised* and *collectivised*. At their core, institutions encompass 'regularized or crystallized principle[s] of conduct, action, or behavior that govern a crucial area of social life that endures over time' (Gould, 1987: 290). This endurance over time suggests the ability of institutions to 'infuse social life with durable norms and dependable structures' (Skowronek, 1995: 93). As sets of relationships, institutional capacity is both dependent on other structures, and at the same time autonomous from them. Institutions 'do not simply constrain or channel the actions of self-interested individuals, they prescribe actions, construct motives, and assert legitimacy' (1995: 94); in other words, to see the (institutional) enabling of social resilience as both a collective and durable enterprise.

At the same time, and as previously acknowledged, it was best to avoid being too starry-eyed about producing and enabling resilience – there were always strings attached, there were always compromises to be made. Li (2010: 80) recounted one version of the compromise between dispossession and protection. Dispossession is real and garners much attention from critical geographers, but protection is real as well – it is not just rhetoric, and not just 'minimal, self-serving, and disciplinary … to manage the chaos created by dispossession, and stave off revolt'. Rather, and harking back to the poverty management framework, there is genuine caring and sustenance of surplus populations on behalf of the voluntary sector, and care and sustenance can ensure not only survival but also potentially a step up (Cloke et al, 2010). Of course this caring and sustenance can become compromised, coercive and abeyance by other means, becoming traps, and thwarting spatial and social mobility. Still, the case studies showed that the voluntary sector provided much-needed support with relatively little exogenous help, although that exogenous help was still crucial; without it, there would simply be too much responsibility for the voluntary sector, but with it, a certain dependency has emerged.

'Everyday' resilience is a potential alternative to spectacular 'resistance' or 'reworking'

The case study material amply demonstrated that voluntary-sector organisations were generally more preoccupied with their own survival, and enabling survival to their clients, than with striving for fundamental transformation. It was frequently difficult to see the voluntary sector involved in spectacular resistance, with the 'right to the city' proving equally unrealistic (Uitermark et al, 2012; May & Cloke, 2014).

Let us not fool ourselves here; while some voluntary-sector action did indeed implicate far-reaching and progressive aims – a focus of Chapter Twelve – the majority of organisations struggled to survive financially while caring for and providing the basics of life to their vulnerable clientele. In turn, this clientele is notoriously disorganised and ill-placed to call for radical transformation, akin to motivating the *lumpenproletariat* to join the revolution. My nuanced approach recognised the importance of voluntary-sector activism, agency and alliances with other sectors in solidifying strategies of resilience. In that spirit, what sometimes appears to be resistance is more likely to be everyday, obdurate resilience and outflanking, with nothing radically overturned nor even directly contested.

Resilience thus emerged as more realistic than resistance or reworking for the voluntary sector. This insight aligns with the sense that, while the voluntary sector ought to move to the margins (Wolch, 1999), it remains mired in a mode of de-contestation vis-à-vis the welfare state and the shadow state, unable to fully escape their gravity but maintaining a modicum of independence (Milbourne, 2013). From the results, it was difficult to envision a voluntary sector-led remaking or resisting of the enforced 'smaller state', shadow state and other neoliberalised co-optations happening on the ground. So it was more realistic to see service hubs as actively resilient, at best unruly and unregulated, but not necessarily remaking or resisting society. As such, understanding the voluntary sector as a resilient entity enables us to move beyond seeing it as inherently (or exclusively) resistant/progressive or seeing it as co-opted into the neoliberal 'shadow state'. Resilience has its advantages and disadvantages, and so acts as a middle path between resistance and co-optation; it also provides the voluntary sector with some much-needed agency, not just as dupes of the (neoliberal) state (Cloke et al, 2010).

Let me deepen the distinction between resilience and an over-used resistance by using the concept of the 'intervenient middle' (Rajan & Duncan, 2013). The intervenient middle concept bolsters Katz's arguments about the need to recognise resilience alongside resistance or reworking. Like most critically minded social scientists, Rajan and Duncan acknowledged that, at the time of writing (2013: 70), the world was 'rife with a million mutinies' – the Arab Spring, Occupy movements, and the like. The highly visible and spectacular nature of these protests predictably grabbed the popular and academic attention. All of this served to further downplay the raw reality of quotidian survival and social change through discrete, everyday and mundane initiatives and survival mechanisms, much in the way that Katz (2004) saw incremental change in Sudan. As Rajan and Duncan stated (2013: 70):

> adopting what might seem to be an overly crass and pragmatic perspective, it appears indeed that for millions of people and hundreds of ecosystems, discrete initiatives to ensure their survival are the only 'revolutions' that will ever happen – at least in their lifetimes. Such initiatives, and the motivations that underlie them, cannot therefore be understood only with recourse to an analytical framework about resistance to big power, technology, state or capital. We argue that in order to be historically significant, social change need not just be about large, transformational events recognisable as revolutionary, but can equally about relatively localised everyday attempts to marginally improve the day-to-day drudgery of life.

In other words, certain trends cannot be easily resisted or reworked – for them, collective resilience is the best possible outcome, or otherwise we are projecting false images of resistance and reworking, bereft of any middling concept. So this intervenient middle is effectively resilience put differently – the ability to survive and outlast/outflank rather than radically overturn and overthrow. This is also akin to May and Cloke's (2014) idea of the 'messy middle ground', in which homeless services combined the desire to control and punish the homeless with ambiguous support, enabling a more nuanced and valorising approach to resilience beyond resistance and reworking

To summarise, sometimes the best we can hope for is the intervenient, messy middle and the defence of a previous status quo; Katz (2004) appreciated that resistance and remaking are not always possible, or even desirable, in order to defend social reproduction and survival. The utility of the 'right to the city' remains limited when dealing with a voluntary sector that rarely heeds the call of urban revolution and the overthrow of entrenched structures. Rather than the expansion implicit in the 'right to the city' (the right to produce urban space according to local needs), the voluntary sector was more interested in maintaining long-term centrality, accessibility, as well as enabling the everyday slog of survival and resilience. If the 'right to the city' can prove useful, it stems more from the 'everyday practice of inhabiting of urban space' (Purcell, 2013: 561), the normative underpinning for service hubs to occupy prime land in the gentrifying inner city.

Resilience can be critical, but perhaps not transformative

Back in Chapters One and Two, I outlined the critical promise of resilience, of how it may work against the current status quo, preserving previous gains from a more equitable era, but most of all acting as an obvious and crucial precondition for survival in the city. Two further examples that resonate with my own case study material can be provided to show how resilience, or more properly the holding on to previous gains, may be a site of struggle. Gilbert (2001) focused on welfare rights organisations, both in the 1960s and the 1990s, that sought to safeguard advances made in struggles over the newly won gains of the 1960s War on Poverty programmes or the threatened loss of those gains 30 years later in the 1996 PRWORA. Similarly, Reese (2011), in her detailed chronicling of the post-PRWORA welfare landscape in the US, identified broad coalitions of welfare rights social movements that continued, even more than 10 years later, to challenge its legacy and legitimacy, limit the damage, and seek whenever and wherever possible to protect holdovers of pre-1996 entitlements from the welfare state. The coalitions were decidedly grassroots and self-organising, and scored some impressive victories by judiciously intervening into the devolved welfare state and local implementations of welfare reform. I can translate these insights to the resilient service hub: it too encapsulates current but especially previous distillations of social struggle. An obvious example was the LGBT component of service hubs in Westminster, Darlinghurst and Hollywood. These components all incorporated the lengthy pre- and post-Stonewall struggle for civil rights, and drew strength from the concentration of clientele, the diversity and solidarity of organisations, and the proximity to political power.

The production of resilience is therefore essential as a platform for survival and thus subsequent resistance, remaking, reworking and transformation. I can now see Katz's (2004) tripartite resilience/ reworking/resistance as a progressive sequence, as well as working alongside or exclusively of one another. Not everything has to be new, and not everything has to be transformative, but staying put is itself a struggle that ought never to be underestimated. There is nothing inherently limiting by being defensive, protective, incremental and place-based and place-bound – a prerequisite that, in and of itself, needs to be (re)valorised rather than seen merely as a stopgap measure (Castells, 1983; Miller & Nicholls, 2013). This aligns with Fainstein's argument (2010: 18) that 'urban movements do have transformative potential despite being limited to achieving change only at the level in which they are operating'. But, as previously mentioned, it is not easy for the voluntary sector, as the building block of the service hub, to transcend its transformational limitations. In Chapter Twelve, I will expand on this proposition that the service hub can be both preservative of former transformation and generative of future transformation by recasting the service hub to 'commons'.

Resilience can usefully be applied to residual arrangements

My results confirmed the incomplete, uneven, sometimes contradictory and always contingent nature of neoliberalism and post-welfarism. As a resilient residual in the interstices of the incompletely neoliberalising post-welfare inner city, the service hub thrives on its centrality, of maximising accessibility to the most clients across urban regions who may, because of gentrification, be increasingly suffering from spatial dispersal (DeVerteuil, 2012). The conspicuous presence of voluntary-sector organisations may act as bulwarks against present and future gentrification. I speculate that gentrification itself cannot proceed until voluntary-sector organisations begin to hide the abrasive presence of the homeless and other surplus populations, but that once services do exist, subsequent gentrification is potentially blunted through spatial resilience. In turn, this blocking action demands the curtailing of the service hub at the very least, and at the very most enabling its destruction as an obstacle to gentrification and an immaculate (yet so far, unattainable) post-welfare city. Service hubs are proof positive that the (uneven) post-welfare city always contains the credible and resilient residues of bygone eras.

I also want to use my results as a springboard to consider several locational issues of a *resilient service hub model* within an emerging *post-welfare geography*, referring back to the post-welfarism outlined in the Introduction. As mentioned there, a distinctly *public* facility location theory has been eclipsed by the rise of the voluntary sector as the main vehicle for service provision to the socially vulnerable. The gradual shift from state provision of welfare to the voluntary sector since the 1980s fundamentally altered the 'public' nature of public facilities, making it even harder to conserve their centrality and accessibility. As I argued in 2000 (66):

> In an era of public divestment and devolution, many 'public' facilities are actually partnerships between a governmental agency and a nonprofit organisation. Should

nonprofit service facilities be located according to the same criteria as public ones? Given the expediency of current shadow state dynamics and welfare reform, do public agencies subcontracting to nonprofits no longer worry about location distributional equity? Finally, given the fact that the voluntary sector is geographically uneven in its development, such that those neighborhoods most in need are often also among the least adequately served, how do trends toward privatisation impact upon the wider geography of human services? Since gaps in funding are sure to create gaps in the spatial extent and coverage of human services, thereby making facility location even *more* important to clients, these are certainly critical questions to interrogate.

Within this new context, the first issue to consider is the utility of the service hub itself – what would be the consequences of its dismantlement across the gentrifying inner city, and the generalised dispersion and suburbanisation of voluntary-sector organisations? This counterfactual question forces me to defend the service hub in several ways. First, I am against dispersion if it means destruction and extinction of certain services or their eventual inaccessibility, which would certainly be the case for places like Skid Row. Some clientele will not go far for services (for example, homeless people on foot), so dispersion and far-flung locations will mean no access at all. Service hubs have taken decades to build up and defend, and once gone they can never be replicated in a gentrifying city (or exclusionary suburbs). Second, I am against dispersion as the benefits of agglomeration – the dense meshing of likeminded and complementary services that breeds accessibility – would be lost if voluntary-sector organisations scattered. Third, dispersion would result in the loss of centrality and visibility so crucial for advocacy and perhaps change – as Harvey (2012) memorably raised the point, no one wants or talks about the 'right to the suburbs'! So we do lose something when dispersing to the suburbs: the built-up legacies, compromises and struggles that mark inner-city service hubs, and the high accessibility and visibility. Critical geographers are well aware that all urban forms under capitalism, whether clustered or scattered, are in some way unequal, but a suburbanisation and scattering of voluntary-sector organisations would be particularly detrimental in the absence of compensating inner-city hubs.

Yet the marooning of the voluntary-sector/public city within the uneven post-welfare inner city raises another prickly issue of accessibility – the dispersion of clientele beyond the inner city, leading to an increasing spatial mismatch. This was recognised by Cordero-Guzman (2005: 896) in New York City, whereby 45% of immigrant-serving organisations were located in Manhattan, but 82% of recent migrants were heading to the other four boroughs (Bronx, Brooklyn, Staten Island and Queens). This creeping dispersion was similarly recognised by many of the organisations that I interviewed, especially in places like Sydney, where surplus populations were so evidently at risk of suburbanisation; some wondered whether, without a nearby clientele, their abeyance roles would disappear. Of course, there is nothing necessarily wrong with suburbs gaining services, as long as it is not an excuse to dismantle irreplaceable components of the inner-city service hub, such as density, proximity and solidarity. Moreover, many suburban areas are criminally under-served by the voluntary sector even as they become poorer, suggesting incipient spatial injustice (Soja, 2010): in Sydney most obviously, but also Outer London where per capita rates of voluntary-sector organisations are much lower than Inner London rates (MacInnes et al, 2011) and far-flung suburbs within Los Angeles County but especially beyond, such as the Inland Empire. This is part of an American trend where more poor people now live in suburbs than in cities, but with the former lacking effective anti-poverty infrastructure (Kneebone & Berube, 2013; Luce, 2013).[1] This mismatch becomes crucial when times are tough and people turn to the voluntary sector for succour – during the 2008 recession, many Latino people working in the under-serviced exurbs of Los Angeles re-centralised to inner-city hub neighbourhoods, where life was more expensive but survival more assured through the dense networks of voluntary, informal and state support (DeVerteuil, 2011b). So a rebalancing of the voluntary-sector geography would be welcome if it became more like the service hub in theory – the promise of agglomerations equitably and efficiently dispersed throughout the *entire* metropolitan area. In the absence of such a pattern, the next best solution is to retain inner-city hubs while striving for a more judicious decentralisation.

Even with suburbanisation of clientele, however, there is something special about inner-city space that is worth hanging on to. The access, density, diversity and proximity of inner-city space enables care and sustenance (Till, 2012), but also makes service hubs defensible and resilient. As Hackworth (2007: xii) noted, 'cities are sites of both the most acute articulation of neoliberalism and of its most acute opposition'. Inner-city space is not a backdrop to resilience but constitutive of it. In the case of Elephant and Castle in Southwark,

DeFilippis and North (2004: 85) underlined all of these characteristics in the defence of social housing:

> At the heart of a global city, population density, geographical proximity, and the palimpsest of layered traditions of urban political action formed a dense and rich sedimented network of information, advice, support, and resources that community activists could call upon.

Ultimately, resilience remains useful enough to retain, but only when carefully defined and applied. Resilience is often overly capacious conceptually, and too often applied uncritically; what is needed (and what I have provided) is a critical co-optation of its production, cognisant of its advantages without throwing out the concept entirely but also sober about its disadvantages, especially with regard to (radical) transformation. This 'critical resilience of the residuals', which essentially combines the last two proposals, is the centrepiece of my conceptual contribution, constituting the key thread throughout this book, proof that a more *flexible critical geography* is not only possible but essential. This flexibility eschews rigid critiques of resilience, while building on work by critical geographers (for example, Katz, 2004) that attempted to incorporate resilience into traditional areas of concern, such as unevenness, accumulation by dispossession and surplus populations. Further, the production of resilience via service hubs exposes and effectively counters the fiction of an immaculate post-welfare, neoliberalised inner city, and valorises the study of slow tectonic shifts of urban space over the acute events that still capture too much of our attention.

But will my 'resilience of the residuals' gain traction among critical geographers? Admittedly, my cepaceous approach may have seemed antediluvian, nostalgic and backward looking, perhaps even a lost cause, limited at best to a stagnant number of Keynesian residuals that are worth saving but invariably threatened with extinction. But resilience need not be conservative or sinister; I have clearly shown that resilience was also a missed opportunity for crucial matters of interest to urban social geographers, including survival, protection, homelessness and im/mobility, and ultimately of why certain urban phenomena persist while others go by the wayside. These matters are applicable to more than just Keynesian relics; they can include emerging urban phenomena that touch on a wide variety of interests. Finally, I admit that the production of resilience and the enabling of survival – a politics of necessity (Zuern, 2011) that largely accept the terms of the debate around neoliberalism ('there is no alternative') and translates redistribution into technical problems – are not enough for a politics of change, especially if considered only as a precondition for transformation that cannot generate its own remakings and resistances. In the next chapter, I supplement resilience with the concept of the 'commons' as a way to recast service hubs in particular (and the voluntary sector more generally) as a potential way-station to a better urban future.

Note

[1] Events in August/September 2014 in the St Louis suburb of Ferguson showed the ill effects of suburban exclusion, in some ways paralleling the Paris unrest of 2005.

TWELVE

Here, now: recasting service hubs in an age of austerity

In this final chapter, I return to lessons generated via the five cornerstones of the book, and then contemplate the transformative promise of service hubs by introducing the notion of 'commons'. From there, I investigate the emergence of what Peck (2012) called 'austerity urbanism', and how this acute version of neoliberalism threatens to corrode some of the resilience of service hubs, particularly in London but also for Los Angeles and Sydney.

Key contributions of the book: returning to the five cornerstones

In terms of thinking about *(incomplete) neoliberalism and the (uneven) post-welfare city as the context and threat*, my results have shown their chronic and pervasive nature via the vehicle of inner-city gentrification, but also their incompleteness and unevenness that allowed for residual arrangement of bygone eras to prove resilient as well as enable resilience. This confirmed the insights that the post-welfare city always contains the residuals of past structures; what I have shown in great and innovative detail is the struggle around those residuals, the actual means and strategies around this struggle and how they differed comparatively. This missing story around resilience constitutes a key contribution, and further de-essentialises rigid notions of neoliberalism and the post-welfare city.

In terms of *resilience*, my results have suggested that it is an important if ignored response to displacing threats, and that the interpretation of its production was long overdue. My innovation of the 'critical resilience of the residuals' represented a critical co-optation of what can be a regressive, at best status quo, term. It also indicated that the active production of service hub resilience is a crucial element in ensuring the survival of both the voluntary sector and of surplus populations in the gentrifying inner city, ensuring centrality and accessibility. Rather than turn to resistance as a reflex action, we can employ resilience and the intervenient middle as a more realistic approach, especially when dealing with structural shifts (for example, shadow state, shrinking state, devolution) that are difficult to remake, especially for marginal agents. Taken as a defence of previously won gains, the production of resilience surely becomes something as positive as resistance, actively shrugging off pervasive territorial stigmatisation and challenges to 'staying put' inherent in the uneven post-welfare inner city.

For the *voluntary sector as the agent*, the overall contribution was quite clear – the sector is conflicted and partially co-opted, but has proven quasi-independent and resilient, a crucial foundation for the everyday survival of surplus populations and an agent of an ambivalent/supportive poverty management. Service hub resilience and enabling of resilience were far-reaching proof of the sector's active yet constrained agency, and occasional unruliness, despite the fact that service hubs were always fragile and 'borrowed places'. In so doing, I have also advanced a more sophisticated perspective on the voluntary sector, not just as a stooge of neoliberalism but more times than not ambivalent of the neoliberal project and frequently supportive of surplus populations. Finally, by placing the voluntary sector as a key agent in the management of social polarisation in global city-regions, I have elevated its role well beyond more mundane concerns of everyday survival.

The main contributions from considering the *inner city as the territorial focus* are several. First, that there are multiple and sometimes contradictory motivations – gentrification-induced displacement and punitiveness, but also offsetting ambivalence and support – at work in inner-city space, illustrated especially well by Downtown, Hollywood, Tower Hamlets and Pico-Union. Second, that the density, proximity, accessibility and centrality of inner-city space necessarily breeds and enables resilience through a variety of strategies, including voluntary-sector clustering inherent in the service hub model, but that these conspicuous hubs also attracted unwanted attention. In particular, the legacies of agglomeration and centrality still matter even in this age of cutting-edge polycentrism and networks/flows; there remains a longing for it on the part of both gentrifiers and voluntary-sector organisations. The service hub is part and parcel of alternative spaces in the inner city, non-commodified spaces that I will return to in the next section.

Finally, *comparison as the method* elevated my study to fully embrace three hallmarks: comparing the unlike to find likeness; the utility of the encompassing comparative approach; and using comparison as a strategy, to shine a light on some current misconceptions around transoceanic welfare state and voluntary-sector regime convergence and divergence, as well as Anglo-American gentrification. My deliberate comparison of humble agents in marginal, overlooked and ordinary places also served to rectify the usual high-end focus when comparing global-city regions. The comparison of voluntary-sector resilience brought in lessons from comparative urbanism to make my study more rigorous and interesting empirically, but conceptually extended the nascent field of comparative resilience (and perhaps the voluntary sector as well?) within a context of managing the social polarisations so inherent to global city-regions.

Service hubs as incremental commons?

Now that the contributions of the book have been reinforced, I wish to consider how the results challenged dominant codes of the uneven post-welfare city, but also supplemented survival and resilience beyond the defensive and the protective, the stopgap and the rearguard, important preconditions as they may be. Alas, the voluntary sector does not offer far-reaching solutions to seemingly intractable social problems, and so its resistance and transformative potential appears blunted. In response, I propose that service hubs can more thoroughly embrace and generate transformative aims if they are recast as 'commons'. To recast the resilient and residual service hub as commons, I must first recast the threat of gentrification-induced displacement as a blatant case of 'enclosure'. Enclosure returns us to Marx's concept of primitive accumulation,

> the actual, and often bloody, practices by which capitalism takes over and commercialises growing areas of human life. This has included the clearing of peasants from common lands, the destruction of artisanal workshops, the canceling of local right to the land, and the destruction of entire homes and villages. (Shantz, 2013: 60)

During this earlier era of capitalism, but periodically resurfacing, 'dispossession and displacement were not simply the consequences of enclosure, they were its very essence, and led to both the commodification of labour power and the commodification of space as a highly valuable asset' (Hodkinson, 2012: 504). Current gentrification-led restructuring of inner-city space is a restored wave of exclusionary and displacing enclosure. Harvey (2012: 80) claimed that 'capitalist urbanization tends to destroy the city as social, political and livable commons', commons that are however perpetually being rebuilt. Gentrification represents a relatively new outlet for the privatisation of inner-city spaces in the post-Keynesian, uneven post-welfare city, manifesting the purifying tendencies of roll-out neoliberalism via direct, physical displacement. Like roll-out neoliberalism, enclosures target the embedded class compromises of Keynesian commons, bringing them into the fold of the market.

But what are 'commons' exactly, and how do they resist enclosure? At an abstract level, the commons represent the promise and practice of 'life beyond marketization, privatization and commercialization' (Jeffrey et al, 2012: 1249), of space that is 'both collective and non-commodified – off-limits to the logic of market exchange and market valuations' (Harvey, 2012: 73). Chatterton (2010: 626) added that commons are 'bounded entities, which exist to nurture and sustain particular groups', collectively owned and shared, 'a byword for resistance against the excesses of contemporary capital encroachment and expansion' (627), which gives the concept a certain Polanyi-esque flavour. As such, enclosures and commons are dialectically related, the dialectic itself dynamic (Jeffrey et al, 2012). Commons are ultimately non-commodified spaces of solidarity that can exist outside of capitalist flows, enclosures and neoliberal governance. Commons are a natural home of collective goods, which are also 'complex goods' in the sense that most urban amenities 'consist of many components that have multiple interactions and have different uses for different people ... [its] provision is engendered through the divergent demands of actors in a socially heterogeneous and fragmented social fabric' (Moyersoen & Swyngedouw, 2013: 155). Common property and social housing are classic commons, and have been the target of enclosures since the 1980s in the UK ('Right to Buy') and the US (Hope VI program), and its equivalent in Australia.

Recast as commons, I propose that service hubs can potentially – and incrementally – be preservative *and* generative, defensive *and* productive, a necessary way-station on the path towards more socially just transformation, rather than merely as 'anti-enclosures', which imply only delaying and obfuscating, but never truly changing, the inevitable outcome of eventual enclosure and displacement (Hodkinson, 2012). As concentrated, non-commodified usufruct enclaves that partially exist outside of neoliberalism, service hubs can become springboards for transformation, greater socioeconomic equality and redistribution, key nodes in an ambivalent/supportive poverty management, envisioning and then constructing a world exceeding neoliberalism and not just in response to it. Normatively, service hubs as commons provides an alternative vision of the 'good city', providing complex goods that embody non-commodified spaces and the potential for progressive aims, questioning and intervening in matters of social justice and transformative politics. My own results suggested a panoply of empirical examples; when taken as a (dense) whole, every service hub had a kernel of potential transformation. Pico-Union was both the stage and generator for voluntary sector-led Living Wage campaigns, immigrant rights and welfare rights, alongside citizenship drives and general community empowerment. In Surry Hills, this included the advocacy work of the Communist Party of Australia and the Wilderness Society, calling for fundamental societal change. On Skid Row, this included organisations that agitated for (and provided) something beyond emergency, band-aid sustenance. It could also include the grassroots nature of many organisations in immigrant enclaves such as Tower Hamlets that served communities under siege but also sought to expand their rights and empower clients, rather than only providing care and sustenance. In Hollywood but also in Darlinghurst, the service hub was a distillation of 45 years of the LGBT civil rights movement, a vehicle for alternative sexuality and citizenship drawing strength from voluntary-sector strategies outlined in Chapter Ten. This sort of commons can act as 'institutional islands of social solidarity' (Wills, 2012: 114), beachheads of de-commodification and potentially of adversarial politics. By their very obdurate resilience, and as defensive and protective anchors that blunt the spread of gentrification, service hubs can undermine accumulation, as prime urban space is given over to non-producing and non-consuming surplus populations and the advocacy of good causes, enabling their survival independent of market forces. With regards to urban space, service hubs as commons can help reject the false choice of complete gentrification versus utter dereliction.

These empirical examples suggested that service hubs were durably generative of social innovations, providing crucial and complex social goods, filling the gaps left by a receding state and hostile market, building up new modes of social reproduction that very much reflect the slow change of daily structures and the commitments of everyday life, 'made up of the quiet moments of re-connecting, of building, of restoring, of constructing. More than a hurling against the walls, they are a shoulder to the wheel. They are a building of commons. In these moments they are more quiet than a scream' (Shantz, 2013: 13). This suggested some overlap between service hubs and community organisations, social movements, collective action/activism, all of which have been associated with commons and public, rather than private, societal aims (Miller, 2006; Miller et al, 2013). Recasting resilient residuals as commons enables the service hub to connect to a variety of similarly minded visions for a more just city (Fainstein, 2010). This can include Castells' (1983) vision of progressive social movements in the city; in the words of Hasson and Ley (1997: 33), '[he] suggested that urban social movements could be at the forefront in laying the foundation for a new democratic and just city, a city in which quality of life, preservation of local and cultural identities, and community participation are taken seriously in decision making'. This can crucially include a vision of less commodified urban future; Brenner et al (2009: 176) saw that 'capitalist cities have long served as spaces for envisioning, and indeed mobilizing towards, alternatives to capitalism itself, its associated process of profit-driven urbanization and its relentless commodification and re-commodification of urban spaces'. But it can also include DeFilippis's (2004) understanding of local collectivist impulses and place-based social change through collective ownership of work, housing and money. Finally, it can embrace Harvey's (2012) implicit recognition of the promise of commons to the right to the city.

However, I duly admit that service hubs constitute imperfect commons due to their extremely slow and incremental nature, but also the conflicted nature of the voluntary sector itself. The sector is sometimes too tied to the neoliberalising welfare state and its pernicious influences, the latter now enclosing in tandem with the market, as well as functioning as abeyance structures that obscure and coerce the poor and foster segregation and dependency. I freely admit that the voluntary sector remains contradictory, asymmetrical and uneven. And while I am inclined to agree with Hodkinson (2012: 516), who argued that the production and reproduction of urban commons offers the best way to appropriate and ensure 'alternative forms of sociality that protect us against enclosures and market forces', through the actions of commonism and mutual aid (see also DeFilippis, 2004), there is the prickly issue of enclavism and localism. In effect, service hubs represent a patchy geography of potential transformation, seemingly akin to other enclaves of non-commodification and solidarity such as community gardens. However, service hubs are more capacious than, for instance, community gardens! They are residues of increasingly lost patterns of redistribution, related to larger structures that 'make live' substantial segments of the urban population, one of many prefigurative enclaves that could be joined across urban space. Besides, neoliberal enclosures proceed as a series of enclaves, and more patchily than some would readily admit.

Service hubs in a context of 'austerity urbanism'

So far I have mostly conceived neoliberalism as a slow-moving, pervasive and chronic threat, potentially corroding and displacing Keynesian residuals such as service hubs via gentrification. Yet since the 2008 financial crisis, neoliberalism has (re)emerged as a shock, an acute threat in its own right, and whose full impacts are still up for speculation. Certainly, my own results were largely collected before the full reckoning of the crisis was felt, and certainly before the cutbacks at the national welfare scale and the emergence of 'austerity urbanism' in response to the financial crisis at the state and then local levels (Peck, 2012). So I am cautious about writing a history of the present, given how quickly politics may change, how difficult it is to see meaningful trends emerge, and how murky the consequences might be for austerity-driven attacks on communities deemed resilient (or not).

Looking back, the 2008 crisis was certainly one of neoliberalism itself, signalling that a certain crossroads had been reached:

> The global economic crisis that began in 2008 can be seen as the culmination of the neoliberal era. Indeed, its roots lie in the relaxation of government regulation and a blind faith in markets that encouraged unparalleled expansion of the financial sector and a vast increase in debt in many countries. (Hall & Lamont, 2013: 21)

But rather than seeing the death of neoliberalism or its reversal, Peck (2010: 109) saw neoliberalism entering a 'zombie phase', reacting robotically to the crises of its own making but staying firmly on the same narrow and forsaken path. In a follow-up piece (2012), he outlined some of these reactions that predictably focused on rolling back the (zombie neoliberal) state once more. Peck developed a concept of 'austerity urbanism' to frame the fiscal retrenchments post-2008, especially in the US. It was a manifestly urban programme, in Peck's words (2012: 629):

> It is ... a distinctively *urban* crisis in the sense that the cities have been hit especially hard by the housing slump and the parallel wave of mortgage foreclosures; in the sense that cities are disproportionately reliant on public services; and in the sense that they are 'home' to many of the preferred political targets of austerity programs – the 'undeserving'

poor, minorities and marginalised populations, public-sector unions and 'bureaucratised' infrastructures.

To Peck's list I can add left-behind (but now increasingly scrutinised) service hubs composed of voluntary-sector organisations, and so the 2008 financial crisis may be a harbinger of further mutation to uneven and emerging post-welfare geographies, challenging well-established patterns of resilience – perhaps even a tipping point, where resilience may yield a critical transition to deformation and entirely new trajectories. These new trajectories are likely to be negative, but could spur the voluntary sector into unlinking the shadow state and occupying the margins (Wolch, 1999). There is certainly pressure to do more with less, which elevates the voluntary sector to even greater importance as the welfare state shrinks yet again, perhaps this time for good (Reese, 2011; Milbourne, 2013). Simultaneously, the voluntary sector takes on an even greater role in plugging gaps that obscure – perhaps wrongly in the eyes of critical geographers – the full impacts, scale and scope of state denial. In Australia, the voluntary sector enjoyed strong support from the Labor Party, especially during Gillard's term of office (2010–13) with the creation of the Australian Charities and Not-for-profits Commission (ACNC), but which is now threatened with closure. But while these may be austere times, they are not as austere as the immediate post-war period was for the UK, for instance, and cannot be considered as purely post-welfare, harking back to Chapter One – important residues of the welfare state remain, more or less intact, in all three national contexts, and promise to remain in the near future.

In more detail, the US context post-2008 is perhaps the most dire, although I am less convinced of a fundamental break than Peck (2012); rather, I see it more as a deepening of austerity urbanism that emerged from the 1980s and 1990s onwards, both federally and in California, particularly in the wake of Proposition 13. Indeed, this path to austerity has been well trodden since at least the Reagan years (1980–88) in places like Los Angeles County (DeVerteuil et al, 2002; DeVerteuil et al, 2003). Further, the debates at the federal and state levels in the early 2010s were familiar as well to those who had chronicled the 1996 PRWORA (DeVerteuil, 2001), swirling once again around the proper size of the federal welfare state and its responsibility to the individual (Staeheli, 2012), and manifesting themselves through large-scale cutbacks to an already residual welfare state under the spectre of widespread municipal bankruptcy (for example, Detroit in 2013). While less a focus than the high-profile fights over public-sector employee pay and pension plans, the 2008 financial crisis did serious harm to local and state budgets for social spending that ultimately trickled down to the voluntary sector, and California was no exception (Reese, 2011; Henriksen et al, 2012). California's fiscal crisis was particularly severe and led to significant cuts to an already frayed welfare system, particularly evident in the 2011 Budget, which attacked welfare to families with children, as well as direct children's assistance (Reese, 2011).

Post-2008 cutbacks in the UK were perhaps more unprecedented than those in the US, given a higher and stronger base of spending. Since the advent of the Coalition government in 2010, the scale, scope and raison d'être for the UK's relatively generous welfare state has been under the microscope, with sweeping cuts in place since 2011 that 'represent perhaps the most radical reshaping of the British welfare system since its introduction post-1945', a re-setting at least as fundamental as the 1996 PRWORA in the US (Hamnett, 2010a; Hamnett, 2014: 490). Of critical importance to surplus populations, voluntary-sector organisations and local welfare settlements were cuts to (1) clients on Housing Benefits, and (2) local councils and voluntary sector funding. For the former, and faced with dramatically rising costs, the Coalition government introduced from 2013 onwards overall caps on Housing Benefits, which involve a subsidy to pay for private rental accommodation in the absence of sufficient state-provided social housing. These caps will disproportionately affect London (given the much higher rents) and will be (and are already as of 2014) particularly consequential for Inner London boroughs such as Lambeth, Islington, Southwark, Tower Hamlets and, above all, Westminster. Data from 2010 (Hamnett, 2010b) indicated that Islington and Tower Hamlets were in the top five in the UK for Housing Benefits recipiency per 1,000 people, while Westminster was the local authority with the highest average weekly amount of Housing Benefit, and housed 23% of all London renters who stood to lose their Housing Benefits or see them capped. Data from 2011 showed that every Inner London borough had at least 22% of its households reliant on Housing Benefits, going up to 46% for Hackney (Hamnett, 2014). By 2014 there was already evidence of thousands of evictions in Inner London, with councils socially cleansing and expunging former tenants to locations as far away as the Midlands and Manchester. The displacement of tenants paralleled the no-service hub scenario: once pushed out, there is no return to the (gentrified) inner city. These cuts will be simultaneously compounded by the advent of the so-called Bedroom Tax, where tenants with under-occupied bedrooms in social housing would have their Housing Benefits penalised by 14% for one extra bedroom, and 25% for two or more (Slater, 2014a). The Bedroom Tax will undoubtedly produce more evictions alongside the Housing Benefits cap, again to the advantage of those seeking gentrifiable areas and properties.

The second important change was direct cuts to local councils and voluntary sector. MacInnes et al (2011: 88) outlined the early cutbacks in 2010 to local councils in London, part of an overall national withdrawal amounting to more than £2.1 billion, a 26% reduction. The greatest budget cuts (more than 5%) once again disproportionately affected Inner London boroughs, with Tower Hamlets, Islington and Southwark all cutting more than 8% of their budgets, which equalled at least £35 million each. The level of cuts is unprecedented, and may have potentially devastating impacts on a variety of groups. Clifford (2012) noted the special vulnerability of organisations that serve the most marginal surplus populations within the most deprived neighbourhoods – that they are most likely to depend on public funds, and therefore most likely to suffer drops in funding in the post-2010 period. This will undoubtedly bring pain to those heavily dependent on social housing in poorer boroughs, such as Bangladeshi people in Tower Hamlets. Milbourne (2013) outlined the various cuts to voluntary-sector funding in 2011 and 2012 in the UK, representing a dramatic shift away from robust and upward-trending state funding since the 1990s and towards a looser system of unfunded (yet potentially greater) responsibilities, despite the rhetoric of the 'Big Society'. The estimated shortfall in statutory funding for the voluntary sector between 2010 and 2012 was £3.3 billion, 'which cannot realistically be recouped through philanthropic donations or social enterprise' (Milbourne, 2013: 225). And so, the greater emphasis on entrepreneurialism and localism could mean greater burdens on voluntary-sector organisations in already deprived areas with great (and probably increasing) need, raising the fear that the UK is rushing headlong to the American model of devolution, stringent differentiations between deserving and undeserving, and greater fiscal unevenness, but crucially lacking the widespread philanthropy found in the US. For all three global-city regions, those well-entrenched and predictably funded voluntary-sector organisations will remain resilient, but the marginal organisations less so.

Finally, the Australian context was, and remains, quite different from some of this potential convergence seen in the US/UK context. Fuelled by a resource boom, the expected cuts to the welfare state and voluntary sector were delayed during the Gillard government (2010–13), although Labour did implement more stringent controls on disability payments and workfare for jobseekers (the 'Work for the Dole' programme as of July 2014) in 2011 (Jabour, 2014; O'Connor, 2014). The proposed 2014 welfare reforms under the Abbott government not only continue these controls but deepen them as well, with suggestions of a UK-style universal credit that would cap overall benefits to below the average wage. While much of the current rhetoric speaks to the need to avoid European (and presumably) UK levels of public debt, the spectre of a leaner and meaner US model also hovers. Since the federal government maintains sole responsibility for individual transfer (welfare) payments, it can compel state governments to toe the line, even if they are the ones who ultimately deliver the programmes (Weller & O'Neill, 2014). For instance, the state government of New South Wales is shifting the homeless management model from crisis to Housing First – which will mean fewer emergency beds in Inner Sydney and a potential scattering of services.

Austerity and cutbacks in the post-2008 period will doubtless chip away at the relationship among surplus populations, service hubs and the voluntary sector, and represent a further unravelling of the post-welfare settlement. In contrast, certain aspects of the global city-region economy have received subsidies and have been doing remarkably well (for example, real estate and finance). After a short lull, both London and Los Angeles have seen gentrification return; for Sydney, gentrification did not go away at all, although residential building approvals in 2012–13 were double the pre-2008 peak (in 2006–07) and more than ten times the post-2008 trough (in 2009–10) (Australian Bureau of Statistics, 2013). Johnstone (2014) identified that the number of AU$1 million suburbs in Sydney had grown exponentially during the extended housing boom, from five in 1993 to 69 in 2003 to 163 in 2013, including all of Inner Sydney. In London, gentrification has continued apace since 2011, consolidating gains made in the 2000s (for example, Brixton and Hackney) and moving to super-gentrification in others (for example, Islington and Westminster), with extensive skyscraper new-build gentrification along the Thames. In Los Angeles, projects are returning to Downtown and Hollywood after a five-year lull, including significant foreign investment. For instance, the tallest building in the western US is currently being built in Downtown with substantial Korean investment. Residentially, there are at least a dozen new high-rise condo towers, and new high-rise projects are on the books in Hollywood.

But rebounding gentrification can no longer be divorced from the downsizing welfare state, the combination of which has actually *worsened* the impacts upon poor people and their ability to hold tight in inner-city locations. Nowhere is this more apparent than in Greater London. Malik (2013) noted that, between 2007 and 2011, Greater London's economy grew by 12.5%, while the rest of the UK stagnated, and housing prices increased at a far faster rate in Inner London when compared to the rest of the UK (Heywood, 2012). Following on from this point, an estimated one-third of London now comprises 'prime' areas where average prices are at least £700,000 (Walker, 2013). Robust as it is on its own (and indirectly supported by subsidies to City banks during the crisis), this resurgent gentrification is now *directly abetted* by the 2013 benefits reform, including the cap to Housing Benefits and the Bedroom Tax, evicting poor tenants and opening up reinvestment opportunities in once untouchable properties and protected neighbourhoods. In a Wacquantian-inspired turn of phrase, this *toxic kinship* of austerity-driven gentrification will further threaten the resilience of service hubs and their clientele in all the boroughs under study, but especially in areas like Tower Hamlets, where Bangladeshi people in particular are heavily reliant on exactly the benefits being cut. As Hamnett (2014: 500) remarked, 'the impact of the Housing Benefit cap will mean that low-income groups are unable to live in private renting in much of inner London'. This might well signal an irreversible spatial gap opening up between inner-city service hub and clientele, especially in high-priced boroughs such Westminster, which in turn might restructure the client/voluntary sector spatial relationship and push London further along towards the inverted Parisian model. The recent shifts also suggested that fourth-wave gentrification, buttressed by a *national* policy shift to benefit gentrifier households, is embedding itself in the UK (Lees et al, 2008).

The last word will be on encouraging urban social geographers, social planners and researchers of the voluntary sector to better understand the future of service hubs in the uneven and restructuring post-welfare inner city. There are issues of what to study, and how to study them, and when and where to study them. There are immediate needs to understand the full implications of this new round of roll-back neoliberalism and welfare 'reform' upon service hubs and their clientele, but also the longer-term impacts of an increasingly 'weightless' voluntary-sector model of delivery that promises more personalised and scattered provision (for example, Power, 2013). There are issues of perhaps how to rebalance voluntary-sector geographies in favour of suburbanising poverty in line with a Parisian model, at least for those cities that are rapidly and fully gentrifying – the suburbs as frontier space of service hub geographies, of geographies of help and the voluntary sector. Conversely, there is also a present need to roll out the concept of 'critical resilience of the residuals', and the notion of commons, to other successful and not-so-successful 'holdouts' in the gentrifying city, which returns us to consider both the long-term 'whether' or resilience (as threatened by austerity urbanism) alongside the more immediate 'how' that has consumed the majority of this book.

Perhaps more radically, we should begin to approach resilience as a *global strategy* in all of its obscure and mundane details, in response to the view that displacement and gentrification have themselves become firmly planetary in scale and scope (Smith, 2002). As such, we ought to extend resilience to places where the public city (and Keynesianism) never existed, such as the Global South and Asian cities. This can widen our purview, including not just places in the Global North such as Christiania in Copenhagen, the Downtown Eastside in Vancouver, San Francisco's Tenderloin and Kensington Market in Toronto, but further afield to Dharavi in Mumbai, Jardim Edith favela in São Paulo (among many others in Brazilian cities), Kamagasaki in Osaka and San'ya in Tokyo, to name just a few. In a world of cookie-cutter regeneration and serially reproduced urban landscapes, it is essential to focus on the resilience of these 'borrowed places' rather than attend to their seemingly inevitable displacement. Equally though, we ought to perform post-mortems on the spectacular failures of long-gone places, such as Kowloon's Walled City, New York's Bowery, neighbourhoods demolished in Beijing for the 2008 Olympics, District 9 in Cape Town, and other alternative and mundane sites of social reproduction, on why they did not prove resilient enough.

References

Aalbers, M. (2010) 'The revanchist renewal of yesterday's City of Tomorrow', *Antipode*, 43(5): 1696–1724.

Abu-Lughod, J. (2007) 'The challenge of comparative case studies', *City*, 11(3): 399–404.

Adger, W. (2000) 'Social and ecological resilience: Are they related?', *Progress in Human Geography*, 24(2): 347–64.

Alexander, C. (2011) '*Making Bengali Brick Lane: claiming and contesting space in East London*', *British Journal of Sociology*, 62(2): 201–20.

Allen, J. and Turner, E. (1997) *The ethnic quilt*, Northridge, CA: California State University at Northridge.

Amin, A., Cameron, A. and Hudson, R. (2002) *Placing the social economy*, London: Routledge.

Ancien, D. (2011) 'Global city theory and the new urban politics twenty years on: the case for a geohistorical materialist approach to the (new) urban politics of global cities', *Urban Studies, 48(12):* 2473–93.

Aplin, G. (2000) 'From colonial village to world metropolis', in J. Connell (ed) *Sydney: The emergence of a world city*, Melbourne: Oxford University Press, pp 56–75.

Arvidson, M. and Lyon, F. (2014) 'Social impact measurement and non-profit organisations: Compliance, resistance and promotion', *Voluntas*, 25(4): 869–86.

Atkinson, R. (2000) 'Measuring displacement and gentrification in Greater London', *Urban Studies*, 37(1): 149–65.

Atkinson, R. (2003) 'Introduction: Misunderstood saviour or vengeful wrecker? The many meanings and problems of gentrification', *Urban Studies*, 40(12): 2343–50.

Atkinson, R. (2011) *Gentrification and displacement: The household impacts of neighborhood change*, Melbourne: Australian Housing and Urban Research Institute.

Atkinson, R. and Bridge, G. (2005) *Gentrification in a global context: The new urban colonialism*, London: Routledge.

Australian Bureau of Statistics (2001) *2001 census.* Canberra: ABS.

Australian Bureau of Statistics (2006) *2006 census.* Canberra: ABS.

Australian Bureau of Statistics (2011) *2011 census.* Canberra: ABS.

Australian Charities and Not-for-profits Commission (2013) www.acnc.gov.au.

Australian Tax Office (2013) www.ato.gov.au/Non-profit/.

Back, L., Keith, M., Khan, A., Shukra, K. and Solomos, J. (2009) 'Islam and the new political landscape: Faith communities, political participation, and social change', *Theory, Culture and Society*, 26: 1–23.

Baker, T. (forthcoming) 'Housing First and the changing terrain of homeless governance', *Compass Geography*.

Baker, T. & Ruming, K. (forthcoming) 'Making "Global Sydney": Spatial imaginaries, worlding and strategic plans', *International Journal of Urban and Regional Research*.

Banham, R. (1971) *The architecture of four ecologies*, New York: Penguin.

Barnes, L. and Hall, P. (2013) 'Neoliberalism and social resilience in the developed democracies', in P. Hall and M. Lamont (eds) *Social resilience in the neoliberal era*, Cambridge, UK: Cambridge University Press, pp 209–38.

Barnett, C. (2005) 'The consolations of "neoliberalism"', *Geoforum*, 36: 7–12.

Barney, P. (2007) *A crisp, new $20 bill/a nickel taken: 'revitalization', gentrification and displacement in Los Angeles' Skid Row*. Master's thesis, Occidental College, Los Angeles, CA.

Baum, S. (1997) 'Sydney, Australia: A global city? Testing the social polarization thesis', *Urban Studies*, 34: 1881–901.

Beaverstock, J., Hubbard, P. and Short, J. (2004) 'Getting away with it? Exposing the geographies of the super-rich', *Geoforum*, 35(4): 401–7.

Beaverstock, J., Taylor, P. and Smith, R. (1999) 'A roster of world cities', *Cities*, 16: 445–58.

Benton-Short, L., Price, M. and Friedman, S. (2005) 'Globalization from below: The ranking of global immigrant cities', *International Journal of Urban and Regional Research*, 29(4): 945–59.

Betancur, J. (2002) 'The politics of gentrification: The case of West Town in Chicago', *Urban Affairs Review*, 37: 780–814.

Blasi, G. and the UCLA School of Law Fact Investigation Clinic (2007) 'Policing our way out of homelessness? The first year of the safer cities initiative on Skid Row'. Unpublished manuscript, 24 September.

Blomley, N. (2003) 'Law, property, and the geography of violence: The frontier, the survey, and the grid', *Annals of the Association of American Geographers*, 93(1): 121–41.

Bode, I. (2006) 'Disorganized welfare mixes: voluntary agencies and new governance regimes in Western Europe', *Journal of European Social Policy*, 16: 346–59.

Bollens, S. (2009) 'Comparative research on urban political conflict: Policy amidst polarization', *The Open Urban Studies Journal*, 2: 1–17.

Bouchard, G. (2013) 'Neoliberalism in Québec: The response of a small nation under pressure', in P. Hall and M. Lamont (eds) *Social resilience in the neoliberal era*, Cambridge, UK: Cambridge University Press, pp 267–92.

Boudreau, J.A., Hamel, P., Jouve, B. and Keil, R. (2007) 'New state spaces in Canada: Metropolitanization in Montreal and Toronto compared', *Urban Geography*, 28(1): 30–53.

Bounds, M. and Morris, A. (2006) 'Second wave gentrification in inner-city Sydney', *Cities*, 23(2): 99–108.

Brandsen, T., van de Donk, W. and Putters, K. (2005) 'Griffins of chameleons? Hybridity as a permanent and inevitable characteristic of the third sector', *International Journal of Public Administration*, 28: 749–65.

Brenner, N. and Keil, R. (2006) *The global city reader*, London: Routledge.

Brenner, N. and Theodore, N. (2002) 'Cities and geographies of "Actually Existing Neoliberalism"', in N. Brenner and N. Theodore (eds) *Spaces of neoliberalism*, London: Blackwell, pp 2–32.

Brenner, N., Marcuse, P. & Mayer, M. (2009) 'Cities for people, not for profit', *City*, 13(2–3): 176–84.

Bristow, G. and Healy, A. (2014) 'Regional resilience: An agency perspective,' *Regional Studies*, 48(5): 923–35.

Brown, K. (2014) 'Global environmental change: A social turn for resilience', *Progress in Human Geography*, 38(1): 107–17.

Brown, M. (1997) *RePlacing citizenship: AIDS activism and radical democracy*. New York: Guilford Press.

Bunge, W. (1971) *Fitzgerald: Geography of a revolution*, Cambridge, MA: Schenkman Publishing Company.

Burawoy, M. et al (1991) *Ethnography unbound: Power and resistance in the modern metropolis*, Berkeley and Los Angeles, CA: University of California Press.

Burrows, R., Atkinson, R., Webber, R., Butler, T., Knowles, C. and Savage, M. (2013) 'Mapping the "alpha territory": The geodemographics of the "super rich" in London'. Presented at the Los Angeles Association of American Geographers annual conference.

Butler, T. (2003) 'Living in the bubble: Gentrification and its "others" in North London', *Urban Studies*, 40(12): 2469–86.

Butler, T. (2007) 'For gentrification?' *Environment and Planning A*, 39: 162–81.

Butler, T. and Robson, G. (2001) 'Social capital, gentrification and neighbourhood change in London: A comparison of three South London neighbourhoods', *Urban Studies*, 38(12): 2145–62.

Butler, T. and Robson, G. (2003a) *London calling: The middle classes and the re-making of Inner London*, Oxford: Oxford University Press.

Butler, T. and Robson, G. (2003b) 'Plotting the middle-classes: gentrification and circuits of education in London', *Housing Studies*, 18: 5–28.

Butler, T. and Lees, L. (2006) 'Super-gentrification in Barnsbury, London: globalization and gentrifying global elites at the neighbourhood level', *Transactions of the Institute of British Geographers*, 31: 222–39.

Butler, T., Hamnett, C. and Ramsden, M. (2008) 'Inward and upward: marking out social class change in London, 1981–2001', *Urban Studies*, 45: 67–88.

Butler, W. (2011) Westminster council U-turn saves soup runs for homeless people. *Guardian*, 2 November.

Byrne, J. and Houston, D. (2005) 'Ghosts in the city: Multicultural redevelopment and urban memory in East Perth', in D. Cryle and J. Hillier (eds) *Consent and consensus: Politics, media and governance in twentieth century Australia*, Perth: Common Cultures Series, pp 319–49.

Cameron, A. (2007) 'Geographies of welfare and exclusion: Reconstituting the "public"', *Progress in Human Geography*, 31: 519–26.

Campkin, B. (2013) *Remaking London: Decline and regeneration in urban culture*, London: Tauris Press.

Carpenter, J. and Lees, L. (1995) 'Gentrification in New York, London and Paris: An international comparison', *International Journal of Urban and Regional Research*, 19: 286–303.

Castells, M. (1977) *The urban question: A Marxist approach* (Alan Sheridan, trans.), London: Edward Arnold.

Castells, M. (1983) *The city and the grassroots*, Berkeley and Los Angeles, CA: University of California Press.

Castles, F. (1996) 'Needs-based strategies of social protection in Australia and New Zealand', in G. Esping-Andersen (ed) *Welfare states in transition: National adaptations in global economies*, London: Sage, pp 88–115.

Castree, N. (2006) 'From neoliberalism to neoliberalisation: Consolations, confusions, and necessary illusions', *Environment and Planning A*, 38(1): 1–6.

Castree, N., Chatterton, P., Heynen, N., Larner, W. and Wright, M. (2010) 'Introduction: The point is to change it', *Antipode*, 41(s1): 1–9.

Caulfield, J. (1994) *City form and everyday life. Toronto's gentrification and critical social practice*, Toronto: University of Toronto Press.

Charity Commission (2014) *Recent charity register statistics*, London: UK Charity Commission.

Chatterton, P. (2010) 'Seeking the urban common: Furthering the debate on spatial justice', *City*, **14:** 625–8.

City of Sydney (2006) Community profiles website, www. cityofsydney.nsw.gov.au/AboutSydney/CityResearch/CityofSydney/ CommunityProfile.asp.

City of Sydney (2008) *Sydney 2030: Green/global/connected*. Sydney: City of Sydney.

City of Sydney (2011) Community directory, www.cityofsydney.nsw. gov.au/.

Clarke, N. (2012) 'Urban policy mobility, anti-politics, and histories of the transnational municipal movement', *Progress in Human Geography*, 31(1): 25–43.

Clerval, A. (2013) *Paris sans le people: La gentrification de la capitale* (Paris without the people: The gentrification of the capital). Paris: Découverte.

Clifford, D. (2012) 'Voluntary sector organisations working at the neighbourhood level in England: Patterns by local area deprivation', *Environment and Planning A*, 44(5): 1148–64.

Cloke, P., May, J. and Johnsen, S. (2010) *Swept up lives? Re-envisioning the homeless city*, London: Wiley RGS-IBG Series.

Cole, M. and Nightingale, A. (2011) 'Resilience thinking meets social theory: Situating change in socio-ecological systems research', *Progress in Human Geography*, 36(4): 475–489.

Community Redevelopment Agency (CRA) Los Angeles (1991) *Hollywood social services plan*. Los Angeles: CRA.

Community Redevelopment Agency (CRA) Los Angeles (2011) www. crala.org/internet-site/.

Connell, J. (ed) (2000) *Sydney: The emergence of a world city*. Melbourne: Oxford University Press.

Connell, J. and Thom, B. (2000) 'Beyond 2000: The post-Olympic city', in J. Connell (ed) *Sydney: The emergence of a world city*, Melbourne: Oxford University Press, pp 319–43.

Conradson, D. (2003) Spaces of care in the city: The place of a community drop-in centre', *Social and Cultural Geography*, 4: 507–25.

Conradson, D. (2006) 'Values, practices and strategic divestment: Christian social service organisations in New Zealand', in C. Milligan and D. Conradson (eds) *Landscapes of voluntarism: New spaces of health, welfare and governance,* Bristol: Policy Press, pp 153–72.

Conradson, D. (2008) 'Expressions of charity and action towards justice: Faith-based welfare in urban New Zealand', *Urban Studies*, 45(10): 2117–41.

Cordero-Guzman, H. (2005) 'Community-based organizations and migration in New York City', *Journal of Ethnic and Migration Studies*, 31: 889–909.

Corry, O. (2010) 'Defining and theorizing the third sector', in R. Taylor (ed) *Third sector research*, London: Springer, pp 11–20.

Cresswell, T. (1996) *In place/out of place: Geography, ideology and transgression*, Minneapolis, MN: University of Minnesota Press.

Daly, M. and Pritchard, B. (2000) 'Sydney: Australia's financial and corporate capital', in J. Connell (ed) *Sydney: The emergence of a world city*, Melbourne: Oxford University Press, pp 167–88.

Davidson, M. (2008) 'Spoiled mixture: where does state-led "positive" gentrification end?', *Urban Studies*, 45: 2385–405.

Davidson, M. and Lees, L. (2005) 'New-build "gentrification" and London's riverside renaissance', *Environment and Planning A*, 37: 1165–90.

Davidson, M. and Lees, L. (2011) 'New-build gentrification: Its histories, trajectories, and critical geographies', *Population, Space and Place*, 16: 395–411.

Davidson, M. and Wyly, E. (2012) 'Class-ifying London: Questioning social division and space claims in the post-industrial metropolis', *City*, 16(4): 395–421.

Davis, M. (1990) *City of quartz*, New York: Verso.

Davis, M. (1998) *Ecology of fear*, New York: Vintage Press.

Davis, M. (2001) *Magical urbanism: Latinos reinvent the US big city*, New York: Verso.

Dear, M. (1980) 'The public city', in W. Clark and G. Moore (eds) *Residential mobility and public policy*, Beverly Hills, CA: Sage Publications, pp 219–41.

Dear, M. and Wolch, J. (1986) *The service hub concept: Exchanging landscapes of despair for islands of hope. Los Angeles Homelessness Project*, Los Angeles, CA: University of Southern California, Department of Geography.

Dear, M. and Wolch, J. (1987) *Landscapes of despair*, Princeton, NJ: Princeton University Press.

Dear, M., Wolch, J. and Wilton, R. (1994) 'The service hub concept in human services planning', *Progress in Planning*, 42: 173–271.

Deener, A. (2012) *Venice: A contested bohemia in Los Angeles*, Chicago, IL: University of Chicago Press.

DeFilippis, J. (2004) *Unmaking Goliath: Community control in the face of global capital*, London: Routledge.

DeFilippis, J. and North, P. (2004) 'The emancipatory community? Place, politics and collective action in cities', in L. Lees (ed) *The emancipatory city?* Thousand Oaks, CA: Sage Publications, pp 72–88.

Dench, G., Gavron, K. and Young, M. (2006) *The new East End*, London: Profile Books.

DeVerteuil, G. (2000) 'Reconsidering the legacy of urban public facility location theory in human geography', *Progress in Human Geography*, 24(1): 47–69.

DeVerteuil, G. (2001) 'Welfare reform and welfare neighborhoods: Institutional and individual perspectives'. Unpublished PhD thesis, Department of Geography, University of Southern California.

DeVerteuil, G. (2003a) 'Welfare reform, institutional practices and service delivery settings', *Urban Geography*, 24(6): 529–50.

DeVerteuil, G. (2003b) 'Homeless mobility, institutional settings, and the new poverty management', *Environment and Planning A*, 35(2): 361–79.

DeVerteuil, G. (2005) 'Welfare neighborhoods: Anatomy of a concept', *Journal of Poverty*, 9: 23–41.

DeVerteuil, G. (2006) 'The local state and homeless shelters: Beyond revanchism?', *Cities*, 23: 109–20.

DeVerteuil, G. (2011a) 'Evidence of gentrification-induced displacement among social services in London and Los Angeles', *Urban Studies*, 48: 1563–80.

DeVerteuil, G. (2011b) 'Survive but not thrive? Geographical strategies for avoiding absolute homelessness among immigrant communities', *Social and Cultural Geography*, 12(8): 929–45.

DeVerteuil, G. (2011c) 'From E1 to 90057: The immigrant-serving non-profit sector among London Bangladeshis and Los Angeles Central Americans', *Urban Geography*, 32(8): 1129–47.

DeVerteuil, G. (2012) 'Resisting gentrification-induced displacement: Advantages and disadvantages to "staying put" among non-profit social services in London and Los Angeles', *Area*, 44(2): 208–16.

DeVerteuil, G. (2013) 'Where has NIMBY gone in urban social geography?', *Social and Cultural Geography*, 14(6): 599–603.

DeVerteuil, G. (2014) 'Does the punitive need the supportive? A sympathetic critique of current grammars of urban injustice', *Antipode*, 46(4): 874–93.

DeVerteuil, G. and Evans, J. (2009) 'Landscapes of despair', in T. Brown, S. McLafferty and G. Moon (eds) *The companion to health and medical geography*, Oxford: Blackwell, pp 278–300.

DeVerteuil, G. and Wilson, K. (2010) 'Reconciling indigenous need with the urban welfare state? Evidence of immigrant-serving non-profit sector services and spaces for Aboriginals in Winnipeg, Canada', *Geoforum*, 41: 498–507.

DeVerteuil, G. and Wilton, R. (2009) 'Spaces of abeyance, care and survival: The addiction treatment system as a site of "regulatory richness"', *Political Geography*, 28: 463–72.

DeVerteuil, G., Lee, W. and Wolch, J. (2002) 'New spaces for the local welfare state? The case of General Relief in Los Angeles County', *Social and Cultural Geography*, 3: 229–46.

DeVerteuil, G., May, J. and von Mahs, J. (2009a) 'Complexity not collapse: Recasting the geographies of homelessness in a "punitive" age', *Progress in Human Geography*, 33(5): 646–66.

DeVerteuil, G., Marr, M. and Snow, D. (2009b) 'Any space left? Homeless resistance by place-type in Los Angeles County', *Urban Geography*, 30(6): 633–51.

DeVerteuil, G., Sommer, H., Wolch, J. and Takahashi, L. (2003) 'The local welfare state in transition: Welfare reform in Los Angeles County', in D. Halle (ed) *New York and Los Angeles politics, society and culture: A comparative view*, Chicago, IL: University of Chicago Press, pp 269–88.

DeVerteuil, G., Hinds, A., Lix, L., Walker, J., Robinson, R. and Roos, L. (2007) 'Mental health and the city: Intra-urban mobility among individuals with schizophrenia', *Health and Place*, 13(2): 310–23.

Duneier, M. (1999) *Sidewalk*, New York: Farrar, Straus, and Giroux.

Eakin, H. and Luers, A. (2006) 'Assessing the vulnerability of social-environmental systems', *Annual Review of Environmental Resources*, 31: 365–94.

Elwood, S. (2006) 'Beyond cooptation or resistance: Urban spatial politics, community organizations, and GIS-based spatial narratives', *Annals of the Association of American Geographers*, 96(2): 323–41.

Engels, B. (1999) 'Property ownership, tenure and displacement: In search of the process of gentrification', *Environment and Planning A*, 31: 1473–95.

Esping-Andersen, G. (1990) *The three worlds of welfare capitalism*, Cambridge, UK: Polity Press.

Esping-Andersen, G. (1996) 'After the golden age?', in G. Esping-Andersen (ed) *Welfare states in transition*, London: Sage Publications, pp 1–30.

Evans, J. (2011) 'Exploring the (bio)political dimensions of voluntarism and care in the city: The case of a "low barrier" emergency shelter', *Health and Place*, 17: 24–32.

Evans, L. (2014) 'The strange saga of the Cecil Hotel', *Downtown LA News*, 17 March.

Evans, P. and Sewell, W. (2013) 'The neoliberal era: ideology, policy, and social effects', in P. Hall and M. Lamont (eds) *Social resilience in the neoliberal era*, Cambridge, UK: Cambridge University Press, pp 35–68.

Fagan, R. (2000) 'Industrial change in the global city: Sydney's new spaces of production', in J. Connell (ed) *Sydney: The emergence of a world city*, Melbourne: Oxford University Press, pp 144–66.

Fainstein, S. (2010) *The just city*, Ithaca, NY: Cornell University Press.

Fairbanks, R. (2009) *How it works: Recovering citizens in post-welfare Philadelphia*, Chicago, IL: University of Chicago Press.

Flood, J. (2003) *The case of Sydney, Australia*. Understanding Slums: Case Studies for the Global Report 2003 (University College London).

Florida, R. (2002) *The rise of the creative class: And how it's transforming work, leisure, community and everyday life*, New York: Basic Books.

Folke, C. (2006) 'Resilience: The emergence of a perspective for social–ecological systems analyses', *Global Environmental Change*, 16: 253–67.

Forrest, J. and Dunn, K. (2007) 'Constructing racism in Sydney, Australia's largest EthniCity', *Urban Studies*, 44(4): 699–721.

Freeman, L. (2006) *There goes the 'hood: Views of gentrification from the ground up*, Philadelphia, PA: Temple University Press.

Friedmann, J. (1986) 'The world city hypothesis', *Development and Change*, 17: 69–83.

Fullilove, M. (2004) *Root shock: How tearing up city neighborhoods hurts America, and what we can do about it*, New York: One World/Ballantine Books.

Fyfe, N. (2005) 'Making space for "neo-communitarianism"? The third sector, state and civil society in the UK', *Antipode*, 37: 536–57.

Fyfe, N. and Milligan, C. (2003a) 'Space, citizenship and voluntarism: Critical reflections on the voluntary welfare sector in Glasgow', *Environment and Planning A*, 35: 2069–86.

Fyfe, N. and Milligan, C. (2003b) 'Out of the shadows: Exploring contemporary geographies of voluntarism', *Progress in Human Geography*, 27(4): 397–413.

Ghai, D. (1996) 'Foreword', in G. Esping-Andersen (ed) *Welfare states in transition*, London: Sage Publications, pp vi–viii.

Gibson-Graham, J.K. (2006) *A postcapitalist politics*, Minneapolis, MN: University of Minnesota Press.

Gilbert, M. (1998) '"Race", space, and power: the survival strategies of working poor women', *Annals of the Association of American Geographers*, 88: 595–621.

Gilbert, M. (2001) 'From the "walk for adequate welfare" to the "march for our lives": Welfare rights organizing in the 1960s and 1990s', *Urban Geography*, 22(5): 440–56.

Glaeser, E., Kahn, M. and Rappoport, J. (2000) *Why do the poor live in cities?* Cambridge, MA: National Bureau of Economic Research Working Paper.

Glass, R. (1964) 'Introduction: aspects of change', in R. Glass (ed) *London: Aspects of change*, London: MacKibbon and Kee, pp xiii–xlii.

Glynn, S. (2005) 'East End immigrants and the battle for housing', *Journal of Historical Geography*, 31: 528–45.

Glynn, S. (2010) 'Playing the ethnic card: Politics and segregation in London's East End', *Urban Studies*, 47: 991–1013.

Goetz, E. (1992) 'Land use and homeless policy in Los Angeles', *International Journal of Urban and Regional Research*, 16(4): 540–54.

Goldstein, A. (2011) *Collaborative resilience: Moving through crisis to opportunity*, Cambridge, MA: MIT Press.

Gorman-Murray, A. and Nash, C. (2014) 'Mobile places, relational spaces: Conceptualizing change in Sydney's LGBTQ neighborhoods', *Environment and Planning D*, 32: 622–41.

Gould, S.J. (1987) 'Institutionalism,' in V. Bognador (ed) *The Blackwell encyclopedia of political institutions*, Oxford: Blackwell Reference, pp 45–7.

Gowan, T. (2010) *Hobos, hustlers and back-sliders: Homeless in San Francisco*. Minneapolis, MN: University of Minnesota Press.

Hackworth, J. (2002) 'Post-recession gentrification in New York City', *Urban Affairs Review*, 37: 815–43.

Hackworth, J. (2007) *The neoliberal city*, Ithaca, NY: Cornell University Press.

Hall, N. and Taplin, R. (2007) 'Solar festivals and climate bills: Comparing NGO climate change campaigns in the UK and Australia', *Voluntas*, 18(4): 317–38.

Hall, P. and Lamont, M. (eds) (2013) *Social resilience in the neoliberal era*, Cambridge, UK: Cambridge University Press.

Hamnett, C. (2003) *Unequal city: London in the global arena*, London: Routledge.

Hamnett, C. (2009) 'Spatial divisions of welfare: The geography of welfare benefit expenditures and of housing benefit in Britain', *Regional Studies*, 43(8): 1015–33.

Hamnett, C. (2010) 'Moving the poor out of central London? The implications of the coalition government 2010 cuts to Housing Benefits', *Environment and Planning A*, 42(12): 2809–19.

Hamnett, C. (2014) 'Shrinking the welfare state: The structure, geography and impact of British government benefits cuts', *Transactions of the Institute of British Geographers*, 39(4): 490–503.

Hamnett, C. and Whitelegg, D. (2007) 'Loft conversion and gentrification in London', *Environment and Planning A*, 39: 106–24.

Hardt, M. and Negri, A. (2009) *Commonwealth*, Cambridge, MA: Harvard University Press.

Harris, A. (2008) 'From London to Mumbai and back again: Gentrification and public policy in comparative perspective', *Urban Studies*, 45: 2407–28.

Hartman, C. (1984) 'The right to stay put', in C. Geisler and F. Popper (eds) *Land reform, American style*, Totowa, NJ: Rowman and Allanheld, pp 302–18.

Harvey, D. (1989) 'From managerialism to entrepreneurialism: The transformation in urban governance in late capitalism', *Geografiska Annaler. Series B, Human Geography*, 71: 3–17.

Harvey, D. (2012) *Rebel cities*, New York: Verso.

Hasson, S. and Ley, D. (1997) 'Neighborhood organizations, the welfare state, and citizenship rights', *Urban Affairs Review*, 33: 28–58.

Henriksen, L., Smith, L.R. and Zimmer, A. (2012) 'At the eve of convergence? Transformations of social service provision in Denmark, Germany and the United States', *Voluntas*, 23(2): 458–501.

Hero, R. and Preuhs, R. (2007) 'Immigration and the evolving American welfare state', *American Journal of Political Science*, 51: 498–517.

Heynen, N. (2006) '"But it's alright, Ma, it's life, and life only": Radicalism as survival', *Antipode*, 38: 916–29.

Heynen, N. (2010) 'Cooking up non-violent civil disobedient direct action for the hungry: Food Not Bombs and the resurgence of radical democracy', *Urban Studies*, 47(6): 1225–40.

Heywood, A. (2012) *London for Sale? An assessment of the private housing market in London and the impact of growing overseas investment*, London: Smith Institute.

Hill, D. (2014) 'Has Southwark found the right answer for London's famous Aylesbury estate?', *Guardian*, 2 February.

Hodkinson, S. (2011) 'Housing regeneration and the private finance initiative in England: Unstitching the neoliberal urban straitjacket', *Antipode*, 43(2): 358–83.

Hodkinson, S. (2012) 'The new urban enclosures', *City*, 16(5): 500–18.

Holling, C. (1973) 'Resilience and stability of ecological systems', *Annual Review of Ecological Systems*, 4: 1–23.

Hopkins, L. (2010) *Mapping the third sector: A context for social leadership*, report prepared for Clore Social Leadership Programme, London: The Work Foundation.

Hopper, K. and Baumohl, J. (1994) 'Held in abeyance: Rethinking homelessness and advocacy', *American Behavioral Scientist*, 37: 522–52.

Horvath, R. (2004) 'The particularity of global places: Placemaking practices in Los Angeles and Sydney', *Urban Geography*, 25: 92–119.

Hubbard, P., Matthews, R., Scoular, J. and Agustin, L. (2008) 'Away from prying eyes? The urban geographies of "adult entertainment"', *Progress in Human Geography*, 32(3): 363–81.

Hubbard, P., Boydell, S., Crofts, P., Prior, J. and Searle, G. (2013) 'Noxious neighbours? Interrogating the impacts of sex premises in residential areas', *Environment and Planning A*, 45(1): 126–41.

Hugo, G. (2008) 'The globalization of an established immigrant gateway', in M. Price and L. Benton-Short (eds) *Migrants to the metropolis: The rise of immigrant gateway cities*, Syracuse, NY: Syracuse University Press, pp 68–96.

Hutton, T. (2010) *The new economy of the inner city*, London: Routledge.

Institute for the Study of Homeless and Poverty (2004) *Homelessness in Los Angeles*. Los Angeles, CA: Weingart Center.

Isay, D. and Abramson, S. (2000) *Flophouse: Life on the Bowery*, New York: Random House.

Iveson, K. (2014) 'Building a city for "the people": The politics of alliance-building in the Sydney Green Ban Movement', *Antipode*, 46(4): 992–1013.

Jabour, B. (2014) 'Australia's "unsustainable" welfare system to be overhauled, says minister', *Guardian*, 20 January.

Jacobs, J. (2012) 'Urban geographies I: Still thinking cities relationally', *Progress in Human Geography*, 36(3): 412–22.

Jarvis, H., Pratt, A. and Cheng-Chong, W. (2001) *The secret life of cities: The social reproduction of everyday life,* Harlow: Prentice Hall.

Jeffrey, A., McFarlane, C. and Vasudevan, A. (2012) 'Rethinking enclosure: Space, subjectivity and the commons', *Antipode*, 44(4): 1247–67.

Jenson, J. & Levi, R. (2013) 'Narratives and regimes of social and human rights: The Jack Pines of the neoliberal era', in P.A. Hall and M. Lamont (eds) *Social resilience in the neoliberal era*, Cambridge, UK: Cambridge University Press, pp 69–98.

Jessop, B. (2002) 'Liberalism, neoliberalism, and urban governance', in N. Brenner and N. Theodore (eds) *Spaces of neoliberalism*, Oxford, UK: Blackwell Press, pp 105–25.

Johnsen, S. and Fitzpatrick, S. (2010) 'Revanchist sanitisation or coercive care? The use of enforcement to combat begging, street drinking and rough sleeping in England', *Urban Studies*, 47(8): 1703–23.

Johnsen, S., Cloke, P. and May, J. (2005a) 'Day centres for homeless people: Spaces of care or fear?', *Social and Cultural Geography*, 6: 787–811.

Johnsen, S., Cloke, P. and May, J. (2005b) 'Transitory spaces of care: Serving homeless people on the street', *Health and Place*, 11: 323–36.

Johnstone, T. (2014) 'Welcome to Sydney's new multi-million dollar suburbs', http://news.domain.com.au/domain/real-estate-news/welcome-to-sydneys-new-milliondollar-suburbs-20140124–31e9a.html.

Jonas, A. (2012) 'Region and place: Regionalism in question', *Progress in Human Geography*, 36(2): 263–72.

Jonas, A. and Ward, K. (2007) 'Introduction to a debate on city-regions: New geographies of governance, democracy and social reproduction', *International Journal of Urban and Regional Research*, 31(1): 169–78.

Katz, C. (2001) 'Vagabond capitalism and the necessity of social reproduction', *Antipode* 33(4): 709–28

Katz, C. (2004) *Growing up global: Economic restructuring and children's everyday lives*, Minneapolis, MN: University of Minnesota Press.

Kearney Consultants (2014) Global cities index, www.atkearney.com/research-studies/global-cities-index.

Keil, R. (1998) *Los Angeles*, London: Wiley.

Keith, M. (2005) 'Racialization and the public spaces of the multicultural city', in K. Murji and J. Solomos (eds) *Racialization*, Oxford: Oxford University Press, pp 249–70.

Kendall, J. and Knapp, M. (1995) 'A loose and baggy monster: Boundaries, definitions and typologies', in J. Davis Smith and R. Hedley (eds) *Introduction to the voluntary sector*, London: Routledge, pp 65–94.

Kenney, M. (2001) *Mapping gay LA*, Philadelphia, PA: Temple University Press.

Kissoon, P. (2010) 'From persecution to destitution: A snapshot of asylum seekers' housing and settlement experiences in Canada and the United Kingdom', *Journal of Immigrant and Refugee Studies*, 8: 144–77.

Klein, R., Nicholls, R. and Thomalla, F. (2003) 'Resilience to natural hazards: How useful is this concept?', *Environmental Hazards*, 5: 35–45.

Klinenberg, E. (2002) *Heat wave: A social autopsy of disaster in Chicago*, Chicago, IL: University of Chicago Press.

Kneebone, E. and Berube, A. (2013) *Confronting suburban poverty in America*, Washington, DC: Brookings Institute.

Knopp, L. (1990) 'Some theoretical implications of gay involvement in an urban land market', *Political Geography Quarterly*, 9(4): 337–52.

Koopmans, R. (2010) 'Trade-offs between equality and difference: Immigrant integration, multiculturalism, and the welfare state in cross-national perspective', *Journal of Ethnic and Migration Studies*, 36: 1–26.

Lalich, W. (2006) 'Developing voluntary community spaces and ethnicity in Sydney, Australia', in C. Milligan and D. Conradson (eds) *Landscapes of voluntarism*, Bristol, UK: Policy Press, pp 209–29.

Land Registry (2008) *UK land registry 1998–2008*, London: Crown Corporation, www.landregistry.gov.uk/.

Land Registry (2013) *UK land registry 1998–2013*, London: Crown Corporation, www.landregistry.gov.uk/.

Landolt, P. (2008) 'The transnational geographies of immigrant politics', *Sociological Quarterly*, 49: 53–77.

Lane, L. and Power, A. (2009) *Soup runs in central London*, London: Centre for Analysis of Social Exclusion, London School of Economics and Political Science.

Larner, W. (2003) 'Neoliberalism?', *Environment and Planning D: Society and Space*, 21(5): 309–12.

Laurenson, P. and Collins, D. (2007) 'Beyond punitive regulation? New Zealand local governments' responses to homelessness', *Antipode*, 39: 649–67.

Law, R. (2001) '"Not in my city": Local government and homelessness in Los Angeles Metropolitan Region', *Environment and Planning C: Government and Policy*, 19: 791–815.

Lawson, V. (2007) 'Geographies of care and responsibility', *Annals of the Association of American Geographers*, 97(1): 1–11.

Lawson, V. (2009) 'Instead of radical geography, how about caring geography?', *Antipode*, 41: 210–13.

Lee, W. (1994) 'Restructuring the local welfare state: a case study of Los Angeles, PhD dissertation', School of Urban and Regional Planning, University of Southern California.

Lees, L. (2004) 'The emancipatory city: Urban (re)visions', in L. Lees (ed) *The emancipatory city?* Thousand Oaks, CA: Sage, pp 3–20.

Lees, L. (2014) 'The urban injustice of New Labour's 'New Urban Renewal': The case of the Aylesbury Estate in London', *Antipode*, 46(4): 921–47.

Lees, L., Slater, T. and Wyly, E. (2008) *Gentrification*, London: Routledge.

Leiter, J. (2008) 'Non-profit isomorphism: An Australian–US comparison', *Voluntas*, 19: 67–91.

Ley, D. (1986) 'Alternative explanations for inner-city gentrification: A Canadian assessment', *Annals of the Association of American Geographers*, 76(4): 521–35.

Ley, D. (2004) 'Transnational spaces and everyday lives', *Transactions of the Institute of British Geographers*, 29(2): 151–64.

Ley, D. and Dobson, C. (2008) 'Are there limits to gentrification? The context of impeded gentrification in Vancouver', *Urban Studies*, 45(12): 2471–98.

Li, B. (2013) *Chinatowns then and now*, New York, NY: Asian American Legal Defense and Education Fund.

Li, T.M. (2010) 'To make live or let die? Rural dispossession and the protection of surplus populations', *Antipode*, 41: 66–93.

Lo, L. (2008) 'DiverCity Toronto: Canada's Premier Gateway City', in M. Price and L. Benton-Short (eds) *Migrants to the metropolis: The rise of immigrant gateway cities*, Syracuse, NY: Syracuse University Press, pp 97–127.

London Tenants Federation, Lees, L., Just Space & Southwark Notes Archive Group (2014) *Staying put: An anti-gentrification handbook for council estates in London.* London: Calverts Co-operative.

Longstreth, R. (1997) *City center to regional mall: Architecture, the automobile, and retailing in Los Angeles, 1920–1950*, Cambridge, MA: MIT Press.

Luce, E. (2013) 'The future of the American city', *Financial Times*, 14–21 June.

MacInnes, T., Parekh, A. and Kenway, P. (2011) *London poverty profile*, London: New Policy Institute.

MacKie, P., Bromley, R. and Brown, A. (2014) 'Informal traders and the battlegrounds of revanchism in Cusco, Peru', *International Journal of Urban and Regional Research*, 38(5): 1884–903.

MacKinnon, D. and Derickson, K. (2013) 'From resilience to resourcefulness: A critique of resilience policy and activism', *Progress in Human Geography*, 37(2): **253–70.**

MacLeod, G. (2011) 'Urban politics reconsidered: Growth machine to post-democratic city?', *Urban Studies*, 48: 2629–60.

Mair, A. (1986) 'The homeless and the post-industrial city', *Political Geography Quarterly*, 5: 351–68.

Marcuse, P. (1985) 'Gentrification, abandonment, and displacement: connections, causes, and policy responses in New York City', *Washington University Journal of Urban and Contemporary Law*, 28: 195–240.

Marcuse, P. (1997) 'The enclave, the citadel, and the ghetto: what has changed in the post-Fordist US city', *Urban Affairs Review*, 33: 228–64.

Marquand, D. (2004) *Decline of the public*, Cambridge, UK: Polity Press.

Marr, M. (2012) 'Pathways out of homelessness in Los Angeles and Tokyo: The multilevel contexts of limited mobility amid urban marginality', *International Journal of Urban and Regional Research*, 36(5): 980–1006.

Marr, M., DeVerteuil, G. and Snow, D. (2009) 'Towards a contextual approach to the place–homeless survival nexus: An exploratory case study in Los Angeles', *Cities*, 26: 307–17.

Martin, N. (2010) 'The crisis of social reproduction among migrant workers: Interrogating the role of migrant civil society', *Antipode*, 42(1): 127–51.

Martin, N. (2011) 'Toward a new countermovement: A framework for interpreting the contradictory interventions of migrant civil society organizations in urban labor markets', *Environment and Planning A*, 43(12): 2934–52.

Martin, R. (2012) 'Regional economic resilience, hysteresis and recessionary shocks', *Journal of Economic Geography*, 12(1): 1–32.

Martin, D. (2013) 'Place frames: Analysing practice and production of place in contentious politics', in W. Nicholls and J. Beaumont (eds) *Spaces of contention: Spatialities of social movements*, Aldershot, UK: Ashgate, pp 85–100.

Martin, D. and Pierce, J. (2013) 'Reconceptualizing resistance: Residuals of the state and democratic radical pluralism', *Antipode*, 45: 61–79.

Massey, D. (2007) *World city*, Cambridge, UK: Polity Press.

Massey, D. (2011) 'A counterhegemonic relationality of place', in E. McCann and K. Ward (eds) *Mobile urbanism*, Minneapolis, MN: University of Minnesota Press, pp 1–14.

Masuda, J. and Crabtree, M. (2010) 'Environmental justice in the therapeutic inner city', *Health and Place*, 16: 656–65.

Mavrommatis, G. (2006) 'The new "creative" Brick Lane: A narrative study of local multicultural encounters', *Ethnicities*, 6(4): 498–517.

May, J. (1996) 'Globalization and the politics of place: Place and identity in an inner London neighbourhood', *Transactions of the Institute of British Geographers*, 21: 194–215.

May, J. and Cloke, P. (2014) 'Modes of attentiveness: Reading for difference in geographies of homelessness', *Antipode*, 46(4): 894–920.

May J., Cloke, P. and Johnsen, S. (2006) 'Shelter at the margins: New Labour and the changing state of emergency accommodation for single homeless people in Britain', *Policy and Politics*, 34(4): 711–29.

May, J., Wills, J., Datta, K., Evans, Y., Herbert, J. and McIlwaine, C. (2007) 'Keeping London working: global cities, the British state and London's new migrant division of labour', *Transactions of the Institute of British Geographers,* 32(2): 151–67.

Mayhew, L. and Harper, G. (2010) *Counting the population of Tower Hamlets: A London borough in transition,* London: Mayhew Harper Associates.

Mayor of London (2011) London key facts, www.londoncouncils.gov.uk/londonfacts/default.htm?category=10.

Mayor of London, Rough Sleeping Group (2013) www.london.gov.uk/priorities/housing-land/tackling-homelessness-overcrowding/rough-sleeping/mayors-rough-sleeping-group.

McCann, E. (2004) 'Urban political economy beyond the "global" city', *Urban Studies,* 41(12): 2315–33.

McCann, E. and Ward, K. (2010) 'Relationality/territoriality: Toward a conceptualization of cities in the world', *Geoforum,* 41: 175–84.

McDowell, L. (2004) 'Work, workfare, work/life balance and an ethics of care', *Progress in Human Geography,* 28(2): 145–63.

McFarlane C, (2010) 'The comparative city: Knowledge, learning, urbanism', *International Journal of Urban and Regional Research,* 34: 725–42.

McFarlane, C. and Robinson, J. (2012) 'Introduction: Experiments in comparative urbanism', *Urban Geography,* 33(6): 765–73.

McGuirk, P. (2002) 'Sydney: the emergence of a world city', *Political Geography,* 21(3): 418–20.

McGuirk, P. and Dowling, R. (2009) 'Neoliberal privatisation? Remapping the public and the private in Sydney's masterplanned residential estates', *Political Geography,* 28(3): 174–85.

McGuirk, P. and O'Neill, P. (2002) 'Planning a prosperous Sydney: The challenges of planning urban development in the new urban context', *Australian Geographer,* 33: 301–16.

McNeill, D., Dowling, R. and Fagan, B. (2005) 'Sydney/Global/City: An exploration', *International Journal of Urban and Regional Research,* 29: 935–44.

Mendes, P. (2009) 'Retrenching or renovating the Australian welfare state: The paradox of the Howard government's neoliberalism', *International Journal of Social Welfare,* 18(1): 102–10.

Merrifield, A. (2013) 'The urban question under planetary urbanization', *International Journal of Urban and Regional Research,* 37(3): 909–22.

Milbourne, L. (2013) *Voluntary sector in transition: Hard times or new opportunities?* Bristol, UK: Policy Press.

Miller, B. (2006) 'Castells' The City and the Grassroots: 1983 and today', *International Journal of Urban and Regional Research*, 30(1): 207–11.

Miller, B. (2013) 'Conclusion: Spatialities of mobilization: Building and breaking relationships', in W. Nicholls and J. Beaumont (eds) *Spaces of contention: Spatialities of social movements*, Aldershot, UK: Ashgate, pp 285–303.

Milligan, C. (1996) 'Service dependent ghetto formation: A transferable concept?', *Health and Place*, 2(4): 199–211.

Milligan, C. (2009) 'Voluntary sector', in R. Kitchin and N. Thrift (eds) *International encyclopedia of human geography*, London: Elsevier Press, pp 165–70.

Milligan, C. and Conradson, D. (2006) 'Contemporary landscapes of welfare: The "voluntary turn"?', in C. Milligan and D. Conradson (eds) *Landscapes of voluntarism*, Bristol, UK: Policy Press, pp 1–14.

Mitchell, D. (1997) 'The annihilation of space by law: The roots and implications of anti-homeless laws in the United States', *Antipode*, 29: 303–35.

Mitchell, D. (2001) 'Postmodern geographical praxis? The postmodern impulse and the war against homeless people in the "post-justice" city', in C. Minca (ed) *Postmodern geography: Theory and praxis*, Oxford: Blackwell, pp 57–92.

Mitchell, D. (2003) *The right to the city: Social justice and the fight for public space*, New York, NY: The Guilford Press.

Mitchell, D. and Heynen, N. (2009) 'The geography of survival and the right to the city', *Urban Geography*, 30: 611–32.

Mitchell, K. (2001) 'Transnationalism, neo-liberalism, and the rise of the shadow state', *Economy and Society*, 30: 165–89.

Mohan, J. (2000) 'Geographies of welfare and social exclusion', *Progress in Human Geography*, 24(2): 291–300.

Mohan, J. (2003) 'Geography and social policy: Spatial divisions of welfare', *Progress in Human Geography*, 27: 363–74.

Moon, G., Kearns, R. and Joseph, A. (2006) 'Selling the private asylum: Therapeutic landscapes and the (re)valorization of confinement in the era of community care', *Transactions: Institute of British Geographers*, 31: 131–49.

Moyersoen, J. and Swyngedouw, E. (2013) 'LimiteLimite: Cracks in the city, brokering scales, and pioneering a new urbanity', in W. Nicholls and J. Beaumont (eds) *Spaces of contention: Spatialities of social movements*, Aldershot, UK: Ashgate, pp 141–62.

Murphy, S. (2009) '"Compassionate' strategies of managing homelessness: Post-revanchist geographies in San Francisco', *Antipode*, 41(2): 305–25.

National Center for Charitable Statistics (NCCS) (2014) www.nccs.urban.org.

National Centre for Social Research (2009) *Profiling London's rough sleepers*, London: National Centre for Social Research.

National Coalition for the Homeless (2009) *Homes not handcuffs: The criminalization of homelessness in US cities*, Washington, DC: National Coalition for the Homeless.

Nelson, C. and Wolch, J. (1985) 'Intrametropolitan planning for community-based residential care: A goals programming approach', *Socio-Economic Planning Sciences*, 19: 205–12.

Nevile, A. (2009) 'Values and the legitimacy of third sector delivery organizations: Evidence from Australia', *Voluntas*, 20: 71–89.

Newman, K. and Wyly, E. (2006) 'The right to stay put, revisited: Gentrification and resistance to displacement in New York City', *Urban Studies*, 43: 23–57.

Nicholls, W., Beaumont, J. and Miller, B. (2013) 'Introduction: Conceptualizing the spatialities of social movements', in W. Nicholls, B. Miller and J. Beaumont (eds) *Spaces of contention: Spatialities of social movements*, Aldershot, UK: Ashgate, pp 1–23.

Nijman, J. (2007a) 'Introduction – Comparative urbanism', *Urban Geography*, 28(1): 1–6.

Nijman, J. (2007b) 'Place-particularity and "deep analogies": A comparative essay on Miami's rise as a world city', *Urban Geography*, 28(1): 92–107.

Nowra, L. (2013) *Kings Cross: A biography*, Sydney: University of New South Wales Press.

O'Connor, P. (2014) 'Australian government prepares sweeping welfare cuts', World Socialist Web Site, wsws.org.

O'Neill, P. & McGuirk, P. (2002) 'Guest Editorial – A contemporary geography of prosperity along Australia's eastern seaboard', *Australian Geographer*, 33: 237–9.

Office of Mayor James K. Hahn (2004) 'Mayor Hahn, Chief Bratton announce successful crackdown on the production and sale of illegal documents in Macarthur Park 9', 11 November, www.lacity.org/mayor/oldpresss/mayormyrpress27425284_11232004.pdf.

Parsell, C., Jones, A. and Head, B. (2013) 'Policies and programmes to end homelessness in Australia: Learning from international practice', *International Journal of Social Welfare*, 22: 186–94.

Pastor, M. (2001) 'Common ground at ground zero? The new economy and the new organizing in Los Angeles', *Antipode*, 33(2): 260–89.

Peach, C. (1996) 'Does Britain have ghettoes?', *Transactions of the Institute of British Geographers*, 21: 216–35.

Peach, C. (2006) 'Islam, ethnicity, and South Asian religions in the London 2001 census', *Transactions of the Institute of British Geographers*, 31: 353–70.

Peck, J. (2001a) *Workfare states*, New York, NY: Guildford Press.

Peck, J. (2001b) 'Neoliberalizing states: Thin policies/hard outcomes', *Progress in Human Geography*, 25: 445–55.

Peck, J. (2003) 'Geography and public policy: Mapping the penal state', *Progress in Human Geography*, 27: 222–32.

Peck, J. (2010) 'Zombie neoliberalism and the ambidextrous state', *Theoretical Criminology*, 14(1): 1–7.

Peck, J. (2012) 'Austerity urbanism: American cities under extreme economy', *City*, 16(6): 626–55.

Peck, J. and Tickell, A. (2002) 'Neoliberalizing space', in N. Brenner and N. Theodore (eds) *Spaces of neoliberalism*, Oxford, UK: Blackwell Press, pp 33–57.

Peck, J., Theodore, N. and Brenner, N. (2010) 'Postneoliberalism and its malcontents', *Antipode*, 41(6): 1236–58.

Peterson, P. (1981) *City limits*, Chicago, IL: University of Chicago Press.

Phillips, D., Davis, C. and Ratcliffe, P. (2007) 'British Asian narratives of urban space', *Transactions of the Institute of British Geographers*, 32: 217–34.

Phillips, R. and Goodwin, S. (2014) 'Third sector social policy research in Australia: New actors, new politics', *Voluntas*, 25(3), 565–84.

Pilgrim, M. (2006) 'London regional governance and the London boroughs', *Local Government Studies*, 32: 223–38.

Popkin, E. (1999) 'Guatemalan Mayan migration to Los Angeles', *Ethnic and Racial Studies*, 22: 267–89.

Power, A. (2013) 'Making space for belonging: Critical reflections on the implementation of personalised adult social care under the veil of meaningful inclusion', *Social Science and Medicine*, 88: 68–75.

Prior, J., Boydell, S. and Hubbard, P. (2012) 'Nocturnal rights to the city: Property, propriety and sex premises in inner Sydney', *Urban Studies*, 49(8): 1837–52.

Purcell, M. (2002) 'Excavating Lefebvre: The right to the city and its urban politics of the inhabitant', *Geojournal*, 58: 99–108.

Raco, M. and Street, E. (2012) 'Resilience planning, economic change and the politics of post-recession development in London and Hong Kong', *Urban Studies*, 49: 1065–87.

Rajan, S. and Duncan, C. (2013) 'Ecologies of hope: Environment, technology and habitation – case studies from the intervenient middle', *Journal of Political Ecology*, 20: 70–9.

Randolph, B. and Holloway, D. (2005) 'The suburbanization of disadvantage in Sydney: New problems, new policies', *Opolis: An International Journal of Suburban and Metropolitan Studies*, 1(1): 31–4.

Randolph, B. and Tice, A. (2014) 'Socio-spatial change in an era of neoliberalism', *Journal of Urban Affairs*, 36(1): 384–99.

Raskall, P. (2002) 'Equity issues in the "new prosperity" of the 1990s: The case of Sydney', *Australian Geographer*, 33(3): 281–99.

Reese, E. (2011) *'They say cutback, we say fightback!' Contemporary welfare rights activism in an era of retrenchment*, New York, NY: Russell Sage Foundation.

Reese, E., DeVerteuil, G. and Thach, L. (2010) '"Weak-center" gentrification and the contradictions of containment: deconcentrating poverty in Downtown Los Angeles', *International Journal of Urban and Regional Research*, 34: 310–27.

Robinson, J. (2002) 'Global and world cities: A view from off the map', *International Journal of Urban and Regional Research*, 26: 531–54.

Robinson, J. (2011a) 'Cities in a world of cities: The comparative gesture', *International Journal of Urban and Regional Research*, 35(1): 1–23.

Robinson, J. (2011b) 'The travels of urban neoliberalism: Taking stock of the internationalization of urban theory', *Urban Geography*, 32(8): 1087–109.

Rose, D. and Lynch, R. (2012) 'Work and play in the city: Some reflections on the night-time economy of Sydney', *Annals of Leisure Research*, 15(2): 132–47.

Roy, A. (2009) 'The 21st century metropolis: New geographies of theory', *Regional Studies*, 43(6): 819–30.

Ruddick, S. (1996) *Young and homeless in Hollywood: Mapping social identities*, New York, NY: Routledge.

Ruming, K.J., Randolph, B., Pinnagar, S. and Judd, B. (2010) 'Urban renewal and regeneration in Sydney, Australia: Council reflections of the planning and development process', *Journal of Urban Regeneration and Renewal*, 3(4): 357–69.

Ruting, B. (2008) 'Economic transformations of gay urban spaces: Revisiting Collins' evolutionary gay district model', *Australian Geographer*, 39(3): 259–69.

Rymer, R. (2001) 'The rules of the Row', *Mother Jones*, March–April: 38–45.

Sakizlioglu, N. and Uitermark, J. (2014) 'The symbolic politics of gentrification: The restructuring of stigmatized neighborhoods in Amsterdam and Istanbul', *Environment and Planning A*, 46: 1369–85.

Salamon, L. (1999) 'The non-profit sector at the crossroads: The case of America', *Voluntas*, 10(1): 5–23.

Salamon, L. and Anheier, H. (1998) 'Social origins of civil society: Explaining the nonprofit sector cross-nationally', *Voluntas*, 9: 213–48.

Sassen, S. (2001) *The Global City*, Princeton, NJ: Princeton University Press.

Sassen, S. (2014) *Expulsions: Brutality and complexity in the global economy*, Boston, MA: Belknap Press, Harvard University.

Scott, A. (2001) 'Introduction', in A. Scott (ed) *Global city-regions: Trends, theory, policy*, Oxford: Oxford University Press, pp 1–8.

Scott, A. and Storper, M. (forthcoming) 'The nature of cities: The scope and limits of urban theory', *International Journal of Urban and Regional Planning* DOI: 10.1111/1468–2427.12134.

Searle, G. (2013) '"Relational" planning and recent Sydney metropolitan and city strategies', *Urban Policy and Research*, 31(3): 367–78.

Shantz, J. (2013) *Commonist tendencies: Mutual aid beyond Communism*, Brooklyn, NY: Punctum Books.

Sharp, J., Routledge, P., Philo, C. and Paddison, R. (2000) 'Entanglements of power: Geographies of domination/resistance', in J. Sharp, P. Routledge, C. Philo and R. Paddison (eds) *Entanglements of power: Geographies of domination/resistance*, London: Routledge, pp 1–42.

Shaw, K. (2005) 'Local limits to gentrification', in R. Atkinson and G. Bridge (eds) *Gentrification in a global context: The new urban colonialism*, London: Routledge, pp 168–84.

Shaw, W. (2007) *Cities of whiteness*, London: Blackwell Press-Antipode Book Series.

Shelter Partnership (2000) *A report on cold/wet weather shelter utilization in Los Angeles County*, Los Angeles, CA: Shelter Partnership, Inc.

Short, J.R. (1989) 'Yuppies, yuffies and the new urban order', *Transactions of the Institute of British Geographers*, pp 173–88.

Skinner, M. and Power, A. (2011) 'Voluntarism, health and place: Bringing an emerging field into focus', *Health and Place*, 17(1): 1–6.

Skowronek, S. (1995) 'Order and change', *Polity*, 28(1): 91–6.

Slater, T. (2004) 'North American gentrification? Revanchist and emancipatory perspectives explored', *Environment and Planning A*, 36(7): 1191–213.

Slater, T. (2006) 'The eviction of critical perspectives from gentrification research', *International Journal of Urban and Regional Research*, 30: 737–57.

Slater, T. (2014a) 'Grieving for a lost home, revisited: The "Bedroom Tax" and displacement', www.geos.ed.ac.uk/homes/tslater/bedroomtax.html.

Slater, T. (2014b) The resilience of neoliberal urbanism, www.opendemocarcy.net/opernsecurity/tom-slater/resilience-of-neoliberal-urbanism.html.

Smart, A. (2001) 'Unruly places: Urban governance and the persistence of illegality in Hong Kong's urban squatter areas', *American Anthropologist*, 103(1): 30–44.

Smith, M.P. (2001) *Transnational urbanism: Locating globalization*. Malden, MA: Wiley Blackwell.

Smith, N. (1996) *The new urban frontier: Gentrification and the revanchist city*, London: Routledge.

Smith, N. (2002) 'New globalism, new urbanism: gentrification as global urban strategy', *Antipode*, 34: 427–50.

Smith, N. (2005) 'Neo-critical geography, or, the flat pluralist world of business class', *Antipode*, 37(5): 887–99.

Smith, S., Pain, R., Marston, S. and Jones III, J.P. (2010) *The SAGE Handbook of Social Geography*, London: Sage Publications.

Soja, E. (1989) *Postmodern geographies*, New York, NY: Verso Press.

Soja, E. (2000) *Postmetropolis*, New York, NY: Routledge Press.

Soja, E. (2010) *Seeking spatial justice*, Minneapolis, MN: University of Minnesota.

Southwark Council (2014a) *Bankside, Borough and London Bridge SPD*, www.southwark.gov.uk/info/200151/supplementary_planning_documents_and_guidance/1246/bankside_borough_and_london_bridge_spd.

Southwark Council (2014b) Aylesbury partner decision, www.southwark.gov.uk/news/article/1647/aylesbury_development_partner_decision.

Staeheli, L. (2013) 'Whose responsibility is it? Obligation, citizenship and social welfare', *Antipode*, 45: 521–40.

Stuart, F. (2014) 'From "rabble management" to "recovery management": Policing homelessness in marginal urban space', *Urban Studies*, 51(9): 1909–25.

Swidler, A. (2013) 'Cultural sources of institutional resilience: Lessons from chieftaincy in rural Malawi', in P. Hall and M. Lamont (eds) *Social resilience in the neoliberal era*, Cambridge, UK: Cambridge University Press, pp 319–45.

Takahashi, L. (1998) *Homelessness, AIDS, and stigmatization*, Oxford: Clarendon Press.

Till, K. (2012) 'Wounded cities: Memory-work and a place-based ethics of care', *Political Geography*, 31(3): 3–14.

Trudeau, D. (2008a) 'Junior partner or empowered community? The role of non-profit social service providers amidst state restructuring in the US', *Urban Studies*, 45(13): 2805–27.

Trudeau, D. (2008b) 'Towards a relational view of the shadow state', *Political Geography*, 27: 669–90.

Trudeau, D. (2012) 'Constructing citizenship in the shadow state', *Geoforum*, 43(3): 442–52.

Trudeau, D. and Veronis, L. (2009) 'Enacting state restructuring: NGOs as translation mechanisms', *Environment and Planning D: Society and Space*, 27(6): 1117–34.

Tyner, J. (2013) 'Population geography I: Surplus populations', *Progress in Human Geography*, 37: 701–11.

Uitermark, J., Nicholls, W. and Loopmans, M. (2012) 'Cities and social movements: Theorizing beyond the right to the city', *Environment and Planning A*, 44: 2546–54.

UK Registered Charity Database (2013).

UK census (1991) *UK census 1991*, London: Office for National Statistics.

UK census (2001) *UK census 2001*, London: Office for National Statistics.

UK census (2011) *UK census 2011*, London: Office for National Statistics.

UK Office for National Statistics for London (2001) www.statistics.gov.uk/focuson/london/.

US Census Bureau (1990) *US census 1990*, Washington, DC: Census Bureau.

US Census Bureau (2000) *US census 2000*, Washington, DC: Census Bureau.

US Census Bureau (2010) *US census 2010*, Washington, DC: Census Bureau.

Vale, L. and Campanella, T. (eds) (2005) *The resilient city: How modern cities recover from disaster*, New York, NY: Oxford University Press.

Van Eijk, G. (2010) 'Exclusionary policies are not just about the "neoliberal city": A critique of theories of urban revanchism and the case of Rotterdam', *International Journal of Urban and Regional Research*, 34(4): 820–34.

Van Hulten, A. (2010) *Global flows, gentrification and displacement in Melbourne's Inner West*. Centre for Strategic Economic Studies, Victoria University Melbourne.

Vergara, C. (1995) *The new American ghetto*, New Brunswick, NJ: Rutgers University Press.

Vicino, T., Hanlon, B. and Short, J. (2011) 'A typology of urban immigrant neighborhoods', *Urban Geography*, 32(3): 383–405.

Voluntary Action for Westminster (VAW) (2009) *The recession yet to come: Planning for resilience in the voluntary and community sector in Westminster*, London: Voluntary Action for Westminster.

Von Mahs, J. (2013) *Down and out in Los Angeles and Berlin: The sociospatial exclusion of homeless people*. Philadelphia, PA: Temple University Press.

Wacquant L. (1999) 'Urban marginality in the coming millennium', *Urban Studies*, 36: 1639–47.

Wacquant L. (2008) *Urban outcasts: A comparative sociology of advanced marginality*, Cambridge, UK: Polity Press.

Wacquant, L. (2009) *Punishing the poor: The neoliberal government of social insecurity*, Durham, NC: Duke University Press.

Walker, B., Holling, C., Carpenter, S. and Kinzig, A. (2004) 'Resilience, adaptability and transformability in social-ecological systems', *Ecology and Society*, 9(2): 5.

Walker, B., Anderies, J., Kinzig, A. and Ryan, P. (2006) Exploring resilience in social-ecological systems through comparative studies and theory development: Introduction to the Special Issue, *Ecology and Society*, 11(1): www.ecologyandsociety.org/vol11/iss1/art12/.

Walker, P. (2013) 'London's world status and house price boom is now hurting the middle class', *Guardian*, 2 August.

Walks, A. and August, M. (2008) 'The factors inhibiting gentrification in areas with little non-market housing', *Urban Studies*, 45: 2594–625.

Walsh, T. (2011) *Homelessness and the law*, Annandale, NSW: The Federation Press.

Walters, P. and McCrea, R. (2014) 'Early gentrification of the public realm: A case study of West End in Brisbane', *Urban Studies*, 51(2): 355–70.

Ward, K. (2008) 'Towards a comparative (re)turn in urban studies? Some reflections', *Urban Geography*, 29(2008): 405–10.

Ward, K. (2010) 'Towards a relational comparative approach to the study of cities', *Progress in Human Geography*, 34(4): 471–87.

Ward, K. (2012) 'Of comparison, learning and models: Thinking through the city', *Political Geography*, 31(1): 20–1.

Ward, K. and McCann, E. (2011) 'Introduction', in K. Ward and E. McCann (eds) *Mobile urbanism: City policymaking in the global age,* Minnesota, MN: University of Minnesota Press, pp 1–16.

Warshawsky, D. (2010) 'New power relations served here: The growth of food banking in Chicago', *Geoforum,* 41: 763–75.

Watt, P. (2009) 'Housing stock transfers, regeneration and state-led gentrification in London', *Urban Policy and Research,* 27: 229–42.

Watt, P. (2013) '"It's not for us": Regeneration, the 2012 Olympics and the gentrification of East London', *City,* 17(1): 99–118.

Webb, L. (2013) *Resilience: How to cope when everything around you keeps changing,* New York, NY: Capstone Press.

Weischselgartner, J. and Kelman, I. (forthcoming) 'Geographies of resilience: Challenges and opportunities of a descriptive concept', *Progress in Human Geography.*

Westminster Council (2004) *An integrated approach to reduce begging in Westminster,* London: Westminster Council.

Westminster Council (2007) *Unitary development plan,* London: Westminster Council.

Westminster Council (2008) *Preferred core strategy option,* London: Westminster Council.

Weller, S. and O'Neill, P. (2014) 'An argument with neoliberalism: Australia's place in a global imaginary', *Dialogues in Human Geography,* 4(2): 105–30.

Williams, A., Cloke, P. and Thomas, J. (2012) 'Co-constituting neoliberalism: Faith-based organizations, co-opting and resistance in the UK', *Environment and Planning A,* 44: 1479–501.

Wills, C., Datta, K., Evans, Y., Herbert, J., May, J. and McIlwaine, C. (2010) *Global cities at work: New migrant divisions of labour.* London: Pluto Press.

Wills, J. (2012) 'The geography of community and political organisation in London', *Political Geography,* 31: 114–26.

Wilson, D. and Keil, R. (2008) 'The real creative class', *Social and Cultural Geography,* 9: 841–7.

Wilson, G. (2013) 'Community resilience, social memory and the post-2010 Christchurch (New Zealand) earthquakes', *Area,* 45(2): 207–15.

Wiseman, J. (1970) *Stations of the lost: The treatment of Skid Row alcoholics,* Englewood Cliffs, NJ: Prentice-Hall.

Wolch, J. (1979) 'Residential location and the provision of human services: Some directions for geographic research', *Professional Geographer,* 31: 271–7.

Wolch, J. (1980) 'Residential location of the service dependent poor', *Annals of the Association of American Geographers,* 70: 330–41.

Wolch, J. (1981) 'The location of service-dependent households in urban areas', *Economic Geography*, 57: 52–67.

Wolch, J. (1990) *Shadow state: Government and voluntary sector in transition*, New York, NY: Foundation Center.

Wolch, J. (1999) 'Decentering America's nonprofit sector: Reflections on Salomon's crises analysis', in H. Anheier and J. Kendall (eds) *Third sector policy at the crossroads: An international nonprofit analysis*, London: Routledge, pp 51–60.

Wolch, J. (2006) 'Foreword: Beyond the shadow state?', in C. Milligan and D. Conradson (eds) *Landscapes of voluntarism: New spaces of health, welfare and governance*, Bristol: Policy Press, pp xii–xx.

Wolch, J. (2008) 'Intransigent LA', *Geoforum*, 39: 543–5.

Wolch, J. and Geiger, R. (1983) 'The distribution of urban voluntary resources: an exploratory analysis', *Environment and Planning A*, 15: 1067–82.

Wolch, J. and Dear, M. (1993) *Malign neglect: Homelessness in an American city*, San Francisco, CA: Jossey-Bass.

Wolch, J. and DeVerteuil, G. (2001) 'Landscapes of the new poverty management', in J. May and N. Thrift (eds) *TimeSpace*, London: Routledge, pp 149–68.

Wood, S. (2012) 'There goes the neighbourhood', *Sydney Morning Herald*, 31 August.

Wright, T. (1997) *Out of place: Homeless mobilizations, subcities, and contested landscapes*, Albany, NY: State University of New York Press.

Wrigley, N. and Dolega, L. (2011) 'Resilience, fragility, and adaptation: New evidence on the performance of UK high streets during global economic crisis and its policy implications', *Environment and Planning A*, 43(10): 2337–63.

Wyly, E. and Hammel, D. (2005) 'Mapping neo-liberal American urbanism', in R. Atkinson and R. Bridge (eds) *Gentrification in a global context: The new urban colonialism*, London: Routledge, pp 55–79.

Yanos, P. (2007) 'Beyond "landscapes of despair": The need for new research on the urban environment, sprawl, and the community integration of persons with severe mental illness', *Health and Place*, 13: 672–6.

Yoon, H. and Currid-Halkett, E. (forthcoming) 'Industrial gentrification in West Chelsea, New York: Who survived and who did not?', *Urban Studies*, DOI: 10.1177/0042098014536785.

Zilberg, E. (2002) 'A troubled corner: The ruined and rebuilt environment of a Central American barrio in post-Rodney King riot Los Angeles', *City and Society*, 14: 31–55.

Zolli, A. and Healy, A. (2013) *Resilience: Why things bounce back*, New York, NY: Business Plus.

Zuern, E. (2011) *The politics of necessity: Community organizing and democracy in South Africa*. Madison, WI: University of Wisconsin Press.

Zukin, S. (1992) 'The city as a landscape of power: London and New York as global financial capitals', in L. Budd and S. Whimster (eds) *Global finance and urban living*, London: Routledge, pp 195–223.

Zukin, S. (1995) *The cultures of cities*, New York: Blackwell.

Index

Note: page numbers in *italic* type refer to figures and tables.

D

Darlinghurst/Kings Cross case study 69,
121, 204
  area profile 136–8
  Darlinghurst gay districts and
  gentrification 138–42
  Kings Cross gentrification and resilience
  123, *124*, 142–7
  transformative potential of service hub
  243
  voluntary-sector resilience 141–2,
  143–7
Davidson, M. 221
day labourers 177, 194–5, 196
Dear, M. 11, 37
deep analogies 78–9, 213–14
DeFilippis, J. 236
Dench, G. 179
dependent city thesis 27
Derickson, K. 34
development aid agency 116
DeVerteuil, G. 44
displacement
  by place type 97–8
  concept of 73–4
  in Downtown LA 155–60
  as enclosure 241–2
  in Hollywood 166, 167–9
  in Kings Cross 145
  operationalising 72–6
  patterns and profile 83–5
  resilience to *see* resilience
  rise of 7–8
  service hubs vulnerable to 53–4, 72
  in Southwark 128, 134–5
  as threat 220–5
  in Tower Hamlets 184–5
  in Westminster 107–9
  see also suburbanisation
displacement pressure 73–4, 83, 97
  in Kings Cross 142–3
  in Los Angeles 85, 155–7, 207
  in Southwark 128
  in Surry Hills 116
  in Westminster 106, 109
diversity *see* population diversity
Downtown Eastside (Vancouver) 39
Downtown Los Angeles case study 67,
68, 149, 205
  area profile 151–3
  gentrification and displacement 65,
  155–60
  and inner-city typology 96
  local policy 149, 154–5
  voluntary-sector resilience 159–64
drug addiction facility 145–7
Duncan, C. 35, 230–1

E

employment agencies 161
enclaves *see* immigrant enclaves
enclosure 241–2
encompassing approach to comparison
79, 214
entrapment 224–5
  in established gentrified areas 99, 110,
  114, 115–16, 117
  in mixed areas 129, 130, 134
Esping-Andersen, G. 3, 88
established gentrified areas 95, 99–100
  case studies *see* Surry Hills; Westminster
  resilience comparisons 203–4
  and tolerance 146–7
Evans, J. 51

F

Fainstein, S. 92
Fairbanks, R. 9, 45
faith-based organisations 50, 182
feeding services 108–9, 122–3, 170
Flusty, S. 11
folk concepts 80
Folke, C. 27
food delivery programme 169
Fullilove, M. 7

G

gay districts 138–40
gay gentrification 139
gentrification
  abetted by policy reform 250
  and austerity urbanism 249–50
  definition of 8, 73
  gay gentrification 139
  impact of 53–4, 73–4
  see also displacement
  models of immigrant community space
  and 173–4
  and neoliberalism in inner city 13
  residues as barrier to 233
  resilience of 221
  in sample cities 62, 64–5, *67*, *69*,
  149–51
    Darlinghurst/Kings Cross 137–8,
    139–40, 142–3
    Downtown LA 65, 155–6
    Hollywood 168, 170
    Pico-Union 65, 195–7
    Southwark 126–8, 129–33
    Surry Hills 111–12, 117, 118
    Tower Hamlets 65, 179–80, 185–6
    Westminster 64, 101–2
  supergentrification 101, 121, 122
  and tolerance 146–7, 203, 205, 221–2
  see also NIMBYism

www.ingramcontent.com/pod-product-compliance
Lightning Source LLC
Chambersburg PA
CBHW060028030426
42334CB00019B/2234